D1371305

edited with an introduction by
EUNICE HANGER

THREE AUSTRALIAN PLAYS

UNIVERSITY OF MINNESOTA PRESS, *Minneapolis*

© Copyright 1968 University of Queensland Press. First published as *Khaki, Bush, and Bigotry: Three Australian Plays*. Printed in the United States of America at North Central Publishing Company, St. Paul

Library of Congress Catalog Card Number: 68-55386

PUBLISHED IN THE UNITED KINGDOM AND EIRE BY THE OXFORD UNIVERSITY PRESS, LONDON, AND IN CANADA BY THE COPP CLARK PUBLISHING CO. LIMITED, TORONTO *acknowledgments*

.

For help in assembling script, original cast lists, and other details, and for permission to print, we thank the playwrights Sumner Locke Elliott and Ray Mathew, and also Judith Wright (Mrs. Jack McKinney), Miss Doris Fitton of the Independent Theatre, and the Mitchell Library, especially Miss Suzanne Mourot.

contents

Introduction 7

Rusty Bugles 23

We Find the Bunyip 107

The Well 203

introduction

In introducing three Australian plays hitherto unpublished, I want to indicate some of the directions our drama seems to have been taking in the last two decades. For these years have certainly given us more than any earlier times.

Since 1945, some important landmarks have appeared, and the most important is this, that professionalism in the writing of plays has become the rule rather than the exception. One can actually, I think, name 1955 as the year in which this is demonstrably so. A number of influences culminate here: since the thirties, play-competitions have been providing lessons in the craft of telling a story in stage-dialogue; some amateur theatres and semi-professional theatres have produced plays that won competitions and also other plays locally written, and the resulting criticism and audience-response have had some effect on new writers; the professional theatres—that is, the Australian Elizabethan Theatre Trust, established in 1955 and based in Sydney, as well as a few satellite theatres partly supported by the Trust, and some few independent of the Trust—have sometimes offered professional return for the playwright's labours: payment of rights, professional production, a run of some length. As a result, the general level of playwriting has been higher, and to the top have floated—struggled rather— a few playwrights whose individuality, peculiar talent, temporary inspiration, or genius has produced what constitutes, in sum, a genuine dramatic literature, small but distinctive.

First, some naturalistic plays have been recognized and success-fully played, passing sometimes into the repertory of published work used by amateurs, done over and over, set for wider reading in schools, studied in courses on Australian literature. *Rusty Bugles* (1948) was the first successful play, and was naturalistic, but for various reasons was never published; then in 1955 came *Summer of the Seventeenth Doll*, by Ray Lawler, and soon after it *The One Day of the Year*, by Alan Seymour. Such plays established the "well-made" play as the popular type and with their numerous imitations constitute the nearest approach we have to a *school*. Meanwhile Douglas Stewart and others, working partly in radio, made more than a partial success of verse drama, using local legend and history for heroic and myth-making factors in such plays as *Ned Kelly*, *The Golden Lover*, *Fire on the Snow*, *Shipwreck*, *Sons of the Morning* (the last is Catherine Duncan's). The atmosphere of particular places, almost enough to constitute a regional drama, has been caught in the speech, imagery, and action of such plays as G. L. Dann's *Resurrection at Matthewtown*, J. Hepworth's *The Last of the Rainbow*, Ray Mathew's *A Spring Song* and *We Find the Bunyip*, Sumner Locke Elliott's *Rusty Bugles*, and *The Season at Sarsaparilla* of Patrick White.

The last-named writer stands apart in the quality of his achieve-ment: though his four published plays break quite new ground in excitingly original ways, they have had relatively little production. This paradoxical phenomenon, which I make no pretension to explain, has prevented White's having the influence he might have had on Australian drama. Apart from his ideas, themes, philosophy, and so on, his impact might have been felt in our theatres through his initiative in using modern stage-equipment, composite set,

8

non-realistic technique of all kinds, and through his awareness of what will "go" on stage—how the playwright can feed the curiosity of a story-loving audience and also feed an audience hungry for poetry, for the unexpected, for what couldn't be anticipated.

There are also many playwrights who don't fit precisely into categories even loosely defined: writers of farce, like L. Collinson sometimes and A. Hopgood always; of fantasy, or pseudo-history, or sheer blatant melodrama, like Ralph Petersen and Hal Porter. The important thing is, I believe, that there are many writers, and in the history of English drama our best times have been times when writers have crowded into a limited area and competed, collaborated, picked each other's brains, and stolen each other's ideas, styles and even lines, as did the Elizabethan gang. We might see a renaissance of such prosperous times, if our theatres were as active as our writers. Some demand for the best, such as the Tudor monarchs seem to have provided in themselves or by deputy, is what I believe would release a damned-up flood of stage drama in Australia at present.

The three plays published in this book represent something of that flood as it appeared to me to be available a few years ago. White's plays had not been seen when *We Find the Bunyip* and *The Well* were first written, though White's *The Ham Funeral* was written earlier. A few facts on these plays and their writers may be appreciated:

Rusty Bugles, by Sumner Locke Elliott, was first produced at the Independent Theatre, Sydney, by Doris Fitton, Director of the Theatre, on 21 October 1948. The story of what happened on that occasion has been told in detail by Leslie Rees in his book, *Towards an Australian Drama* (pp. 169-173). Miss Fitton conveys with entertaining terseness her memory of the sequence of incidents:

> The production was proceeding smoothly and everyone in the cast happily anticipated a successful show when Frank O'Donnell, the first "Mac", happened to discuss his part over a cup of coffee with a journalist.
>
> A few lines from the script were printed in an evening paper. By next morning all news editors smelt a sensation.

9

Within 48 hours reverend gentlemen were writing protesting letters to the press.

The Chief Secretary's Department cried out for censorship, and a copy of the play was forwarded to it.

On the first night a number of police stood at the back of the audience.

The Chief Secretary called for censorship.

A slightly censored version was staged on the second night with police present again.

The Chief Secretary made no comment.

The original version was played on the third night and ever after and everyone was happy.

The author has lived since 1948 in New York.

We Find the Bunyip, by Ray Mathew, was a runner-up in the competition won by *Summer of the Seventeenth Doll*. It was first produced at the Independent Theatre in Sydney by Geoffrey Thomas, playwright and producer, who at that time was trying to create a playwrights' theatre, and was working with actors uncorrupted by training in plays of English or American origin. This first production in 1955 was only a two-night stand. The play was not done again till 1963, when Brisbane's Twelfth Night Theatre, with the Director Joan Whalley producing, presented it first at a theatre week-end school in Lismore, and later at the Theatre in Brisbane.

The author has lived in England since 1962.

Jack McKinney's play *The Well* was first produced in Brisbane by Twelfth Night Theatre in 1959. The first act has been published as a one-act play in *Australian One-Act Plays* (Adelaide: Rigby Ltd., 1962, Vol. I).

The author died in Queensland in December 1966.

All three plays have now had a number of productions, and have proved themselves on stage, *Rusty Bugles* in professional theatre, the other two in a number of Little Theatre productions. In book form, handy for rehearsal, they will be more readily accessible to the amateur player than in script, and perhaps a wider recognition of their merits may lead to their being reconsidered by professionals of stage, radio, TV—*Rusty Bugles* has had recent productions on radio and TV—and film.

Meanwhile a weightier argument has prompted this publication. We have three scripts that could be lost, and that should be preserved in solider form than script because they have a claim on our interest as dramatic literature, something to be savoured, read and re-read, not forgotten after use for one "nice night's entertainment".

Rusty Bugles was the first full-length play that convincingly set unmistakably Australian characters in a setting unmistakably Australian, to behave as they did because they were where they were. These characters are not stereotypes of army plays from just anywhere. They are Australian soldiers (diggers), unlike any other set of soldiers anywhere in the world—some would say, Thank God! They have grown up in the cities and towns of Australia; the train has brought them to camp in the Northern Territory, and they want just one thing, to get out of it and back. The story is a merry-go-round, bringing them back at the end for another wet season. Back they come, swearing or silent with misery, to confess a kind of comfort in the familiarity of the old faces, in the sharing of their despair.

It's a play of atmosphere, and of inaction rather than action— some say, a documentary more than a play. Let's not quibble over words. The response of the soldiers to inaction is itself a continuous movement, now slow, now violently swift. The fluctuations of mood take us from sheer high-spirited or even farcical comedy to biting satire of dogs in office, to the pathos of broken home and faithless love, to the loneliness of the frustrated spirit. The audience response often teeters on the border that separates mirth from pathos, as when the men make their phone calls. Not much happens; but that is the point, and the men's boredom doesn't become boredom for an audience, because it is the source of constantly fluctuating moods and relationships.

The ebullient Ot, who tells everyone all his affairs, is expecting to go on leave in a few weeks: the sympathetic newcomer, Rod, and the cynical Gig Ape are present.

ROD: Getting married this leave, Ot?
OT: You said it. Just got to talk to Mum first. I'm Mum's only interest see? But Mum's a sport. Good old Mum.
GIG (*singing*): Home to Mum, home to Mum . . .

11

The casual, unemphatic sympathy evoked by this technique of individualizing characters by tiny touches—like "Mum's only interest"—makes the next scene notably poignant: Ot comes slowly into the tent reading a letter—his girl has got married to someone else, and now he doesn't want to go on leave. An even fiercer irony near the end of the play lets Keghead, one of those about to go on the next leave, say:

> Thank God we'll never come back to this joint—that's one thing certain—

and falter on the last word as he sees in the doorway Mac and the others, who left a few weeks ago with the same words on their lips.

The lively image, often familiar but sometimes original and always fresh and vital, appears in the talk of those of the men who are least inhibited. Someone is

> nutty as a fruitcake;

the officer who suddenly wakes up in the telephone scene, because he thought he "heard his name called", is mocked for his airs:

> Heard his name called! Thinks he's bloody Joan of Arc!

And on the other hand the pathetic Y.M.C.A. sergeant, Bill, is made convincing by having only the flattest, most lifeless clichés in which to offer the "boys" a game of euchre:

> Makes something to do . . . you know . . . makes it a nice bright evening, doesn't it? . . . you know . . . nice and bright.

The "boys", of course, prefer to do their money at the two-up school.

The trend in contemporary drama is well away from the totally naturalistic, towards which writers of this century marched rather doggedly until they became aware of the dead end. *Rusty Bugles* was written when the trend was at its height, the other two plays of this volume some years later; but one can't get away from talking naturalism if one is to talk about these three plays at all. Each has passages where for a moment the sense of bare truth is breath-taking—a veil has been drawn from a face, a person is seen defenceless. For me this is naturalism at its best, the *best* that justifies the method.

I think of some superbly prepared and realized comic moments in *Bunyip*, as when the Gink stands in the pub-kitchen with a book of raffle-tickets in his hand, unhopefully offering them for sixpence; Mrs. Pocks and Tony go on playing that game of gin-rummy that slithers the first act along on crazy rollers; George sits with his head on the table, full, morose, resentful of life; Blanche and Snow whisper frustratedly of love; Denise sews her dress. It's a Saturday night, any Saturday night in the country-town pub. Gink asks again:

Would you like a ticket in a raffle? They're only sixpence.

But no one does. In the silence George lifts his head and accuses:

Ought to be ashamed of himself.

And when they stare he says it again:

. . . ought to be ashamed of himself . . . *It's to bury his father* . . .

Someone repeats it:

To bury his father.

And Gink confirms it:

The raffle's to bury my father.

adding in a moment, reasonably:

He's got to be buried.

In *The Well*, Ted is exasperated by the mystery that has suddenly come into his life regarding his daughter Mary, and by the way his wife and Mary seem to gang up on him with that feminine solidarity most men have stubbed their toes on at times. The persistent blocking that greets his questions—"a bit of bother" . . . "what d'yer mean, bother?" . . . "oh nothin' " . . . "coulda been"— brings on an attack of mild swearing:

13

Christ! If wimmin ain't mysterious!

and at last culminates in the sublime illogic of

A man had any bloody sense he'd be in the madhouse.

It is sometimes by poignancy that these writers achieve the moments of truth. I think of Mrs. Pocks accepting, after a moment of shock, the fact that Blanche *has* to get married, and furiously seizing her cards to embark on the game of patience that is her form of drug; turning on Snow, Blanche's lover, in what is now only a pretence of the snubbing she has always subjected him to; and reversing her

Don't call me "ma"—

by now giving orders to a prospective son-in-law, grudgingly accepted, but accepted.

MRS. POCKS [*to* BLANCHE]: Well, stop your crying. It's too late to cry, now. You should have cried then, and he might have left you alone. But I doubt it. [*She looks fiercely at* SNOW.] What are you crying *for*? You're getting married, aren't you? You want to marry him, don't you? Isn't that what you want? Stupid as they make them!

BLANCHE: Snow . . .

MRS. POCKS: Snow! Snow! I wonder he's got the hide to look me in the face after what he's done—

SNOW: I'm not looking you in the face, Lil—

MRS. POCKS: No! That's men all over. And don't call me Lil! You'd better start calling me ma . . . [*She plays cards.*]

SNOW: Gee, thanks, Lil—ma.

[MRS. POCKS *winces, but says nothing.*]

The Well, with more of a story, in a sense, strikes me as the least usual of these plays, perhaps because of its unashamed presentation of sheer, downright, pig-headed stupidity. Reading it now, one can hardly believe this was written before Pinter had made any impact here. The slow speech, the slow uptake, the cautious, repetitive response, the ready misunderstanding (so hard to clear up)—it could all delude one at first reading into accusing: "Imitation

14

Pinter". But it isn't non-communication: the characters communicate all right when they want to, and when they are uttering their slow, seemingly unresponsive repetitious questions and evasive answers their thought goes underground and emerges later in a pricklier form. It happens in the second scene of Act Two, when Ted is slowly getting round to telling his wife of the fun his union mates have been having at his expense, because Mary has been seen with the boy from "next door". The whole duologue takes place slowly, without quick picking up of cues, as each of them fends off the moment when this thing will have to be brought into the open between them.

> WIFE: Mary wants ter leave her. Get another job.
> TED: Does she? Why?
> WIFE: I dunno. Sick of it—I s'pose. I dunno.
> TED: Yer don't know? [*Pause.*] I do.
> WIFE: Know what?
> TED: Why she wants ter leave.
> WIFE: Why?
> TED: *You* know why.
> WIFE: What d'yer mean? I know?
> TED: Course yer know.
>   [WIFE *takes down kitchen clock and winds it.*]
> It's fast. Quarter've an hour.
>   [WIFE *turns hands back. Puts clock back on mantelpiece.*]
> TED: Man bein' made a bloody fool of.
> WIFE: What d'yer mean?
> TED: Mean? They're all talkin' about it.
> WIFE: About what?
> TED: About him [*jerks head in direction of next door farm*] and her.

One knows that it is all artifice; that only writing *designed* to produce an effect of naturalness draws from us this tribute of recognition— a sense of truth, a renewed awareness of something known and forgotten, known and not-known. It isn't a plain copy of life, but a selective imitation. But in comparison with the method of Patrick White's drama, for instance, or of Mathew's own in *Sing for St. Ned*, these are naturalistic plays in speech, action, setting,

15

characters. The passages I have quoted indicate the *sine qua non* of the naturalistic writer—an ear for the speech rhythms of a kind of people a writer knows intimately, an eye for what such people do with their heads, hands, and feet, and a sensitive nose for atmosphere. All this, too, one could say of Lawler and Seymour. Yet something seems to distinguish these plays from the *Doll* and *The One Day*, the best of our *well-made* plays to date, just as something separates these plays from the essentially non-naturalistic style of *The Season at Sarsaparilla*.

They have a timeless quality. The episodes they present invite us to feel that so it has been, is, and will be for many a long day, if not for ever. This is the unsaid something that comes over, from the stage or from the script of each play. *Rusty Bugles* gets it largely from construction: action goes round in circles, precisely because that is the misery of it all, as any man will tell you who was in one of the inaction stations during the 1939-45 war. He will tell you with wry laughter how he *recognizes* truth in this play, and that it is this circular movement, not forward nor back but round, that most tellingly re-creates the soldiers' lives in the days when life had only one aim—to get off that treadmill. So this circular structure gives the play the sense of *forever*.

Bunyip looks like a straight three-acter but plays like a merry-go-round: gin-rummy and grumbling, frustration, dreams and sentimental memories, birth, marriage, death, and love-making are steps on another treadmill that again is only sometimes funny.

Locke Elliott and Mathew are in the middle of their careers and can speak for themselves of what truth in play-writing means for them. Jack McKinney's death in December 1966 has left me with a responsibility to make available some of his lively writing on this subject. I have therefore devoted the rest of this introduction to *The Well* and to his notes about it.

Jack McKinney, author of *The Well*, had a very short "career" as a playwright. He began writing plays only in 1959, seven years before he died. I don't think he ever wrote another play as good as this one, which was his first, but he did write others, mainly one-acts. (By the way it should be recorded that he had much earlier written scripts for radio, a novel, and some miscellaneous work sometimes involving dialogue, which partly accounts for the

16

extraordinary talent he displayed—out of the blue, as it seemed—for dialogue.)

At this point I have a confession to make. He wrote *The Well*, which he called, in the first draft, *Truth Lies at the Bottom of a Well*, as a tragic play. It was a Romeo and Juliet love story in which the lovers jumped into the well in despair because Mary was pregnant and Charlie under age, and because they were ignorant of what they could do and the feud seemed hopeless. Their deaths brought the two families to a wordless recognition of their folly and presumably to some sort of reconciliation—the last scene was a mimed "discovery" scene, with no words spoken. The shock of this ending after the high comedy of the first act seemed to me to outrage the form, and McKinney accepted my judgment. I don't think he had realized just how funny the first act was. Anyhow he rewrote the last act and modified the play in one or two earlier places to fit with a happy ending. To this day I'm not sure I was right to interfere, being normally convinced that writers know, at the ends of their fingers, more about what they're doing than the brash critic and the omniscient theatre-producer.

Be that as it may, McKinney professed himself happy in the change, and we got the play on at Twelfth Night Theatre. Later he entered the first act in a one-act competition and won it. It's a classic one-acter, with the cow down the well, and the reluctant neighbours who suddenly turn so efficient when they realize it's *their cow*. But the second act plays just as well—less hilariously but with curiously touching effect in the studies of inarticulate, suffering, worrying man and wife. The "business"—with tea-towels and cups and pathetic embroidery—is incredibly well-written: only when you come to play it do you realize how exactly the actors can follow the writer's detailed direction, and how meaningful it is.

The McKinney dramaturgy was no accident: Jack McKinney was forever—once he began play-writing—jotting down on sheets of green note-paper ideas that he would send with a proviso that no answer was needed—he was just working things out. A propos of a one-act called *No Pauper Was I*—a gently wrought evocation of an incident in the life of the poet Shaw Neilson—he wrote:

I find myself working on the theory that if the characters are

17

real people, and not just there to tell a story, the thing has a chance of going over, even for those who don't quite see the point. The theory seems to be that life is interesting in itself.

If the characters are only there to tell a story—*Tea and Sympathy*—it is only action that will justify them. Insufficient action and the thing fails. But if the characters are there primarily because they are real people in their own right—real people in a real human situation—then (so runs the theory, which I am only now getting clear in my own mind) the thing should be able to sustain itself with a minimum of action. And if then there is a story or idea implicit in the thing—those people in that situation—that is something to the good, an extra which those who get it will have free of charge, so to speak, and those who don't won't miss it.

That's the theory. But I've never known a theory to quite work out.

Asked for something as a programme note for *The Well*, he wrote, again working it out as he went, so that it wasn't a programme note but an essay:

How this play came to be written—

It all came about in a rather haphazard way. During a wet weekend at a lake-side cottage in the Queensland wallum country, I read one of those realistic novels in which everybody was very abrupt and blunt and down-to-earth and there was a general air of no-damned-nonsense. But the whole thing was a fake. It was a tough-guy story with a soft sentimental writer. All those bold blunt characters had been talking one way and acting another.

"But", I found myself asking, "could the author have done any different? Could a set of semi-illiterate, near-inarticulate characters, if they were presented with truth, with genuine not fake realism, be made the vehicle of a story?"

"Well why not?" I found myself arguing. "They're human beings, whether they can express their thoughts or not—whether they have any thoughts to express or not. They suffer all the basic emotions that we all suffer. Being less articulate they are merely less apt at concealing what is going on inside them.

"In fact," the argument continued, "mightn't their very inarticulateness make them the ideal vehicle for a story? Not, of course, in the way that the characters brought together by a playwright are made to say the things that will tell the story he has in mind. These inarticulate people couldn't be made to do that because they didn't have the necessary words. The story would have to be one which they, being the sort of people they are, will be acting out with complete innocence of what they are doing. They would have to *be* the story, not to *tell* it."

And then it occurred to me: perhaps, because of their very want of thought and words, because of their very spiritual nakedness, they might have something to tell us about ourselves, about our own inner workings, of which we are usually quite unconscious.

But this at once raised another point. If these people *were* to disclose anything of interest about themselves and us, there would be no taking sides on the part of the author; I couldn't either like or dislike any of my characters. I mustn't suggest in any way that *these* were "goodies" and *those* "baddies" (even if, presumptuously, I thought I knew). There could be no favouritism. The facts—these people as they actually are and do—must be presented without any interference on my part, and the audience allowed to judge for themselves.

(For, without any deliberate intention on my part, the thing was already falling into shape as a play.)

That of course might impose an unusual responsibility on the audience. The accepted convention is, I think, that the author shall give a clear lead at the outset as to what sort of play it is going to be, and which way the audience is to let its sympathies flow. In this case, that wouldn't be playing fair, either with the audience or with the characters in the play. The audience and the characters must work the thing out together, so to speak, the character doing and saying what he must as the sort of person he is in those given circumstances, the audience coming to their own conclusions, without any interference from the author, as to what it all amounted to.

There seemed to be some doubt, for a time, as to whether the play was a tragedy or a comedy. But that is easily understood, for after all Tragedy and Comedy are twins, and in real life it is often difficult to tell one from the other.

"The character doing and saying what he must as the sort of person he is in those given circumstances." Jack McKinney had a serene respect for individuals as individuals; his creative gift was precisely the capacity to *realize*—to render on paper—individuals, doing and saying what they must, not for a plot or a laugh or a tear but because they were that sort of person in that situation. If a plot or a laugh or a tear came out of what they said or did, that was, as he said, a bonus. And it was almost bound to come, if he rendered them with truth, because that was life. In a way it all sounds fairly simple, but it is a thing that each writer discovers for himself, if he discovers it at all; and certainly many of our playwrights never discovered it, never discover it. Mathew said it in his own way once, declaring that it was when he began plotting that truth seemed hard to keep hold of. Louis Esson, to go farther back, used to quote Tolstoy's criticism of something of Gorky's: "You invented that." It is probably significant that McKinney loved to read the letters of Chekhov.

By comparison with this direct, unforced method, the plays of plot, craft, and cunning tend to seem artificial. I mean, of course, among plays that are primarily naturalistic: we are not coming into competition with the great verse dramas. Indeed we are not coming into competition at all: there is room for many kinds of play, the well-made, the comedy of manners, the poetic, the farcical, the absurd, the protesting, the cruel, the epic.

Again, on this last, McKinney had something fascinating to say, his own intense concern with philosophy taking him quickly to a point for which others grope for years. He had been working on a redraft of *The Well* in the light of the experience of production, and in the light of criticism, enthusiastic but probing, from poet Tom Shapcott and others, and talking of the pleasure he had felt at the audience-response to the play:

. . . in fact it seems to me that everybody did [that is, did "see the play we put on"] except the two professional critics in the audience. It would almost seem that the effort to exercise the critical function inhibits the exercise of the critical function."

But then he began to talk of production.

Look, as I finished the job a strange idea occurred to me. The play is meant to be a piece of pure realism—as-pure-as-possible realism, that is. It was meant to achieve the utmost of audience participation, in contradistinction to Brecht's "alienation" principle. It was to be realism-for-truth's-sake—not realism for realism's sake, as with Tennessee Williams. I have the feeling that the "alienation" principle, by preventing the onlooker from feeling the situation in his blood, allows him to evade the challenge that the situation presents—or should present. It seems to me that Brecht's much-discussed principle, though interesting as a technical innovation, misses its point. (Am I presumptuous? But anyway . . .)

However I begin to think that the realistic approach may suffer from a corresponding defect—as a vehicle of truth, that is. The more realistic, the more the onlooker gets to feel and know the persons in the play and their predicament, the more he is induced to see it as a *particular* case. The very sharpness of focus prevents him from seeing—rather feeling—its wider implications. The more clearly he sees the particular the less able he is to see the universal of which it is an instance. So he too, like the "alienated" onlooker, misses the real point.

Well, what I suddenly saw was the possibility of combining the two principles in the one production and so, perhaps, overcoming their defects. It was Bob Dick's skeleton set (on which I congratulated him) that gave me the idea. Why not a particularised realistic, concrete action against an impressionistic, abstract setting? I mean, carry this right to its logical limits. The props (stove, table, chairs etc.) would be treated realistically, but not only would the set be abstract in the extreme—merely a hint of doors, windows, walls etc.—so that you would have a concrete action standing out starkly against an abstract background, *here* everything (action, word, gesture) in sharp focus, *there* everything vague and indeterminate; but, further, the players, when they went "off", would not leave the stage, they would stand about in the indeterminate surround, awaiting their next entry, or simply watching the other players, themselves in full view of the audience—the alienation principle at work—one minute they are persons, involved in the action of the play, the next they are part—a privileged part—of the audience. Is it fantastic?

But that isn't all. There is no real curtain, to mark the interval between scenes: only a very open-gauze curtain—a mere symbol curtain—behind which, though not with the clarity of the action of the play itself, the scene-shifting can be seen by the audience, so that the spectacle they see is not only the play itself but the presentation of the play. But further, the actors themselves help with the scene-shifting and can be recognized through the gauze of the curtain by the audience, so that, as it were, they can be seen *preparing their own destiny*, as we all do, unwittingly, prepare our own destiny.

Do you see what I mean? Realism, brought to the sharpest possible focus because contrasted with an abstract background, leading to the utmost of participation; and alienation, deliberately counteracting the realistic spell. (Charles Blackman complained that *The Well* was too short—he became so absorbed in it that it seemed to last only five minutes, he said.) The particular and the universal reinforcing and complementing one another.

Then McKinney went on to wonder how theatre-in-the-round, which he had read of but not seen, might fulfil his requirements. Without it he had, of course, worked himself back to the Elizabethans and the Commedia dell'Arte.

If any director does try a production of *The Well* along the lines its author here suggested, I hope he will make known the result and his deductions from this. Jack McKinney didn't kid himself— that would have been his expression—on being a theatre man. "It was just an idea," he would say; "I had to get it out of my system." But what was a conclusion for him might well be a beginning for someone else. That was the kind of a person he was: that was the kind of play he wrote.

Eunice Hanger
Department of English
University of Queensland

SUMNER LOCKE ELLIOTT

rusty bugles

characters of the play
in order of appearance
and original cast

The play was first produced on 21 October 1948 at the Independent Theatre, Sydney, with the following cast in order of appearance:

DES NOLAN (the Gig Ape):	John Kingsmill
VIC RICHARDS:	Ivor Bromley-Smith
SERGEANT BROOKS:	Sidney Chambers
ROD CARSON:	Ronald Frazer
ANDY EDWARDS (the little corporal):	Robert Crome
ERIC OTFORD:	Alistair Roberts
MAC:	Frank O'Donnell
OLLIE:	John Unicomb
CHRIS:	Kevin Healy
DARKY MCCLURE:	Lloyd Berrell
KEGHEAD STEPHENS:	Ralph Peterson
CORPORAL:	(Doubled)
KEN FALCON ("Dean Maitland"):	Michael Barnes
FIRST PRIVATE:	Jack Wilkinson
SECOND PRIVATE:	James Lyons
BILL HENRY (YMCA sergeant):	Frank Curtain
PRIVATE:	Peter Hartland
JACK TURNER (Sigs corporal):	(Doubled)
SIGS PRIVATE:	(Doubled)
SAMMY KUHN:	Kenneth Colbert

The entire action takes place at an Ordnance Depot about seventy miles south of Katherine, in the Northern Territory of Australia, in the year 1944.

The play was produced by Doris Fitton, and the scenery executed by Steve Hodgkinson.

This is a documentary. It is not strictly a play. It has no plot in the accepted sense. Its characters are drawn from life—they all existed, and I knew and loved them well. Their names have been altered, but I think in every respect they have been reproduced exactly.

The events of their lives whilst they were cut off from home, family, and normal life, and which have been here reproduced, are authentic, and no one event in the play is fictional. In some cases for convenience of stagecraft some events have been condensed into a shorter time period.

The play is set in the great Northern Territory of Australia during the winter months of the year 1944. From early April until about the beginning of October is the dry season, hot during the day and cold at night, the ideal climate for winter. The six months' action of the play is exactly the time that I myself spent in the Territory on this lonely strip of barren and seemingly endless sandy waste of ant hills and stunted trees—thick, hot red sand in the winter time and a sea of mud during the dreaded "Wet", which begins in October and lasts until March. We lived in wet weather huts and worked in iron buildings shaped like igloos. We were the ordnance clerks, storemen, drivers, and engineers of one of the largest supply depots in the North, during the latter part of the war. We never saw a single Jap plane, we were never bombed, machine-gunned or sniped at like our pals in New Guinea, who were never free of excitement, we thought. We were the backwash. No one knew we existed and yet we did—several hundred of us in this wasted red dust bowl where some of us had already been for three years, and long awaited leave seemed ever further away.

These boys were the ones who had to fight ANOTHER kind of enemy . . . boredom. They groused and complained a lot but they had reason. They used bad language like all soldiers and like all soldiers they sat and dreamed about LEAVE.

I have tried to reproduce six months at a Northern Territory Ordnance Depot as I knew it. I have not restrained anything. It is all there . . . even the bad language to a large extent because it is utterly dissociated from the story. From those who may be shocked I ask forgiveness and tolerance because I, too, was shocked at first, until the constant repetition drove all obscenity from the words and rendered them eventually as harmless as "bread and butter".

To these hard-headed, swearing, grubby, generous friends I dedicate *Rusty Bugles* . . .

ACT ONE

scene 1

The interior of a wet weather hut at Kallereena, an Advance Ordnance Depot in the Northern Territory, an autumn night in the year 1944.

A "Ferris" lamp hangs from a wooden beam and casts a hard white light on six rough camp-stretchers. Dimly outlined is a tin sloping roof and the hessian walls which are open at the bottom. An entrance is gained by the open framework of a door at each end of the hut, one entrance only being visible in this act. Each bed has a mosquito net hanging over it, some clumsily rolled on ropes at each corner of the bed. The bed at the end nearest the door has an occupant asleep with his net pulled down like a large meat safe around him. The floor is of rough white pebbles. Beside each bed is a soldier's box. Some of the boxes are open, their contents strewn over the floor . . . tins . . . empty bottles; and newspapers untidily bestrewn, for it is late in the evening and inspections are over for the day. Beyond the entrance a lamp is hanging from the branch of an enormous tree and vague figures pass in silhouette around a table where the "swy" game is in progress. The voices of the callers drone on just near enough to be unpleasantly distracting.

The hut is almost deserted. VIC RICHARDS *in his "long-uns" and long-sleeved jersey, with bare feet, is sitting astride the end of his bed hitting nails into the canvas with the heel of his boot. On the bed opposite,* DES NOLAN, *known as the* "GIG APE", *is stretched in an uncomfortable position on his back, trying to get the best light for reading. Occasionally he reaches over and gropes on the floor for a bottle of violently colored liquid with which he slakes his thirst.*

A minute passes . . .

VOX [*off*]: A quid he heads 'em. Up and do 'em, spinner.
    [*Slight pause and then a roar of approval from crowd.*]
    Heads pay . . . Pay the heads . . . Heads they are . . .
    [VIC *continues to hammer in the nails.*]

29

VOX [*off*]: I'll spin 'em for a quid . . . Get set in the guts . . . Come on now . . . Another two bob for the guts . . . Who'll be in the guts? . . .

[GIG APE *sighs and turns a page.*]

VOX [*off*]: Get set on the side . . .

[*The subdued murmur of voices continues.* VIC *gets one nail and starts on another.*]

GIG [*quietly*]: Give it a rest.

VIC: What?

GIG [*yelling*]: I said give it a rest! . . . Wot's up with you?

VIC: What's wrong?

GIG: I'm trying to read, that's what, and you're hitting bloody nails in the bed. That's what!

VIC [*springing up*]: Yeah—well I've had getting into bed and scratching my legs every time.

GIG: Why don't you get another bed well—galah.

VIC: Bit of a galah yourself, aren't you?

GIG [*turning back to his book*]: Aw . . . get ripped.

VIC: Get ripped yourself. [*He starts to whistle and continues to knock the nails in a little harder this time.*]

[SGT. BROOKS *comes in. He is thirty and sullen and without humour. He is wearing his hat and is dressed in long pants, jersey, and webbing belt and gaiters. He is followed by a tired and dirty soldier*—ROD CARSON. ROD *is in travel-stained summer dress and carries full equipment, rifle, and webbing. He is carrying a full kit-bag on his shoulder. He stands behind* BROOKS *in the shadow, shifting the bag to an easier position on his shoulder.*]

[VIC *glances up.*]

BROOKS: You got a spare bed in here?

VIC: No.

GIG: We got ten in here already.

BROOKS: Not since McCarthy went to hospital you haven't.

VIC: We got our mob in here . . . We don't want any RSD mob in here. [*He goes on hitting nails.*]

BROOKS [*pointing to an empty bed next to* VIC]: Who's in there?

VIC: That's Occa Stevens.

BROOKS [*to* ROD]: O.K. Bring your things in here . . . You can have that bed for tonight.

[ROD *moves up with his kit into the light.* VIC *and* GIG *look up.*]

VIC [*to* BROOKS]: What are you trying on? That's Occa's bed.

BROOKS: Occa's been transferred over to "A" Company, hasn't he? [*Sourly*] Whaddye trying to do, keep the whole bloody place to yourself?

VIC: We got our own mob in here.

[ROD *starts to put his kit back on his shoulder.*]

BROOKS: Who's your hut corporal?

VIC: Andy Edwards.

BROOKS: Where is he?

VIC. How do you expect me to know where he is?

GIG: He's over at the school.

[BROOKS *gives them a dirty look. Goes to the door and yells.*]

BROOKS: Andy Edwards . . . Andy Edwards there?

VOX [*off*]: Went mad and they shot 'im.

VOX 2: Went through like Speed Gordon.

BROOKS [*to* ROD]: Wait here a sec . . . [*He goes out.*]

[ROD *puts down his pack and takes off his hat and wipes his head. His face is travel-stained and weary. He looks sick at heart. He gives* VIC *a sickly little smile.*]

ROD: H'lo.

VIC: How are you? [*without a smile.*]

GIG: Just march in, did you?

ROD: Just came in.

GIG [*excitedly*]: Gees! . . . Hey! . . . are you replacements?

ROD: I don't know.

GIG: Where're you from?

ROD: Sydney.

VIC: You didn't come in on the train?

ROD: No, they brought us up from Larrimah by utility. [*He sits on the bed exhausted.*] I've been eighteen days travelling.

GIG: Are you on your own?

ROD: No, five of us came up together.

GIG: FIVE!

VIC: Is that all?

ROD: Yes, that's all. Why, how many were you expecting?

GIG [*scathingly*]: Only about five hundred, that's all. Only about five hundred.

VIC: Any more coming after you?

ROD: Not that I know of. We were just an isolated draft from Sydney. Why . . . have you been expecting replacements?

GIG: Have we? [*He laughs raucously.*] Those bludgers promised us two-year blokes we'd all be out of here in March.

ROD [*taking out a wilted packet of cigarettes*]: How long have you been here?

GIG: Oh, I'm only a newcomer . . .

ROD: How long?

GIG: Fourteen months. [*Pointing to* VIC] He's been here just on thirty. [*Pointedly*] Thanks mate, I could do with a tailor-made.

ROD: Oh sure. [*Offers him a cigarette.*]

[GIG *takes one. Proudly* ROD *hands the packet to* VIC *who takes one and nods without smiling.*]

GIG: 'Owd you come to get sent to this bastard of a place?

ROD [*shrugging his shoulders as* GIG *lights his cigarette*]: One of those things.

GIG: Gees, you certainly got rotten stinking luck. This is the greatest bastard of a place on earth. You never get out of here, mate—I'm drumming you. [*Laughs.*] Gees . . . you wait and see.

[BROOKS *returns, followed by* ANDY EDWARDS *who is a minute little bloke but cocky with the deliberate assurance of the very small.*]

BROOKS [*to* ROD]: This is Corporal Edwards . . . He'll look after you . . .

ANDY [*sprightly*]: Well, well—pleased to meet you mate.

BROOKS [*to* ROD]: You got any blankets?

ROD: Yes. Carrying them.

BROOKS: O.K., then . . . You can get your soldier's box and the rest from the Q store in the morning. You'll be reporting to Headquarters at about nine o'clock so you won't be on parade in the morning. Just report up to the R.S.M.'s tent . . . The boys will show you where to go. [*He goes out.*]

ANDY: Just get in, did you?

ROD: Yes, my name's Rod Carson.

ANDY: I'm Andy Edwards and this is Vic Richards and Des Nolan. [*Points to* GIG] He's the Gig Ape. [ROD *forces a smile.*] Yeah, I'm tellin' you . . . the greatest gig ape in the territory. Only fourteen months here and he's troppo . . . Know what he does this morning? . . . Gets out of bed at reveille and goes off to shave with his spoon and fork.

[GIG APE *laughs*.]

I'm telling you . . . the greatest . . .

GIG: Yeah . . . a bloke'ud have to go troppo in a hut full of drongoes like youse.

ANDY: The Gig Ape, eh . . . [*Getting* GIG *in a stranglehold by the neck*] The old Gig Ape . . .

GIG [*struggling with him*]: Yeah, you dirty little sawn-off troppo runt.

[*They wrestle fiercely*.]

VIC: Aw, cut it out. [*He gets up irritably and starts making his bed*.]

ANDY: Give us some lolly water. [*He picks up* GIG APE'S *bottle and takes a long swig*.] Gee . . . it's that stinkin' citronella stuff again. How are they . . . [*Puts bottle back under bed*.]

[ROD *has commenced unpacking his kit bag and has produced some grubby-looking shorts and underclothes and odds and ends of socks, a mirror, and shaving kit*.]

They give you any tea?

ROD: Yes, I had tea before I left Larrimah. We were coming up on the train in the morning but there was a truck leaving and I think they wanted to get rid of us.

ANDY: How many of you came up?

ROD: Five.

ANDY: Five! [*Turns round to* GIG APE] FIVE!

GIG: Five . . . only five come. He reckons there are more on the way though.

ANDY: More coming, are there? [*He sits on bed R. Back*.] Got any good guts on replacements?

ROD: 'Fraid not. We were just pitched out on our own in Sydney.

ANDY: Sydney, eh? How is the Big Smoke?

ROD [*nostalgically*]: I'd give all my deferred pay to see it right now.

GIG [*laughing*]: Gees, listen to him. He's only just come and he wants to see the Big Smoke again already.

ROD [*to* ANDY]: You from Sydney?

ANDY: No, Perth. [*Getting up*] How are you off for blankets?

ROD: O.K. They gave us blankets in Brisbane.

33

ANDY: Oh, came up by Isa, did you?

ROD: Townsville, Mount Isa, Camooweal . . . eighteen days. Five days and nights from Mount Isa in a convoy. Mostly Air Force blokes going back to Darwin from leave.

GIG: The Blue Orchids are curl the Mo . . . Leave!

ANDY: Leave, what's that?

[*Suddenly from outside in the distance come three ominous clangs from an iron rail being struck against a swinging iron sleeper.*]

VOX [*loudly, far away*]: Belt it.

ROD: What's that? Lights out?

ANDY: Three bells before. You've got a quarter of an hour.

[ROD *starts getting out pyjamas. Takes off his webbing.* GIG APE *is undressing.* VIC *takes toothbrush and mug and goes off outside.*]

VOX [*off*]: Two bob we head 'em . . . Come on . . . Last go tonight. Last go tonight . . . Who'll be in it . . . Two bob in the guts.

[ANDY *starts making his bed.*]

ANDY: You'll need all your blankets.

ROD: Does it get cold here?

ANDY: Gees . . . does it! Round about three in the morning, from now till about September.

GIG: Wait till you've done a flamin' guard.

ROD: Do you get guard duty much here?

GIG: Do you? Every five or six nights. I copped picture night last Thursday and I'll cop it again Saturday week, too. Hey, Andy, if we get that Betty Grable pitcher that night, I'm goin' to swop with Ot.

ANDY: Don't give us 'em. Catch young Ot missing Betty Grable. [*He whistles.*]

GIG: Ot don't always go to the pitchers anyway. Last time he stayed in and done all his washing. What did he do that for, then?

ANDY: Makin' up his losses. See how young Ot makes out tonight.

[ERIC OTFORD *comes in. He is tall and gangling, has violent red hair and freckles.*]

OT: Done the lot . . . Done the flamin' lot . . . Yeah, done me thirty quid. How's a bloke's luck . . . I start out headin' 'em and then . . . [*He stops, seeing* ROD.]

ANDY: This is er . . .

ROD: Rod Carson.

34

ANDY: Yeah . . . Eric Otford . . . usually referred to as Ot.

OT: How are you? [*He comes over and shakes hands excitedly.*] Hey . . . are you in with the replacements?

GIG and ANDY: There are only five.

OT: And the rest.

ROD: 'Fraid not.

OT: FIVE!

ROD: That's all.

OT: Well, how flamin' are they, the rats. [*To* ROD] Hey are they sending any more up after you?

ROD: Not that I know of.

GIG: Where you from? First Base Ordnance?

ROD: No, I wasn't in Ordnance . . . I was in a liaison office in Barracks. [*Smiles ruefully.*] Base bludger, I'm afraid . . . but they kicked me out . . . I was A1.

ANDY: Fancy copping Ordnance.

GIG: You'll be here for the rest of your flamin' life.

OT [*leaping upon him*]: The Gig Ape . . . the Gig Ape . . .

[*A tussle ensues and the* GIG APE *gets a beating on the head.*]
[*Outside the voices subside and the lamp moves off. It comes nearer the tent and a voice says:*]

VOX: I'll see you in the morning then, Alan . . . Goodnight.

[MAC *comes in. He is a heavily built man in his late thirties.* ANDY *bristles.*]

ANDY: Finished blood suckin' the poor for another night . . .

MAC: Aw, get ripped, you rotten little sawn-off runt . . . I lose more than they ever make. Hello. Hello . . . Who's deigning to offer their company to the poor bastards at Kallereena?

OT: This is Rod Carson. Rod, meet Mac, the biggest bloodsucker.

ROD: Rod Carson's the name.

MAC: Who stuck you up here, mate?—and I'll go for 'em.

[*There is loud laughter.* GIG APE *succeeds in getting into bed unmolested for a moment.*]

Ever been North before?

ROD: First time.

MAC: Gees . . . Wait until you've done a Wet, mate. Just wait. I done four.

ANDY: My fat aunt you done four—you done two.

MAC [*roaring*]: I done four. I came here in 1940.

ANDY: Yeah, and you had one whole Wet away having twins.

MAC: I had two bloody months away in '42 and two months away last August. This is me third flamin' round and you're a new-comer. One of the rookies . . . come here in '42.

ANDY [*twisting the subject*]: Yeah . . . don't forget you're hut orderly tomorrow and you better clean up some of the mess you made with all your tins of salted peanuts. Wimpy will be on your back tomorrow.

MAC: Yeah, with you. You rotten little pimping sawn-off runt. [*Then casually*] Have a drink of lolly water?

ANDY: No thanks, pet.

MAC: How'd you do tonight?

ANDY: Only stayed in for a few rounds. Made ten bob.

MAC: Good enough.

[*Two bells heard*]

MAC [*yelling*]: Belt it. Belt the rotten flamin' bell. [*Then quietly*] Who's Orderly Officer tonight?

GIG: The Crab.

MAC: The filthy rotten Crab, he'd better not come the raw prawn on us. Better get your nets down tonight, mate. Hey, and if he cops us with that Ferris Lamp here we'll all be on an A4 tomorrow. [*Imitates the Crab*] Er, Private Nolan, this practice will cease forthwith; now I've warned you and I don't intend to warn you again. You will attend hygiene parade for a week . . . Next case.

[*Roars of laughter greet this. VIC returns and goes to his bed. He undresses to his underwear and singlet and hops in. Pulls out a book from under the pillow.*]

ROD: Where can I get a wash? [*Rises.*]

ANDY: I'm going over to the showers now. Take you over.

ROD: Thanks. [*Picks up towel, toothbrush, etc.*]

MAC [*holding the lamp down to his soldier's box*]: Eh . . . Who's got down on me Violet Crumble Bars? . . . One of 'em's gone. I had eight.

ANDY: Blame the white ants. [*To ROD*] Eat anything. Ate right through the leg of my bed one night. Collapsed. Stand too long in one place and they'll eat you up to your knees.

MAC [*attacking* ANDY]: It was you, you rotten little . . .

ANDY: Aw, get ripped. They'd break my plate.

MAC: You're the only one that would pinch a man's tucker from his box. Next time have a read of my letters too, eh?

ANDY [*to* ROD]: Come on . . . [*To* OT] Put out the Ferris.

    [OT *is lighting a hurricane lamp.*]

    [*Ferris lamp out.*]

GIG: Hey Andy, the waterbag's empty.

    [ANDY *gets the waterbag and he and* ROD *exit. Centre.*]

MAC: The little Corporal got down on my Violet Crumble Bars. [*He sits heavily on his bed and starts counting chocolate bars.*] I'll fix him . . . filthy little sawn-off pimp, you wait. [*Yells outside*] A great thing when a man can't trust his own bloody pals.

OT: There it is under the bed. [*He stretches*] Hey, how'd the new bloke be?

GIG: Decent enough.

VIC: Yeah, well we got our own mob in here. He's in Occa's bed.

MAC: Since when have you and Occa been pals?

VIC: He's one of our mob, isn't he?

MAC: He's gone over to "A" Company.

VIC: Yeah, well I don't like all sorts coming into our hut.

    [*He kicks* ROD'S *shaving mug off his bed where* ROD *had placed it. It breaks.*]

OT: That's a clever bloody thing to do.

    [*There's a moment's silence.*]

VIC: Yeah, well why doesn't he leave things on his own bed. [*Turns over and pulls his net down.*]

MAC [*singing airily but out of tune*]: "By the shade of the old apple tree there's a tear in her dress I can see. I can see da da da and a lot of whacko diddle de . . ."

    [OLLIE *and* CHRIS *appear in the doorway. They are both privates—both twenty and both crazy.*]

CHRIS: Hey, we got two of the new replacements in our hut.

OT: We got one in here.

OLLIE: They're only flamin' base bludgers . . . gee . . . you oughta hear them talk.

CHRIS: Cripes, you know what one of them asks Smokums, "Ow long before we get leave?"

[*Shouts of laughter from all.*]

'Ow is the bastard . . . only here five minutes and asks when he's goin' to get leave.

OLLIE [*rolling with glee*]: Yeah but the other one—big lanky drongo he is too—looks up and asks me, "Is there hot showers?"

GIG: Tell the bludgers they'll be in plenty of hot water once Wimpy gets the old claws on them.

[*Hoots of mirth all round.*]

OLLIE: Smokums takes off the old specs and says: "Youse'll be lucky if you get out of here under five years." Gee you ought've seen their faces.

MAC [*fumbling in soldier's box*]: What rotten bastard's taken me glass? . . . Where's me glass?

GIG [*reaching down beside his bed*]: Here y'are.

MAC: Wouldn't ask a bloke before you take his things, would you?

CHRIS: Ollie and I have picked out our replacements . . . We're goin' to put the screw on Red Robbie tomorrow to get us on Leave Draft.

GIG: Yeah? There's only five of these new drongoes come up and it's only us two-years blokes'll be goin'.

OLLIE: When did you come up here?

GIG: June '42.

OLLIE: Oh, get ripped—you wasn't here when the dunny blew up.

GIG: Oh, wasn't I?

[*One bell.*]

VOICES OFF: Get those lights out.

CHRIS [*to* OLLIE]: Come on, lights out.

OLLIE: Where's the new bloke? I wanna see the new bloke.

GIG: He's out getting a hot shower and a Turkish bath with a manure cure.

[*Shrieks of laughter.*]

VIC [*putting head out of net*]: Oh turn it up . . . How's a bloke to get any sleep?

CHRIS: See y'after. Onya. Onya.

OLLIE: Onya.

OT [*yelling after them as they go*]: ONYA ONYA YOU BEAUT. [*Finishes undressing and with one bound is in bed. The next he is standing on his head on the stretcher.*] How am I? How am I?

MAC: Wot you've got don't look no better upside down.

[ANDY *and* ROD *return carrying the lamp and the waterbag.*]

ROD: Not much of a shower, is it? [*Looks at* OT *suspended in mid air.*]

ANDY: Oh don't mind Ot. He's on the exercises just now. It's always something new.

[OT *returns to normal side up. Starts arms out exercises squatting in bed.* ROD *goes to his bed and picks up broken mug. Looks at it frowning and upset.* ANDY *is undressing.* MAC *is sitting on his bed drinking lolly water out of his glass.*]

Here . . . you better have the lamp . . . and don't be long . . . We'll get copped for having the light still on. [*He comes over.*] Something broke?

ROD: It's my shaving mug.

ANDY: Gee they're hard to get up here too . . . 'Owd you do that? . . .

ROD [*glancing at next bed. Pause. Everyone watches him*]: I must have knocked it off the bed in the dark.

ANDY: Well don't be too long . . . You can unpack the rest of your gear in the morning . . . They always give you the first day off to do your washing . . . the grudging bastards . . . [*Gets into bed.*] And don't forget you're on the roster to clean up the hut tomorrow, sweetheart . . . [*to* MAC].

[MAC *belches loudly.*]

OT [*pummelling chest . . . loudly*]: Ahhhhhhhhh . . .

VIC: Pipe down, Otford. Give it a rest, Tauber.

OT [*lying down in bed*]: Ahhh. The old bed, she's not too bad . . . Hey . . . I'm on flamin' guard tomorrow night.

MAC: Thank flamin' hell for that.

OT [*dreamily*]: Oh well, I guess the little Rosebud's laying down right this minute in Kalgoorlie thinking of me.

MAC: Aren't the Yanks in Kalgoorlie?

OT [*ignoring this*]: The old Rosebud, eh . . . About time I had a letter from her. 'Owd it be, 'owd it be to be with her now, eh? Gee, a bloke wouldn't know what to do after all this time.

MAC: You little perv, you. [*Gets into bed heavily, belching.*]

ANDY: Dirty old galah. Why don't you ever wash your face before getting into bed?

[*Silence for second. Only light coming from lamp, where* ROD *is unpacking.*]

39

VOX [*off*]: Get me out of this place.

[*Sleepy laughter.*]

MAC [*giggling*]: That's Ollie. He's a card all right. [*Snore or two.*]

ANDY: Bloody Gig Ape's off. Back bettin' 'em on the tote in Perth.

MAC: I suppose you think Perth discovered the tote.

ANDY: Aw, get ripped, you dirty Queensland dope.

MAC: Get ripped yourself. [*Pause . . . agreeably*] G'night, Andy.

ANDY: G'night, Mac.

[*Torch and* SGT. BROOKS *enter.*]

BROOKS: Who's still got a light on in here?

ROD: I have—sorry.

BROOKS: Didn't you hear one bell?

ROD: Yes.

BROOKS: Don't you know that means lights out? You get the lamp out.

ROD: I'm just getting my things out.

BROOKS: You don't need a light for that. You get that lamp out.

ROD: I'm just getting my things out.

BROOKS: You don't need a lamp for that. I'll have the Orderly Officer on me.

ROD: Sorry.

BROOKS: You're in camp now, not the Hotel Australia.

ANDY: Aw, give him a break—wot's wrong with you?

BROOKS: I don't want any backchat from you, Edwards . . . You're hut corp. and you ought to see the lights are out.

[ROD *turns light out.*]

And make sure the hut is better cleaned out tomorrow than it was yesterday or you'll all be copping C.B. for a week.

[*Goes out. Lights out. Wrathful murmurs.*]

ANDY: Get back to the snake pit where you belong. [*To* ROD] Don't mind that big bullying galah. You better get some sleep now.

ROD: Thanks, Andy.

ANDY: Goodnight.

[*Train whistle.*]

VOICES OFF: Here come the replacements! . . . Here they come!

(*End of Scene*)

ACT ONE

scene 2

Outside one of the ARMCO huts. Morning, two weeks later. We see only the corner of the sloping tin roof of the hut, a tree, and some large red anthills. There are a couple a wooden boxes outside the door and a waterbag hanging from a branch of the tree. As the lights go up DARKY MCCLURE *is sitting on a box, his back to the tree, making a fishing line. After a moment* ROD *comes out of the narrow doorway and goes to the waterbag. He fills his cup and drinks. Pauses and gasps for breath, wipes his forehead, resting his arms on the tree.* DARKY *looks up. He is a big, bulky, bright-eyed youth of twenty-one, full of poise and self-sufficiency.*

DARKY: Borrow your mug?

ROD: What? Oh sure. [*Laughs a little nervously as he is still on edge with strangers.*] It's hot this morning.

DARKY [*filling the cup*]: Hot? You haven't done a Wet yet, sport.

ROD: That's what everyone tells me. Wait until you've done a Wet, wait until you've done a Wet.

DARKY: Cripes, I done bloody three Wets. [*Drinks and spits water on the ground.*] Something died in that. [*Hands back his mug to* ROD.] Hey, do you work in Headquarters?

ROD: Yes, right here.

DARKY: In Q or Admin.?

ROD: Oh, bit of both. They found out I was a typist.

DARKY: Have you typed out my charge sheet?

ROD: What's your name?

DARKY: McClure.

ROD: McClure.

DARKY: Brian Benedict.

ROD: Oh yes, I remember . . . Yes, I typed it . . . Now I remember. I say, that isn't a very serious charge is it?

DARKY: Any charge that Wimpy Murdoch makes against you is a

41

death sentence unless you know how to toss him. Like I do.
I been on sixteen charge sheets since I come to this death valley.
I got out of twelve of them.

ROD [*impressed*]: Imagine that.

DARKY: Yes sir, I got out of twelve of them.

ROD: You must be pretty slick. They all say Captain Murdoch's
the Himmler of the Territory.

DARKY: That's understatin' him . . . I'm telling you once you get
into that old Wimpy's black books it's goodnight. He sent three
men up to Brooks Creek for having extra shirts in their kit bags.

ROD: Brooks Creek?

DARKY: That's the Stalag of the Territory, mate. Once you get
there it's all U.P. They have a suicide a day there . . . I'm telling
you . . . Make you do everything at the double . . . run to mess . . .
run back . . . run carrying a big friggin' log on your back . . . run
to the dike . . . Cripes, you should see them when they come back.

ROD: Have you been there?

DARKY: No, but my mate has. He's gone South now. He's nuts.
He's nutty as a fruit cake. Honest, I'm telling you if you don't
know how to toss Wimpy Murdoch you're not in the race. He'll
never give up. If you beat him he'll get you for something. Take
my cobber for instance. He gets copped writing a green envelope.

ROD: How do you mean? Giving away security and that sort of
thing?

DARKY: And the rest. My mate Sharpey writes to a Federal Member.
They shoot you for that up here if they cop you . . . I'm telling
you, true as I sit here. Sharpey writes green envelopes so's they
won't read it up here, but it gets intercepted down at Base
Censor, see, and they send it back to the Colonel . . . Well . . .
Was it on . . . They gets Sharpey in there on the mat and Wimpy's
ordering the truck for Brooks Creek and Sharpey throws him.

ROD: How do you mean?

DARKY: Sharpey says: "All the things in that letter that I've said
about this camp is true and you'll have to prove they're not before
you can charge me." See he writes all about the food and the
stink-hole outside the Mess and no leave for twenty-three months
. . . Well, it's all true, see, and the Colonel knows that he can't
bloody well disprove it . . . so Sharpey's got them see . . . Gets

42

off with a reprimand, scot free. Wimpy's tearing his hair with rage.

ROD: Gosh!

DARKY: But he gets Sharpey . . . He waits . . . sweatin' on him until he gets him . . . Cops him two nights later over at the pictures when he's supposed to be on guard and takes his stripes off him . . .

[*Enter* KEGHEAD, *worried and depressed. He is breathless.*]

KEGHEAD: Haven't they called you in yet?

DARKY: No.

KEGHEAD [*sits on box*]: Cripes, I'm sick . . . Gee, I've got a stomach ache that'd frighten your mother-in-law.

ROD: What's wrong?

KEGHEAD: Dysentery.

DARKY: Dysentery, my fanny.

KEGHEAD [*almost weeping*]: I tell you I got dysentery. I ought to know, oughtn't I? And now they put me on guard for you. What you up for this time?

DARKY [*laughing*]: Procuring a vehicle without permission and driving same out to the Red Lily Lagoon through the Elsie.

KEGHEAD: Cripes, you're mad.

DARKY: Had a damn good day. Did some shooting and fishing.

KEGHEAD: How'd you get copped?

DARKY: Dunno. Someone give me away. Bet it was bloody Brooks— he'd hear from Transport the truck was out.

[*Whistle.*]

ROD: Morning coffee.

KEGHEAD: Now we won't get in the Orderly Room till after tea.

DARKY: What's hurting you?

[*Enter* ANDY *and* VIC *with mugs. Then* GIG.]

GIG: Keghead.

[*Enter* CHRIS *and* OLLIE.]

Keghead. Keghead.

[*They rush at* KEG, *pull his hat off and tread on it.*]

KEGHEAD: Aw, get out will you . . . Look at me hat . . . How's a man's hat? I ask you . . . New yesterday from the Q Store, and look, me best puggaree . . . Cripes.

ANDY: Who's on the tea? . . . Who's on the tea?

VIC: Oh I am, sorry . . . [*Exit and enter again with dixie.*]

ANDY: Look out, Keghead, some biscuits in here somewhere. [*Produces box inside the butter box.*]

GIG: Aw, you can keep those flamin' things. Concrete. [*They drink their coffee.*]

OLLIE: How are they . . . In the flamin' hot weather they give you flamin' hot coffee to drink.

CHRIS: This isn't the flamin' hot weather, you flamin' drongo.

OLLIE: Aw, get ripped. [*Chases* CHRIS *off-stage.*]

ANDY: Well, Darky, old Wimpy'll be on your tail this time.

GIG: You won't get out of this one.

DARKY: Who says I won't?

ANDY: Old Wimpy's sitting in there with the glasses on the end of his conk . . . always a bad sign . . . getting ready to polish you off and incidentally, I saw on the . . .

[*He stops as* BROOKS *and a serious-looking* CORPORAL *enter. They are walking in step and go and get coffee.*]

BROOKS: And so I said: "But look here, sir, if you indent on a ledger account form, how are you going to show your discrepancies?"

CORP.: I bet that had him thinking.

BROOKS: Yes, that's what I said: "How are you going to show your discrepancies?"

[ANDY *pulls a face. Everyone is interested.*]

And so he said: "Well, what about your CRV's?"

CORP.: Good God, he didn't . . .

BROOKS: Yes, what about your CRV's. [*As they exit*] Now if he knew the first thing about Ordnance Ledgers he'd know that you can't do that. Each Sub-Unit must have its a/c number . . .

[*They have gone inside.*]

ANDY: He never talks about anything else.

KEGHEAD: Born crawler.

GIG: Cripes, this place is bad enough without a crawler.

VIC: Aw—give it away, someone's got to be keen.

ANDY: All right, no one's stopping you.

VIC: You blokes give me the tom-tits. Always bellyaching about something, aren't you? You wouldn't know yourselves if you really had something to bellyache about, would you?

ANDY: What's biting you?

VIC: Nothin's biting me except you always got some complaint. What the hell . . . You eat and sleep, don't you? . . . No one's firing at you. You got it a good deal better than those poor runts up in Lae, and all you talk about's going home to Mum.

[*All astounded at this lecture.*]

Wait until you've had something to hit you and smash your life to pulp.

[*Pause. Whistle blows.*]

ANDY: All right, blokes . . . back to the factory.

[*All go inside with exception of* KEGHEAD, DARKY, VIC, *and* ROD. ROD *has risen and is staring at* VIC. *He is suddenly touched and moved with the feeling of being near tragedy . . .* SGT. BROOKS *appears at the door.*]

BROOKS: Sergeant Stephens.

KEGHEAD: Yes.

BROOKS: Got your hat on?

[KEG *puts it on scornfully.*]

[*To* DARKY] All right, Corporal McClure . . . stand up. Put away that fishing line. [*Calls inside*] Private Nolan . . . are you ready?

GIG [*off*]: Just gettin' on me hat.

[GIG *appears in hat and full webbing equipment. Wearily, as though they have been through this so many times,* KEGHEAD *and* GIG APE *place themselves one before and one behind* DARKY.]

BROOKS: Attention.

[*They come wearily to attention.*]

[*Yelling*] Smarten up there, Corporal McClure . . . You're on a charge and don't forget it. Quick march.

[*They march off, with* SGT. BROOKS *following.* VIC *turns and looks for a moment at* ROD. ROD *smiles.* VIC *crosses him and goes into hut.*]

[*Blackout.*]

(*End of Scene*)

ACT ONE

scene 3

Sunday morning, a few days later. The hut again. The lazy vacuum of Sunday has spread over the camp in soporific haze. The hut is very untidy—boots, papers, and dirty clothes litter the floor. All the beds are unmade. A fiercely yellow sun beats down outside on the red anthills and stunted scrub. On a clothes line outside the door hangs a varied assortment of washing—shirts dripping, with their arms hanging down, and socks and shorts and underwear.

The scene opens: KEN FALCON, *a thin unshaven boy with a very serious face, is sitting on the end of his stretcher looking out the door.* OT *and* GIG *are lying on their backs.* GIG *has a copy of Army News, the small one-sheet newspaper of the Territory troops. On his bed in the corner,* MAC *is lying reading a "Western" and eating salted peanuts out of a tin beside him. For a while no one says anything. After a count of ten* OT *says:*

OT: How long do you reckon it would take a joker to walk from here to Adelaide, eh Gig?

GIG: . . . What?

OT: How long do you reckon it would take to walk from here to Adelaide?

GIG: I dunno. [*Pause.*] 'Bout three months, I reckon.

OT: Aw, get out.

GIG: Bet it would.

OT: Why would it?

GIG [*sitting up in bed*]: Well . . . we're 'ow far from Alice?

OT: 'Bout six hundred miles.

GIG: Yeah and Alice is about a thousand miles from Adelaide . . . Oh, go easy, you wouldn't do it under six months with your feet.

OT [*putting his feet directly over his head and regarding them*]: Wot's wrong with my feet?

GIG: They stink.

46

OT: Shut up!

GIG: Shut up yourself. Has the mail come in?

OT: Too early yet.

GIG: There'd better be a couple for me.

OT: The little Rosebud'll come good again today. [*Puts feet down. Pause.*] What do you bet me I couldn't do it under a month?

GIG: Do what?

OT: Get to Adelaide?

GIG: You're a mug liar . . . You couldn't walk . . .

OT: I never said anything about walking. 'Owd a joker be for getting onto a convoy at Larrimah?

GIG: Yeah . . . You'd never get as far as Larrimah before they found you was missing. Look at Darky McClure . . . He tried to go through . . . He only got as far as the turn-off to Maluka's Grave.

OT: Ah, he hasn't got the sense of a friggin' flea.

GIG: Hasn't he, by George? . . . He got out of his latest charge.

OT: Did he? How'd he get out of that? . . . He was a cert to go up for that, wasn't he? . . . Being up at Red Lily Lagoon in a stolen truck.

GIG [*laughing*]: He told them that he seen the Colonel up there too.

OT: He didn't, did he? . . . And what did Wimpy do?

GIG: Just had to severely reprimand him.

OT: Oho . . . you beaut.

MAC: Don't worry . . . Wimpy'll be sweating on him . . . I bet you Wimpy will get Darky one of these days . . . It's a moral.

[ROD *comes in dressed in shorts and carrying a towel and soap and a small brush.*]

ROD: Any mail in yet?

OT: No. Done your washing?

ROD: Yes. [*Sighs and sits on bed.*] You know I always look forward to Sundays, and when they come . . . I don't know . . . it's a long day to fill in.

OT: I'm going to be busier than a bed bug today.

MAC: When did you ever have anything to do, you little bludger?

OT: I tell you I'm up to the neck today. I got to wash three pairs of shorts and all me sox, me two long-uns and half a dozen shirts, and then I got to scrub all me webbin' . . . I'm going to do all me webbing, take a sling off me rifle and do 'er over properly . . . then polish me two pairs of boots. Then I got to go over to the canteen and get a packet of biscuits and some toothpaste and a new shavin' mirror . . . come back and wash me hair . . . have a shower and go on guard at half-past five. Gee . . . I'm goin' to be busy . . . Yes, I'm going to have to get at it quick smart.

[*Gets up and starts to collect washing.*]

GIG: You were on guard night before last.

OT: I know.

GIG: Well you can't be on again tonight, can you?

OT: I'm doing Ollie's for him.

GIG: Wot for?

OT: Why not, he's payin' me fifteen bob for it . . . [*Winks.*] Ah . . . the big save job's on now . . . Yes, got to raise twenty quid by the time me leave comes.

MAC [*belching*]: Don't think you're getting any leave, you dirty little sawn-off runt.

OT [*hotly*]: Oh yes I am. I asked Captain Wall and he reckoned all the two-year blokes would be on leave by July . . . Well, this is May, isn't it? I reckon about July or August . . . about ten weeks and I'll be on the Spirit of Protest.

MAC: Gawn . . . they got older men than you here. I'm pretty near three years.

OT: You've had leave, but.

MAC: Last August and I'll be due in July.

OT: Oh git out, wot about us wot's never had leave?

MAC [*argumentatively*]: Yeah, well you're not getting away before me. Andy and me are about the two longest records in the place.

OT: Oh get ripped—Darky McClure was here with the first draft in 1942 when they were flamin' bombing Darwin to guts.

MAC: Yeah? I heard the Crab say the Colonel said there was only eight goin' a week and that Andy and me was one of the first eight.

OT: Don't come the raw prawn. What does the Crab know, and anyhow you don't think he'd tell you, do you?

ROD: Vic seems to know more about leave than anyone . . . He works on Field Returns.

OT: Yeah, but he won't tell you anything . . . He's one of those keen bastards.

[*Enter* ANDY.]

MAC: I'm willing to bet you anything you like that I'm out of this place before any of you.

OT [*angrily*]: Ohh . . . listen to him . . .

GIG: Don't give us that.

[*Wild argument.* ANDY *walks in holding a bundle of washing.*]

ANDY: Break it up . . . break it up, boys. Hey Mac, Keghead's looking for you—there's a convoy just come in . . . All traffic personnel wanted.

MAC: Oh rip that . . . This is Sunday. A man's got to have a rest day, hasn't he?

ANDY: Except of course when he's been spine-bashing the whole week. [*Moves just outside door and moves washing on line to make room for his own.*]

[ROD *lies down on bed with magazine. Silence broken only by* ANDY'S *humming. Then train whistle. Instantly voices come from everywhere.*]

VOICES: Here comes the replacements! . . . Here they come! . . .

[KEN FALCON *gets up and goes out.* ROD *raises his head and watches him.*]

ROD: He's a queer bloke, isn't he?

[OT *looks up from where he is holding a bundle of washing.*]

I mean Ken Falcon . . . the end bed.

OT: Oh, him.

ROD: I've never heard him speak . . . have you?

OT: Oh. [*Thinks.*] Yes, I heard him speak once.

ROD: What did he say?

OT: Pass the jam.

[GIG APE *thinks this vastly funny. Silence for a moment. Then* MAC *yells and sits up on his bed.*]

MAC: Come off it, you dirty little sawn-off runt-eyed . . .

ANDY [*outside—innocently*]: What's up with you?

MAC: My washing . . . You find your own line . . . you dirty little crabby pox-eyed . . .

ANDY: Aw, what's wrong with you? . . . I only shifted them along

49

the line a bit . . . [*Starts hurriedly shifting them back. A pair of enormous underpants fall on the ground.*]

MAC [*black with rage*]: Pick 'em up . . . [*Rushes to door and picks up underpants now covered with red dust.*] Look at them . . . you dirty little mug runt.

ANDY: All right . . . all right . . . I'll dip them for you.

MAC: Dip 'em . . . I'll bloody well dip you [*grabs* ANDY].

ANDY [*squirming*]: You know you're not to take up all the line . . . You got to leave a bit of space . . . Read your hut orders.

MAC: Hut orders . . . Do you think I'd read a lot of bull cooked up by you and your friend Wimpy . . . you dirty . . .

[VIC *appears other side of doorway.*]

VIC: Mac . . . Keghead's looking for you.

MAC: Struth.

[*He disappears in one second, leaving* ANDY *tottering against the side of the hut.*]

GIG: The big spine-basher . . . Why don't you knock him, Andy . . .

OT: He's just a great big lazy runt . . . I wish we didn't have him in the hut.

GIG: He never pulls his weight. You have to do all his duties for him.

OT: He never does a guard.

GIG: I swept up the hut for him on Tuesday.

OT: You stupid gig ape . . . what did you do that for? . . . Let him cop it if the Crab comes around on inspection.

GIG: Yeah, and let the whole of me cobbers cop C.B. on a picture night . . . Not me . . . not with Rita Hayworth on.

OT [*laughs*]: How is he . . . Rita Hayworth.

GIG: Strike me . . . a man couldn't do her over much . . . not much.

[KEGHEAD *appears at the door looking very harassed.*]

KEGHEAD: Where's Mac?

OT: Not 'ere.

KEGHEAD: Any idea of where he might've went?

ANDY: Search us.

GIG: He knows you're after him anyhow.

KEGHEAD: He does, does he? Well, when he comes back you tell him he's wanted round at the traffic railroad right away. We got to load a couple of hundred bales of shorts and gas capes . . . 'Ow is it trying to find them on a Sunday. Wouldn't I cop a Sunday Orderly Sergeant and on top of that wouldn't it have to be an urgent convoy too. [*Moves off.*]

OT [*calling after him*]: Hey Keghead, when you going home?

KEGHEAD: Oh, don't talk about it. [*Exit.*]

ANDY: He's a funny bloke. Well I'm goin' over to see if the mail's come.

GIG: Hey Andy, get me a couple of fourpenny stamps, will you?

OT: Yes, Andy, me too, get me a telegram form, will you?

ANDY: What am I . . . a blooming pack horse or something? [*Exit.*]

GIG: What do you want a telegram form for?

OT: To send a telegram, you big gig ape.

GIG: Gwan . . . When did you ever know anyone?

[OLLIE *and* CHRIS *appear in doorway.*]

OLLIE: Onya. Onya. Onya.

CHRIS: Hey . . . are you gig apes goin' to church?

OT: No, are youse?

CHRIS: Yeah. Be in it?

OT: No, I got me washing to do . . . I got a full day on me hands. What do you want to go to church for? There's goin' to be a bit of a kick with the ball before dinner.

CHRIS: We're goin' to church.

OT: Cripes, what's making you two sinners turn over a new leaf?

OLLIE: Gawn . . . We had our choice of church or hygiene duty. [*Looking back*] Hey, Smokums . . . Onya. Onya.

[MAC *drifts back looking sulky and unsure of himself. Everyone ignores him.* OT *collects washing. There is silence for a bit.* MAC *pulls his shirt down and twists his neck to see his back and shoulders. Much eyeing going on for a while.*]

GIG: Pooh . . . you stink . . . I bet you haven't had a shower the whole week.

MAC: Shut your trap.

OT: Cripes, he's on to the old dermo again.

GIG: He's not, is he? [*Watching* MAC] Hey . . . are you trying to work up the old dermo again?

MAC: Shut your ugly big trap.

OT: Don't try to kid us, you dirty old cow . . . trying to get South again on your dermo.

MAC: Well?

OT [*to* ROD]: How is he. Do you know what this bastard does?
Tries to cop everything that's going around to get himself
marked tropically unfit . . . Goes without a shower for a week
and rubs himself with a towel . . . works up a proper case of
dermatitis . . . and gets into hospital for a week . . . He's done it
twice already.

MAC [*glowering*]: Shut your filthy little trap, Otford.

OT: They send you South if you get dermo more than three times
bad enough to put you in hospital.

MAC: And I'll get it again, don't you worry.

OT: We know you will.

MAC: I'm due for leave anyhow.

OT [*angrily*]: You are not . . . I'm due before you . . . and . . .

VIC [*loudly*]: Aw, shut up . . . Can't you talk about anything else?
[KEN FALCON *comes into hut. Looks at others unsmiling, then
sits on bed.*]

OT [*gaily*]: Good day, Dean Maitland. The good old Dean, eh?

GIG: Chatty, ain't he?
[OT *lies prostrate on his bed, wiggling his toes.*]

OT: Hey, Gig.

GIG: Yeah.

OT: How's the bloody war goin'?

GIG [*tossing him Army News*]: You can read it.

OT [*picking it up. Reads laboriously and without interest*]: Eighth
Army starts big offensive in Italy. [*Then excitedly*] Hey listen,
Gig . . . Evergreen's been scratched for the Maiden Handicap.
[*Nostalgically*] I rode that bastard in his first race. I used to work
for his trainer.

ROD: Were you a jockey, Ot?

OT: Yep. Gave it up.

ROD: Oh, why?

OT: The Rosebud don't like it. Gave it up for her and took a job
in a garage. [*Nostalgically*] Evergreen, eh. Mug Alcock rode him
after me . . . ruined him.
[ANDY *enters with a large bundle of mail. Several tins.*]

ANDY: Gig Ape . . . [*Throws him two letters.*]
[*Everyone sits up in a great state of excitement.*]

Rod . . . Rod again . . . Gig Ape . . . Ot.

OT: Rosebud! . . . [*Kissing the letter, dancing, then kissing* GIG APE.] You little smacker!

GIG: Get ripped.

ANDY: Mac [*gives* MAC *letter*] . . . Gig Ape again . . . [*Smells it*] Pooh!

GIG: Give us it . . . Never mind the comedy . . . Give us it.

ANDY: And a cake for you too [*hands* GIG *a tin*].

GIG: You little beaut!

ANDY [*handing* ROD *a bundle of papers*]: Rod.

ROD: Thanks—good . . . reading matter.

ANDY: Vic [*hands* VIC *a letter*].

　　[KEN FALCON *half rises looking at* ANDY.]

　　The rest is all for me.

　　[KEN *sits back again disappointed. They are all deep in their letters immediately. From outside the clanging of three gongs sounds. No one moves.*]

OT: You little beaut. [*Reads a second, then screams*] Oh, you beaut! . . . [*Kisses the letter.*] The Rosebud says she's only waiting for me to come home.

GIG: How's this? Me brother's home from New Guinea on twenty-four days' leave.

ANDY: How long's he been up there?

GIG: Not much more'n a year.

ANDY: There you are see. I tell you those runts are better off than we are. We're the bloody forgotten army here.

OT: How's that . . . I kiss your photo every night and pray that you will soon be back at our place . . . [*Kicks legs wildly.*] Ohhhhh, the little Rosebud. "Mum says tea of a Sunday night isn't the same without you're there making us all have a good old laugh."

GIG: Aw, shut up . . . How can I read my letter with you maggin'.

OT: "P.S. If you're not using your cigarette ration how's about sending me yours." How is she.

　　[*Silence for a second.*]

MAC [*sitting up suddenly*]: Cripes, I'm going to have another baby!

　　[*Roar of laughter greets this.*]

ANDY: That'll be your ninth, won't it?

MAC: Alice has just wrote to me . . . that's me eldest girl . . .

ANDY: Good Lord . . . How is he . . . The ninth, eh?

OT: Layin' it on a bit, aren't you.

GIG: Gee . . . nine kids . . . The Army must be payin' you more than the bloody Colonel.

MAC [*getting up, very pleased*]: You'll be surprised to hear, Dad, that Mum has been real sick again and I found out yesterday that she's going to have another baby in December . . . [*he stops*].

[*The sudden realization comes over them all.*]

ANDY: December. [*He laughs a little nervously*] You must of read wrong.

MAC: That's what she says—December . . .

ANDY: December.

MAC: That means she's only just started.

OT: Wot's up?

GIG: Oh shut up, you big ape.

MAC: I haven't been home since August . . . [*A long pause. He stands there unable to comprehend . . . just a big dumbcluck.*]

ANDY: Have you read all the letter?

[MAC *shakes his head.*]

ANDY: Let's see . . . let's see, eh? [*Gently takes the letter out of* MAC'S *hand. Reads*] "Dad I think you ought to try to get leave to come home . . . Mum has been going away for a week at a time and I think she's been staying over with Jim McMurtrie at the shop . . . I told her I was going to tell on her to you if she didn't behave herself and come home and look after the kids. She reckons she is going to write to you and tell you about it but she don't want to look after us any longer and reckons I can look after the kids now I'm sixteen . . .

[*A gurgling comical sob breaks from* MAC.]

I wasn't going to tell you before that this has been going on a long time, Dad, but I must now . . . and you must get home . . ."

[*Everyone looks embarrassed. They all pick up their letters, trying to look unconcerned.*]

There's a bit more . . . you'd better read yourself, it's a bit private.

[MAC *stands there dumbly holding the bottle of lolly water he had been drinking. Suddenly two gongs sound outside.*]

ROD [*quietly*]: Anyone going over for mess?

[*They reach quietly for their mess tins under their beds.*]

Coming, Mac?

[*A peculiar almost animal scream bursts from* MAC. *Suddenly he turns and smashes the bottle against the doorpost and, leaning against it, sobs.*]

MAC: That lying bitch . . . that bloody lying bitch, I'll cut her throat . . . that bitch . . .

ANDY: Hey, cut that out . . .

[MAC *collapses heavily on the bed groaning weakly.* ANDY *folds up the letter carefully and sits beside him saying nothing. The boys pick up their mess gear as though nothing had happened.*]

OT [*gaily*]: Who's coming over for the good old M and V?

[*They move out chattering and talking.* ANDY *continues to sit beside the moaning heaving* MAC.]

[*The lights fade.*]

(*End of Scene*)

ACT ONE

scene 4

The YMCA hut. Seven o'clock at night a few days later. The room is just an ill-lit tin shed with a few dead-looking ferns hanging in pots. A door to the left leads into the canteen where the noise of evening sales is still going on, with the clang of a cash register every now and then. A door to the right leads to BILL HENRY'S *room and is covered by faded dirty curtains. A rickety, sad-looking piano is pushed against a wall. Various desks and writing materials are scattered around. Notices reading: "WRITE TO MUM FIRST" and "YOUR FIRST DUTY IS TO BE A CHRISTIAN". A few faded pin-up girls are peeling off the wall. Hanging near the exit which is to the verandah to the back is a waterbag. As the lights go up* BILL HENRY, *the YMCA Sergeant, is pumping up a Ferris lamp which is near him on a table. A bookshelf behind has about thirty mildewed library books. A pale-looking* PRIVATE *in long pants and with sleeves rolled down is peering at the titles.* TWO PRIVATES *enter from the canteen and cross towards the verandah. They carry bottles and parcels.*

FIRST PTE.: Only one bottle of lolly water per man. I ASK you!

SECOND PTE.: The friggin' factory's broken down again, I suppose.

BILL [*he has a chirpy little voice*]: Even' gents. Staying for a hand of euchre later? Nice little euchre party going this evening.

SECOND PTE.: No thanks. Got our washing to do and some letters to write.

FIRST PTE. [*as they go out*]: The bastard's given me honeysuckle balls again.

SECOND PTE.: Didn't you ask for them?

FIRST PTE.: No. They get stuck in my plate.

[*The* PRIVATE *is peering at the books.*]

BILL: Found anything you like?

PRIVATE: Not yet. [*Laughs.*]

BILL: Here's a beaut. I read this myself the other day . . . Now you might just like this . . . I'd say it was unusual, you know.

PRIVATE: "Law of the Pampas."

BILL: Real good yarn you know . . . unless you'd like something on the romance. What about this? [*He reaches down a yellow-back novel.*] "Rosemary's For Remembrance" . . . Nice type of book that . . . very flash writer that . . . I know that writer well . . . yes . . . know him well . . . read all his books . . . [*Peering at the title in the bad light*] Sylvia Meadows . . . real good writer that.

PRIVATE [*nervously*]: I don't suppose you'd happen to have anything by Bernard Shaw?

BILL: Who's that?

PRIVATE: Bernard Shaw.

BILL: Bernard Shaw . . . [*Dubiously*] You might find something by him. The mystery section's the top shelf.

[KEN FALCON *comes in. He wanders desolately over to the table and picks up some dog-eared, very old magazines which he begins to peer at in the poor light.* OLLIE *and* CHRIS *come out of the canteen carrying lolly water bottles and packets of soap, etc.*]

BILL: Game of euchre starting at twenty hundred hours, boys . . .

OLLIE: No thanks, Bill.

CHRIS: What's the pictures on Thursday night, Bill?

BILL: I dunno that youse'll be getting any.

CHRIS: What!

OLLIE: Stone the bloody crows. We haven't had any for a fortnight.

BILL: I heard the unit was broke down between Pine Creek and the Katherine.

CHRIS: Oh, how are they.

OLLIE: It's going it a bit thick. Gee, it's all right for those galahs up at Pine Creek.

CHRIS: They got sheilas up there.

OLLIE: I haven't seen a sheila for seventeen months.

CHRIS: Yes you have. You seen that abo skirt. Up at the compound.

OLLIE [*laughs*]: Lulubelle . . . how'd she go, eh?

[GIG APE *comes in from the verandah.*]

CHRIS: You'd better hurry if you want any lolly water.

GIG: Nope, I only want washin' soap.

OLLIE: Heard the late good guts on the leave?

GIG: No.

OLLIE: June. First week in June the replacements are comin'.

GIG: First it was March, then April, then May . . . now it's June. I don't think they'll ever friggin' come.

OLLIE: We heard the good oil today from the Crab.

CHRIS: Yeah, from the Crab. We all get home by June . . . Ollie and I'll be in the first draft.

GIG: That ought to put me in the second or third . . . Gees, I bet Vic Richards knew about that and never told me.

BILL [*hopefully*]: Euchre party tonight, gents . . . all welcome.

GIG: No thanks. I got some letters to write. Hey, did you hear about Mac?

OLLIE: Hey, is that right about Mac's old woman in the family way from the local butcher?

GIG: Yeah. He's put in for compassionate leave.

CHRIS: Fat chance. I couldn't even get home when me sister died.

OLLIE: You got home . . . you got home.

CHRIS: Oh yes; after they frigged me around for so long I got home the day after the funeral.

[ROD *comes in.*]

ROD: Goodnight.

CHRIS and OLLIE: Goodnight.

BILL: Euchre game on tonight, laddie . . . eight o'clock.

ROD: No thanks. Can I just write some letters here?

BILL: Always welcome . . . You'll find paper over there.

GIG: Yeah . . . Well he's put in for it and Wimpy took him before the Colonel.

CHRIS: Before the old Stinkbum? . . . What for?

GIG: You know . . . declaration or some other friggin' thing.

OLLIE: Cripes, if I was married to Mac I'd have frigged off long ago. Imagine having that in bed with you.

[ANDY *and* MAC *enter at this moment. They stop talking as the little corporal and the big lump pass.* MAC *is now in a bad state of dermatitis and has triple dye painted purple in large patches over his face and neck.*]

OLLIE: 'Night, Mac.

MAC: G'night, Ollie . . . 'night, Chris.

CHRIS: 'Night, Mac.

[*They watch him with interest as he goes into canteen with* ANDY.]

OLLIE: Big lump, ain't he?

CHRIS: That don't mean anything.

[*They move towards the verandah.*]

[*To* GIG *as they leave*] We're going to turn on a bit of supper tonight.

OLLIE: On Chris's cake and my bottle of beer . . . Coming over?

GIG: I wouldn't mind. O.K. See youse later.

[CHRIS *and* OLLIE *go out.* GIG *passes* ROD *who is settling down to write in the bad light.*]

She still love you?

ROD: What? Oh . . . oh, yes. [*Laughs.*]

[GIG *goes into canteen.*]

BILL [*to* PRIVATE]: Find what you want?

PRIVATE: I can't find Bernard Shaw in here at all.

BILL: Here's somethink on the same lines. History of Economics . . . how about that?

PRIVATE [*laughs*]: Yes, O.K.

BILL [*holding out tattered exercise book*]: Write your name and number there, please.

[KEGHEAD *comes in looking very dreary. He spots* ROD.]

KEGHEAD: Goodnight.

ROD: Oh hello . . .

[KEGHEAD *sits down.* KEN FALCON *looks up and moves a bit further away. The* PRIVATE *takes his book and exits.*]

KEGHEAD: 'Night, Bill.

BILL: Oh goodnight. Game of euchre on tonight . . . Be in it?

KEGHEAD [*yawning*]: Don't think so.

BILL: Why not? Makes something to do . . . you know . . . makes it a nice bright evening, doesn't it . . . you know . . . nice and bright.

KEGHEAD: Oh yes. [*Yawns.*] I dunno . . . Can't be bothered doing anything these nights. [*To* ROD] How do you fill in your evenings here?

ROD: I find something to do. Make myself do something . . . write up, play quoits, or . . . do something.

KEGHEAD: I can't do anything in this bastard of a place . . . you know . . . like I can't settle down to do anything of an evening.

ROD: You ought to try.

KEGHEAD: You wait till you've done a couple of Wets up here . . .

You'll find you can't do anything either.

ROD: But you ought to try . . . I mean you go to pieces that way.

KEGHEAD: I dunno . . . [*Yawns again.*] Cripes it's only eight o'clock . . . and I'm ready to go to bed. At home you know I used to be a bit of a nightbird . . . always wanting to go out to parties and social evenings and that sort. Molly and me used to go out on an average of four evenings a week . . . that's my wife see . . . she likes a good night out . . . we get on well because of that, but cripes what good will a man be when he gets out of this rathouse.

ROD: Yes.

BILL [*chirpily*]: You ought to come over to one of our discussion nights.

KEGHEAD: Rip that.

ROD: What are they, Bill?

BILL: Oh we've been trying to get up a bit of a debatin' society . . . I've been talking to some of the RSD blokes and Occa Stevens is going to be in it.

KEGHEAD: That ratbag!

BILL: We're going to have a bit of a discussion Friday night over in the men's mess at eight o'clock. Should coal-mining be nationalized. I'm speaking for and Occa's speaking against.

KEGHEAD: That oughtn't to be hard for him. He's always against everything. [*Yawns.*] Gee, a man'll go mad in this joint—honest, if they don't get me away this month I'm going on the biggest jack-up they ever saw.

[ANDY *and* MAC *enter from the canteen carrying lolly water and parcels.*]

ANDY: Keghead . . . Keghead.

KEGHEAD: Aw, give it away.

ANDY: When are you goin' home?

[*This stock joke always gets a laugh.*]

[BILL *and* MAC *laugh.*]

KEGHEAD: Get ripped.

BILL: Nice little euchre game on tonight, gents . . . make the evening nice and jolly . . . you know . . . nice and jolly . . . be in it?

ANDY: We're going over to the swy.

KEGHEAD: Had any news, Mac, about getting your compassionate?

MAC [*worried*]: No . . . It's got to go to Melbourne and back for O.K.

or some bloody thing . . . and those galahs wouldn't know if you was sending 'em up. Bastards. [*He spits.*]

BILL: Hey. Hey . . . no spittin' in here.

MAC [*lunging to the door*]: Aw, get ripped, you and your comic turnout.

[MAC *lunges to door and out into the night followed by the giggling* ANDY.]

BILL: He don't uphold the camp spirit . . . I got no time for them that don't uphold the camp spirit. What I say is no matter where you are youse can still behave like a sport.

KEGHEAD: You wouldn't expect him to understand that. Big bludger. I ought to know, he works for me.

ROD: Oh well, he's in pretty bad trouble right now.

KEGHEAD: He's not the only poor bastard. What about Ernie Gray over at No. 1 Depot? Got a poor luny mother off her rocker going into the nuthouse and he can't get down to find his sister a home. I tell you these runts up here wouldn't care if you lost your whole family. It's friggin' galahs like Mac that make it hard for blokes who've got a dinkum excuse.

ROD: Sure Mac is in trouble. I saw the letter.

KEGHEAD: Aw, cut it out. I wouldn't put it past him to rig that up.

BILL: Me either. He tried to get a transfer from up here last year and his wife was sending him urgent telegrams all the time. The baby fell in a pot of boiling fat.

KEGHEAD [*yawns*]: Stinkbum's awake up to him.

BILL [*laughs*]: Aha, he's awake up to everyone, is the Colonel. Down here the other night making sure we wasn't playing cards for money. I says: "Here are the beans, Sir. Just playing for beans," I says. "No gambling goes on in the YMCA hut," I says. Can't say the same for the Red Shield because I don't know. "Play the game's our spirit," I says.

[GIG APE *enters from the canteen with* DARKY MCCLURE *carrying lolly water bottles.*]

DARKY [*singing*]: "Bless 'em all, bless 'em all, the long and the short and the tall, you won't leave the Territory this side of posterity, so cheer up my lads bless 'em all."

BILL [*chuckling*]: Hello, Darky . . . so you cracked it again I hear.

GIG: Lost his stripes too.

KEGHEAD: Hey Darky, did you lose your stripes?

DARKY [*gaily*]: You can't ever win a point from Wimpy Murdoch. I get out of the charge for the stolen truck . . . get right out of it. Wimpy sweats on me see . . . waits his chance . . . puts on a hut raid the other night and finds me mosquito net's not down and I lose my stripes.

[*They all laugh.* ROD *looks up from his letter.*]

ROD: Really?

DARKY [*going to the piano*]: You just wait till Wimpy gets onto YOU.

KEGHEAD: How are they. How ARE they. Sweating on a man even when he's in bed. [*Groans.*] Oh, I tell you they'd drive a man troppo if the place didn't first. [*Gets up yawning.*] Think I'll do me dough over at the swy . . . nothing else for a man to do.

[DARKY *starts playing the piano softly. He plays well, but it is hopelessly out of tune. He plays "Time on My Hands".* KEN FALCON *gets up and wanders drearily over to the piano and stands looking down at* DARKY *enjoying the music.* GIG APE *goes over to* BILL *with a tattered book.*]

GIG: Hey Bill, have you got any more pervy stories like this one?

BILL [*taking it*]: The Postman Always Rings Twice. Oh, there's a big waiting list for that. Eh, what have you been doing with it . . . drop it down the dike?

GIG: No . . . but you can't keep anything clean in this place. [*He starts hunting for a book on the shelves.*]

[*Canteen door suddenly closes and the light goes out inside.* KEGHEAD *also leans on the piano.*]

KEGHEAD: You ought to hear Molly play that . . . Aw cripes, it's friggin' lovely.

ROD: Time on my hands. [*He laughs but no one else sees point.*]

BILL: Hey Darky, what about helpin' us to get up another concert one of these days?

DARKY: Nothing doing. I'm going South.

KEGHEAD: That's what YOU think. Aw, that's a friggin' lovely tune.

BILL: We got some new talent in here. [*Gets a little book.*] There's a bloke come in from No. 3 Depot last night can play the harmonica . . . and there's a bloke does Donald Duck from RSD. Come on Darky be a sport . . . we haven't been able to get up a concert for about four months.

DARKY: Oh, what do you think I do with my time? [*He switches to the melancholy "As Time Goes By".*]

KEGHEAD: Oh, I love this.

[DARKY *plays for a second.*]

[*Turns to* ROD.] Friggin' lovely. [*Long pause.*] Molly plays that.

BILL [*to* ROD]: How about our new friend here . . . can't you do anything?

ROD: I'm afraid not.

BILL: Aw, come on . . . you don't have to be bashful . . . The boys don't care if you aren't any good. It makes a bit of a jolly evening you know. [*Looking in book*] Ernie Gray reckons he'll do a bit of magic for us.

KEGHEAD: Oh . . . not again.

BILL: I got some sketches here too . . . [*Showing* ROD] See . . . there's a little sort of play here. I've seen this go down real well . . . I've seen this go down myself. The husband and wife change places you see . . . All you need's a bit of a bed rigged up.

ROD: Oh yes.

BILL: Makes a bit of laugh, see? Oh, you got to do something for your mates now and then.

ROD: Oh, I'll give it a go.

BILL: That's the spirit. I'll put your name down. We're having a meetin' over here and auditions in a week or two. I'll let you know . . . Oh yes and we got a bloke here from No. 2 who can whistle on a gumleaf . . . He's not too bad either. [*Pause.*] I don't mind singing again myself.

[KEGHEAD *makes a face.*]

I got up a new song this week. The wife sent me up a bundle of some of my old songs.

[*He hops over to the desk and produces a tattered copy of some songs. Starts going through them.* DARKY *stops playing and peeps at some of them.*]

DARKY: Give us a look . . . "On The Road To Mandalay" . . . "Sylvia" . . . "My Love Is Like A Red Red 'frigging' Rose". How IS he. Haven't you got anything new?

BILL: The wife and I don't go in much for new stuff. I always fancy myself as a ballad singer. [*To* ROD] Know this?

ROD [*taking it*]: "Sweet Alice Ben Bolt." [*With revulsion*] Oh yes.

BILL: I like the old ones myself. I always say they can have this swing. I like the old ballads.

DARKY: Struth, they stink. Haven't you got "Sunday, Monday and Always"?

KEGHEAD: I like that "Jealousy". Oh, it's bloody beautiful. You ought to hear Molly on that. She can put in all the side pieces too, you know. Dum da da dumdada da da da da, it's all over my jealousy.

DARKY [*sings*]: "It's all over my underpants."

KEGHEAD: That's right . . . Be bloody coarse, you galah.

DARKY: Get ripped. What's this one? "Don't be afraid to come Home."

BILL [*proudly*]: I sung that on me last leave up at the Church Social. [*Clears throat and sings*]
"Don't be afraid to come home.
Those who love you . . . won't turn you awaaay.
Tho' you've made the mistake that thousands have made
Whatever you've done, you've paid, yes you've paid.
Don't be afraid to come home.
Tho' friends spurn you wherever you go . . .
For if God can forgive you . . . then why should not I?
Don't be afraid to come home."
[*He finishes with dramatic crescendo.*]
　[*There is a slight pause as he regards them.*]

KEGHEAD [*briskly*]: Well . . . going to do me money at the swy! [*Exits.*]

ROD [*trying not to laugh*]: Yes . . . it's quite a song, isn't it?

DARKY: Cripes! [*He gives the song to* BILL.] That stinks.

BILL: Course I've got others that might go better. They always like that one though . . . it's poignant.

DARKY: Poisonous, you mean. [*Gets up suddenly.*] Hey Gig Ape, come on . . . I'll give you a game of billiards . . . Let's get out of this morgue.

GIG [*taking book*]: I got one, Bill . . . "Lady Chatterley's Lover".

BILL [*downcast*]: O.K. [*Gathers up music.*] Must you go, Darky?

DARKY: Yeah. Coming over to the Red Shield for some billiards, Rod?

ROD: No, I'll finish my letters first.

DARKY: Come on then.

[*He pushes* GIG APE *roughly towards door and they go out pushing and laughing.* KEN FALCON *stands looking down at the piano. Then he wanders over and stares at the pin-up girls mournfully.*]

BILL [*hopefully to* ROD]: Do you play the piano?

ROD: Sorry, no. [*He goes to table starts writing again.*]

BILL: Oh well. Not often you can get up a bit of a singsong. I got to find an accompanist for the concert. [*He closes piano disconsolately and goes back to his desk.*]

[ROD *angrily brushes away the flying ants from his face.*]

ROD: Flying ants bad tonight.

BILL: Yes.

[KEN FALCON *sighs loudly.* ROD *looks up and smiles at him. He stares at* ROD. *Doesn't reply.* BILL *starts entering notes in his exercise book. He hums "Don't Be Afraid to Come Home" tunelessly.*]

BILL: 'Fraid the euchre's going to be a frost again.

[*Long pause.* ROD'S *pen scratches in the quiet.*]

You can't compete against Mac's two-up school. [*Long pause.* BILL *hums a little again.*] One bloke made sixty quid in an evening other night. [*Pause.*] Oh well . . . it's a funny life all right. [*He whistles mournfully.*]

[*The lights fade.*]

(*End of Scene*)

ACT ONE

scene 5

On the roadway near the vehicle park. A few nights later. It is nearly four o'clock in the morning. The moon is on the wane. We see the dark outline of trees and scrub. A figure can be seen sitting on a box. After a second the light from a guard torch illuminates the darkness. The man looks at his watch and sighs. Suddenly he becomes alert. His figure stiffens. In the frosty air footsteps are coming down the road. After a second the figure stands. It is VIC RICHARDS.

VIC: Who's there?

ROD [*voice in distance*]: It's Rod Carson. [*His torch enters the scene. The light flashes into* VIC's *face.*] Who's that? Vic, is it?

VIC: Yeah, it's me. Where are you on?

ROD: Number Three Sub. Depot. I usually walk down here once during the shift to see who's on. Hope you don't mind.

[VIC *resumes his seat on box. The torches go off.*]

It gets pretty lonely up there. I get talking to myself. Gosh the time passes slowly. Cold, isn't it?

VIC: It's not warm [*his voice does not encourage conversation*].

ROD: I've got the willies a bit tonight. [*Laughs shortly.*] I heard the dingoes a while ago. Sounds like a lot of kids being scalded to death. [*Pause.*] Think the old Crab will come around at this hour of the morning? It's almost four.

VIC: The Crab'll come around any time.

ROD: Conscientious blighter, isn't he? [*Pause.*] Gosh, what stars! I've never seen nights like these down South. It's as though they were blazing right into you. They're like drops of ice. [*Pause.*] I always feel there's something insane about walking up and down a road at four in the morning with the rest of the place asleep. Makes you feel a bit unreal, doesn't it?

VIC [*shortly*]: Yeah.

ROD: Though I expect you old timers are quite used to it by now.

It must be hell doing guard in the Wet.

VIC: Yeah.

[*Pause.*]

ROD [*hoisting his rifle onto his shoulder*]: I can't see much sense in it myself. It's crazy. We stand around for four hours in the middle of the night in the middle of the Never Never, ten thousand miles away from anything, to guard a few old sheds . . . from what? [*He laughs.*] It's a bit of a joke. [*Noticing* VIC'S *silence.*] Perhaps you'd rather not talk—you must be tired.

[VIC *says nothing.*]

I really came down to see if you had a fag.

[VIC *searches in his pocket.*]

VIC: Here.

ROD: Where? Oh, thanks. I've got a match.

[*For a second their faces are lit with the flare of a match.*]

S'pose we'll cop it if the Orderly Officer does choose this shift to come around.

[*Their cigarettes burn in the dark.*]

Vic . . . you don't like me for some reason.

VIC: Did you come down to ask me that too?

ROD: No, but I suppose this is as good a time as any to have it out. I wondered just what you have against me.

VIC: I haven't got anything against you.

ROD: Then could you leave off regarding me with such suspicion? I didn't ask to come up here.

VIC: None of us did.

ROD: Well?

VIC: Well, that's no reason for fraternization is it?

ROD: I thought it might be.

VIC: I don't particularly care to make friends with anyone here. I get on with them all right, but as for friends . . .

ROD: What's the matter with you?

VIC: The way I feel about the whole place . . . about the army and life in general.

ROD: You mean you hate it.

VIC: I dunno that I hate it any more than being out of it. But I'm just not one of these jokers that can make the best out of things that are just a racket—and the army's a racket . . . the whole war's a racket . . . same as anything else.

ROD: Same as everything?

VIC: Yep. I haven't had any chances like you.

ROD: I don't know that I've had so many chances.

VIC: Don't give me that. You've had a good education. I can tell that by the way you talk and the sort of things you read.

ROD: I don't know that education counts for much these days.

VIC: You've had a good job, haven't you? You're a writer, aren't you?

ROD: If you could call being a junior reporter that. You get all the kicks and none of the featuring.

VIC: You'd turn over a pretty good screw, wouldn't you?

ROD: I wouldn't say that.

VIC: Go on! You'd do about fifteen quid a week, wouldn't you?

ROD [*laughs*]: Crikey, I wish you meant it! I turn over four quid a week and work practically twenty-four hours a day for it.

VIC: Still it's a job. You got something to go back to.

ROD: Possibly. I still don't see that's anything to hold against me.

VIC: I never said I hold it against you personally.

ROD: What's your grudge? The world?

VIC: Far as I can see it's all a lot of empty damn promises. By the time we get out of this mess the jobs will all be gone anyhow. You see I've never really got anything out of it. I never even got what I wanted out of the war. I never wanted to get stuck up in an Ordnance dump like this. My cobber is up at Lae right now getting stuck into the Japs.

ROD: You mean you'd rather be there?

VIC: Wouldn't you? Fat lot of heroism there is about sitting here with a sandy rifle and twenty rounds guarding a shed full of soyer stoves. Filing vouchers by day. I'm able-bodied, aren't I? I got a right to get into the fight if I want to. Two years here . . . two bloody years and I'm not even a returned soldier when it's over.

ROD: I guess you're browned off.

VIC: Sure. [*Spits.*] I know their promises. When you get your next leave you'll be reposted elsewhere, they say. Oh yes, says Mr. Forde . . . no more Northern Territory Personnel who've done over two years to be reposted there . . . But we'll all come back, don't worry . . . and stay here. How long do you think this is going on for? My guess is years. We haven't even licked the Germans yet.

ROD: Oh, I don't know. I think maybe we'll have a lash at Europe sometime this year. It must come eventually.

VIC: So must old age.

ROD: Maybe it will all be over sooner than we think.

VIC: That'll be the day! Welcome home, Digger . . . bands and streamers, sweeping up the mess at the abattoirs . . . MAYBE.

ROD: Haven't you ever thought of going in for their Post-War Education Scheme?

VIC: I'm twenty-nine. Bit late to start thinking of the University, isn't it? I left school at thirteen to go into a factory because the old man had more of a liking for the rich ruby than for work.

ROD: You got a girl.

[*A pause.*]

VIC: Yeah.

ROD: Going to marry her?

VIC: There's only one thing stopping that. Little matter of having to keep her.

ROD: That's tough. Maybe she'll wait.

VIC: Maybe she believes in Santa Claus. She's been waiting four years now. Those blondes don't last forever.

[*There is silence for a second. Their cigarettes glow.*]

ROD: It's cold.

[*In the distance a truck is heard starting.*]

There's a truck leaving the guardhouse . . . It must be four. Thank God that's over for another night. I'd better get back to my post. [*He stubs out his cigarette with his boot and hoists his rifle onto his shoulder.*] Be seeing you.

VIC: Yeah.

[*The faint moonlight has faded to blackness as the scene closes.*]

(*End of Act One*)

ACT TWO

scene 1

Scene: The hut. Night, a fortnight later. The lights go up on ANDY, GIG APE, *and* KEGHEAD *grouped around* ANDY'S *bed. They are drinking cocoa out of their mugs.*

ANDY: I knew an old bride once who had twins at fifty-eight.

KEGHEAD: Depends on the constitution.

ANDY: She had one on the Tuesday night and the other Wednesday midday and never missed a meal.

[*There is a suitable pleasurable reaction to this.*]

GIG: There was a friggin' sheila in our street went down to the amusement park and had four go's on the big dipper and went home and had a friggin' baby and done the friggin' washing the next day. 'Ow WAS she?

KEGHEAD: Just goin' on the big dipper would give my Molly twins. Wouldn't have to do a thing.

ANDY: I remember one night a few years back meeting a redhead skirt in a hamburger's . . . oho, was she a wonderful piece . . . "Got a cigarette dear?" she says. "Got the makings," I said, and she gave me one of them looks you know that you can't mistake . . . "I'll bet you have," she says. Weeeeellll! Was it ON!!

KEGHEAD: Must have been a bit hard-up takin' on a little runt like you.

ANDY: My fanny!

[OT *rushes in with a bucket full of wet clothes. He is stripped to the waist and perspiring.*]

GIG: How's the laundry going?

OT: Struth! I done fifteen pair of shorts and eleven shirts and I still got four more buckets to go. [*Picking up a piece of paper from his bed*] Let's see . . . Occa James . . . he's done . . . Ernie Green . . . he's done all except for his sox . . . Willie Fong.

ANDY: There's a cup of cocoa going.

OT: Keep one hot for me, will you? I got to get this finished.

KEGHEAD: I dunno wot you want to go washin' everyone's clothes for. You're mad.

OT: Five bob a go . . . Wot's wrong with that? Worth fifty bob to me towards me engagement ring.

GIG: Eh . . . 'ow's Vic and Rod goin' with that toast?

OT: Dunno. Haven't got time to see. [*He dashes out again.*]

ANDY [*laughing*]: Struth, he's a dag.

KEGHEAD: Mad. He's mad. Started a garden.

GIG: Down by the showers . . . yes.

ANDY: He's keen, you know. You got to hand it to him.

GIG: Goes down and rakes all the soil up after he comes back from work. He's got cabbages in and lettuces. Willie Fong's got a pal up at the River sends him down plants.

ANDY: Got a new idea every day, young Ot. He's give up the exercises now. Hasn't got time.

KEGHEAD: He's keen on that girl of his though. Doin' everyone's guards for 'em. He done six guards last week at a pound a go. He's minting money.

ANDY: They'll cop him sooner or later and we'll all get it in the neck for palmin' off our guards.

[VIC *comes in with a plate of toast. He seems much more energetic and his eyes are bright.*]

VIC: Righto blokes . . . get into it. Here's the first batch.

GIG: Cop the toast, will you! Cop it!

VIC: Rod's gone over to the kitchen to pinch some butter and there's some Gravox in my tin . . . spread over it. How's the cocoa going?

OMNES: Great. She's the pickin's.

VIC: Just sing out if you want some more . . . We got the water on. How many of you? [*He counts.*] Where's Dean Maitland?

ANDY: On guard tonight.

VIC: O.K. . . . won't be long with the rest. [*He goes out.*]

KEGHEAD: Where's Mac?

ANDY: Dunno, but I hope he keeps clear of us. Struth, he's in a rotten state.

KEGHEAD: Dermo?

ANDY: All over him now. Cripes, he's got it bad.

KEGHEAD: He'll be in hospital. You see.

GIG: He's been tryin' for it for six months. He's pulled everything to get South.

ANDY: Yeah, but he's scared of the doctor now. He don't want to go to hospital with all this trouble at home.

KEGHEAD: Any news of his compassionate leave?

ANDY: Nope.

KEGHEAD: Cripes, it's going on for three weeks, isn't it?

ANDY: Easily that.

KEGHEAD [*moaning*]: Oh they'd give you the tom-tits. Their bloody red tape. I've had them. Honest to goodness, I've had them.

ANDY: Mac's tryin' to get rid of his dermo now. Serve the big bludger right if they popped him into hospital.

[ROD *and* VIC *come in carrying a plate of butter and more toast with a billy of hot water.*]

ROD: Here it is. The cup that cheers.

KEGHEAD: Good on youse.

GIG: Keep a bit hot for young Ot.

[*They sit and cut the toast, spreading the butter.*]

ROD: Just passed the Leave Draft as I left the kitchen. The RSM was giving 'em their papers.

GIG: Lucky bastards.

KEGHEAD: Who's goin' besides Darky McClure?

GIG: Chris and Ollie and old Sappy Smith and Jim Austen and Pudgy.

KEGHEAD [*moans*]: Gee, it'd be hard to take. Gettin' on that train at four o'clock in the morning.

ANDY: *I* should have been on this draft.

KEGHEAD: Get ripped you should. I've been here longer than you. If I'm not on the next one . . . straight to the Colonel.

ANDY: That'll get you just nowhere.

[CHRIS *and* OLLIE *appear in the doorway. They are dressed in full kit with hats.*]

CHRIS: Onya. Onya. Onya.

OLLIE: Frig the Territory. We're on our way.

ANDY: Lucky runts.

KEGHEAD: Are you just off?

OLLIE: We got to take our gear down to the railhead. We got to sleep there tonight. The train comes in about four.

KEGHEAD: You HOPE. My guess is it mightn't be here till Sunday.

CHRIS: Get ripped. Well so long, fellers . . .

KEGHEAD: See you when you get back.

[*They shake hands.*]

OLLIE: The Colonel come down and told us we'd all be posted down South. How is it we won't have to come back.

ANDY: Good luck to you.

KEGHEAD: You'll be back.

CHRIS: Got a promise this time.

KEGHEAD: Whaddye bet me you won't be back?

[*The boys shake hands with everyone.*]

ANDY: Eh Chris . . . I got a letter here I don't want the censor to see. How about postin' it for me in Adelaide?

VIC [*laughing*]: I guess it's to that woman he keeps.

KEGHEAD: Yeah. 'Ow's that little piece of yours goin', Andy?

ANDY [*mock drama*]: Oh, she never misses a mail . . . Y'orta read the letters . . . Oh, Andy . . . [*everyone laughs*] I wake up at night missin' your arms around me.

KEGHEAD: Christ, she must be hard-up!

ROD: Put your arms around me, honey . . . hoold me tight [*sings*].

[CHRIS *takes the letter.*]

CHRIS: Wait till the wife cops you out.

ANDY: Aha . . . but she never won't! [*Skips around* CHRIS.]

KEGHEAD: Get onto him, will you? Like a dirty-minded little faun!

DARKY [*off. Loud and drunk*]: Up the Territory . . . Up Wimpy Murdoch . . . Up the M and V . . .

CHRIS: Listen to Darky.

[OT *appears in the doorway with a bundle of washing. He dumps it into the bucket.*]

OLLIE   Onya, Onya. Onya.

    [*together*]:

CHRIS   'Ow's our form . . . be on us.

OT: Struth! Goin' South . . . going to be a couple of Queen Street Commandoes.

OLLIE: True as God we're not comin' back.

CHRIS: None of us on this draft is comin' back. Hey, youse'll be sweet.

OT: Good luck to youse. Good luck! [*He shakes hands with them.*] Youse done your term . . .

CHRIS: Be funny to be out of the old place.

OLLIE: Don't forget to write us a note of how youse are all gettin' on.

KEGHEAD: You won't have to worry, Ot. They'll be back. I heard that story before.

CHRIS: Oh get ripped.

> [DARKY *enters singing. He is in a state of great dishevelment and is carrying a bottle of some evil-looking liquid.*]

DARKY [*singing*]: Sorry that I'm goin' but ish makes no diffrencsh now . . . and up Wimpy Murdoch . . . Whacko . . .

VIC: Good on you, Darky . . . getting away at last.

ANDY: Good on you, Darky.

> [*They help him to a bed.*]

DARKY: My fren's . . . my good fren's . . . distinguished company . . . I am leaving for the great South land . . . and I say frig 'em, frig 'em. [*Gaily*] Hooray to all the bastards.

CHRIS: Come on, you big ape . . . put that jungle juice away . . . We got to be getting our gear down to the truck.

DARKY: Frig the gear. [*Attempts to stand.*] My fren's and I call you my fren's . . .

CHORUS: Because you ARE my friends.

> [*Everyone laughs.*]

ANDY: Give him some black coffee.

DARKY: I don' wan' coffee . . . I just wanna tell you all my fren's now that I'm leavin' this bastard of a place that it's no refle'tion on you that I'm leaving . . .

> [*In an effort to embrace them all he nearly falls off the bed.* CHRIS *and* OLLIE *hold him up. He catches hold of* ANDY'S *hand.*]

My good fren's . . . we're all cobbers, aren't we?

ANDY: Sure, Darky.

CHRIS: Oh, come on Darky for the love of Mike—we'll miss the truck.

DARKY [*twisting free and getting to his feet to embrace* ANDY]: All cobbers see . . . and I tell you it's . . . it's not goin' to be the pickin's being away from you all . . . Now I mean it . . . honest I mean . . . I know what you all thinkin' . . . that mad bastard McClure he's . . . bup . . . on the jungle juice . . . but honest,

Andy . . . and Keghead . . . [*Falling almost into* KEGHEAD'S *arms*] I mean it . . . won't seem the same . . .

OLLIE: Come on Darky.

[*They try to get hold of him.*]

DARKY: Goin' to miss the old mess bell . . . and the swy game and . . . [*Getting maudlin and tearful*] Goin' to be . . . lonely down South . . . missin' all this bastardry . . . 'ow's a bloke goin' to be . . . [*His head on a level with* KEGHEAD'S *belt*] I'm on a level . . . You're my best friend . . . I mean it . . .

KEGHEAD: He hasn't half been on the jungle juice . . .

ANDY: Better get him up to the Orderly Room or youse'll miss the truck.

DARKY [*spinning round to* ANDY]: My little Andy . . . you're my best cobber, ole chap . . . Now honest, I mean it . . . Mad Darky they say . . . but when a pal's a pal . . . [*Weeping*] Honest I'll write to yer, Andy . . . a pal can't say more . . . [*To the others*] Can't say more, can you . . . [*Suddenly spies* GIG APE] My old fren' . . . my dearest old fren' . . . Gig Ape . . . finest man in the Territory . . . I'll write to yer . . . A pal can say no more, can he . . . I mean it . . . goin' to be . . . [*drooping*] kinda . . . lonesome . . .

[*He collapses forward as* OLLIE *and* CHRIS *catch him. The bottle falls out of his hand.* KEGHEAD *is the first to catch it. He puts it to his nose.*]

KEGHEAD: Crikey. Don't light a match near this.

GIG: Better chuck that away.

KEGHEAD [*putting it in his hip pocket*]: I'll put it where it'll be safe.

CHRIS: Give us a hand, Ot.

[OT *takes* DARKY'S *legs and with* CHRIS *and* OLLIE *they get him outside as* MAC *squeezes past them into the hut. He is covered in purple triple dye and is in a state of wild excitement.*]

MAC: Hey Andy . . . give us a hand, will you . . . I got to turn me things in.

ANDY: Whaddye mean . . . turn your things in?

MAC: It's through . . . me compassionate's through. Wimpy says I got to go on the draft tonight.

KEGHEAD: Tonight!

VIC: How can you get out tonight?

MAC: They just sent a signal from Norforce, Darwin.

VIC: But who's going to make out your Mob 3's this . . .

MAC: Young Beanie's gone back to HQ. I got to pick 'em up at ten o'clock in the duty truck.

KEGHEAD: ANOTHER one goin' South . . . How are they. I'll never git out of this place . . .

[*Suddenly three great clangs of the gong are heard.*]

VIC: Three bells. Come on, Rod, we'd better clear up some of this mess.

ROD: Give us a hand, Gig.

[*They go out with the plates, etc.*]

ANDY [*to* MAC, *who is frenziedly throwing things right and left*]: You better just pack what you want and leave us the rest . . . We'll hand your gear and stuff in for you tomorrow.

MAC: Wouldn't it rip you? Three bloody weeks making up their mind and they decide to send me at a minute's notice . . . Oh, they'd give you the tom-tits.

ANDY [*on his knees*]: Here—you'll need a clean towel and change of shirt.

MAC [*irritably*]: Leave them alone . . . I know what I want.

ANDY: I'm only tryin' to give you a hand.

MAC: I know, I know. [*Wriggling his back*] I'm in agony.

KEGHEAD [*dourly*]: You oughtn't to be goin' down the way you are.

MAC: You keep your great big trap shut, Keghead. I'm going South because I got trouble at home . . . Whether I got dermo or not don't come into it.

KEGHEAD: Cripes, you're never satisfied. How long you got?

MAC: Thirty days, that's all—and travelling time . . . I won't have time to fix me affairs in that time. [*Throwing sox wildly about.*] See if you can find me razor . . . It's here somewhere . . . I got to get to the Orderly Room by ten—it's quarter to now.

[OT *comes in.*]

OT: Is Mac here?

ANDY: Yeah, did you hear the big news? Mac's going tonight with the draft.

OT: Yeah? Well the doctor wants to see him right away . . . at the R.A.P.

MAC [*pausing in the middle of rolling things in a shirt*]: The Doctor.

OT: Right away. He's just been up to see the Colonel about you.

MAC [*frightened*]: Wot's he want? . . . Tell him I haven't got time . . . I got orders to pack.

OT: He's seen the Colonel about you . . . He's just come back from the Colonel's tent . . . You're to go over at once.

[SGT. BROOKS *appears in doorway*.]

BROOKS: Mac here?

MAC: Yes.

BROOKS: Got a bit of bad news for you. You're on your way to hospital.

[*The sox roll out of* MAC'S *hand. He stares at* BROOKS.]

Better get a pair of pyjamas and toothbrush and come over right away.

MAC: They can't do that to me . . . I've had orders from Norforce . . . I'm to leave tonight on the train. I been waiting weeks for this.

BROOKS: Looks like you'll have to postpone it.

MAC: I can't . . . My kids are in trouble . . . Look here . . .

BROOKS [*steadily*]: Perhaps you should have thought of that before you started any tricks with yourself. [*He turns and walks out.*]

[MAC *turns to* ANDY *shakily.*]

MAC: I'm goin'—to the Colonel.

ANDY: I'll come up with you.

MAC: They can't stop me goin' . . . can they?

ANDY: 'Course not . . . if LHQ grant it . . . you're sweet.

KEGHEAD: Don't be too sure of that. I wouldn't bet on goin' now at all.

ANDY: Shut up, Keghead. Come on, Mac . . .

MAC [*as they go out*]: They can't stop me . . . just on account of a bit of dermo . . . It isn't fair . . . They can't stop me . . . can they?

[*They go out.* KEGHEAD *follows behind, taking a swig of the jungle juice. The hut is empty for a moment. Then from the next hut comes the sad, sweet, lonely sound of someone playing a harmonica.* VIC *and* ROD *come in slowly, carrying the plates they have cleaned. They put them back in their kit bags. They sit on the end of their beds and smile at each other. Then* VIC *reaches behind him and takes out a battered copy of Voltaire.*]

ROD: One of the books I lent you?

    [VIC *turns the cover round.*]

  Voltaire. How are you getting on with him?

VIC: He's not bad, is he? Struth, what words!

ROD: You really like him—no kidding?

VIC: Dinkum.

    [*Two bells sound.* ROD *starts brushing his hair.*]

ROD: Two bells. Wonder where everyone is.

VIC: At the swy, I s'pose.

    [*Harmonica plays on. It has a lonely, sad sound.*]

ROD: There's Ernie Green on the harmonica. [*He puts down his brush to listen.*] Crikey it's a lonely sound.

    [VIC *puts up his head to listen.*]

  It's like all the loneliness in this whole place welling up out of the earth . . . isn't it?

VIC: Yeah. All the loneliness in the world . . . and a million years old.

    [ROD *looks at him sharply but he has returned to his book.* ROD *goes back to brushing his hair. The harmonica continues sadly in the background.*]

    [*The lights dim very slowly.*]

                                                      (*End of Scene*)

ACT TWO

scene 2

Scene: Corner of the switch room at Signals. Three months later. The curtain rises on the corner of the switch-room in the Sigs building. It is past midnight on a Saturday in September of the same year. The building is corrugated iron, dusty and cobwebby. There is a large telephone switch and a long counter. Behind the switch JACK TURNER, *a corporal in Sigs, is sitting trying to keep awake. On the counter stretched out asleep is* SGT. BROOKS *covered with an overcoat. Next to the switch an open doorway leads out into the night. It is bright moonlight.* KEGHEAD *sits on the floor, leaning against the door. Opposite him sits* ROD *yawning behind a copy of Army News.* OT *is asleep on the floor on a groundsheet and in the shadows beyond the door is the shadowy figure of* KEN FALCON. *The whole scene emphasizes an atmosphere of tired static waiting. Ten seconds or so pass after the curtain rises.* KEGHEAD *yawns.*

KEGHEAD: What's about the time?

ROD: Quarter to one.

KEGHEAD: Quarter past Melbourne time.

    [*There is a long pause.*]

ROD: Who's that sitting outside?

KEGHEAD: Dean Maitland.

ROD: Does he ring up much?

KEGHEAD: 'Bout once a month.

    [*Long pause.*]

  How's the war going?

ROD: Monty's going through France like butter.

KEGHEAD: Oh, the Jerries'll make a stand, you'll see. We'll have a two-year stalemate.

ROD: That's right—look on the bright side.

KEGHEAD: We haven't started yet. You wait. I'm tippin' Hitler will use gas. [*Pause. He turns to call up* JACK.] Hey Jack, don't that friggin' thing ever ring?

JACK [*sourly*]: You'll hear it when it does.

KEGHEAD: How ARE they. Bloody well go to sleep down at Alice.

JACK: Think I want to sit up all night?

KEGHEAD: This is the last time I ever ring up Molly.

ROD: You've been saying that ever since I came up here in March.

KEGHEAD: Yeah, well I mean it. [*Groans.*] Oh, a bloke will go mad waitin' around here. Think of all those lucky runts asleep over there.

ROD: Oh, it's worth it if you can get three minutes at home.

KEGHEAD: You'll give the game away by this time next year.

ROD: That's if I'm still here.

KEGHEAD: You'll be here.

ROD: I don't bet on anything.

KEGHEAD: Ahh, don't give me them. You only come up here in March—you got another year to go before you'll get leave.

ROD: A lot can happen in a year.

KEGHEAD: Bloomin' optimist, aren't you? Why don't you pull your head in?

ROD: Why don't you?

> [KEGHEAD *does. There is another silence. Suddenly there is a slight buzz from the telephone. Instantly they are all alert.* BROOKS *rises up on one elbow.*]

JACK [*lifting receiver*]: Larra . . . Larra . . . hello . . . Alice . . . hello . . . Alice?

> [*Pause. He puts the phone down. They all relax again.*]

KEGHEAD: Saturday night down there. Dancin' down at St. Kilda Palais. [*He gives a long sigh.*]

> [ROD *drops the paper and stares ahead.*]

KEGHEAD: Has Andy heard from Mac?

ROD: Yeah.

KEGHEAD: Has he got his divorce?

ROD: I think the papers are filed.

KEGHEAD: Wouldn't blame any dame walking out on that big fat bludger. Struth, he used to give me the tom-tits.

ROD: I think Andy misses him.

KEGHEAD: No one to have a decent brawl with.

> [*Pause.*]

ROD: Have you heard from Darky?

KEGHEAD: Only a postcard. A dirty one too.

ROD: Any good guts about what's going on in Melbourne?

KEGHEAD: He'd seen Chris and Ollie. They reckon fifty replacements get here this month.

ROD: Oh yeah?

KEGHEAD: It's right. Coming up from Adelaide.

ROD: Wish they meant it.

KEGHEAD: By gee, they'll have a ruddy jack-up here in the Transport Section if they don't. Ernie Green's done two years straight next Friday.

[*Again the phone buzzes. All stop talking.*]

JACK: Hello Larra . . . yes, Larra . . . say again . . . Oh, that you George . . . Yeah . . . Who's it for? . . . Mr. Larcombe? . . . He's up at Pine Creek till Tuesday . . . What's it about? . . . Oh, Field Returns? . . . That'll do on Monday, won't it? . . . O.K. How's the game up there? . . . No . . . still here . . . I don't know . . . I say I don't know . . . Supposed to have left in August . . . O.K. [*Hangs up.*]

KEGHEAD: Wasn't that Alice?

JACK: No, Katherine.

KEGHEAD: What the hell's wrong with Alice?

JACK: Dunno. The line may be bad tonight.

[*A* SIGS. PRIVATE *enters with a mug of steaming tea.*]

SIGS. [*handing mug to* JACK]: Here's yours.

JACK: Ta.

SIGS.: Calls started yet?

JACK: No.

SIGS.: Got many tonight?

JACK: About ten.

SIGS.: Good on you, Jack. Well, I'm going to bed. [*He goes out.*]

[*The boys watch* JACK *drink the tea, enviously.*]

KEGHEAD: I could do a mug of tea meself right now.

BROOKS [*sitting up drowsily*]: Someone call me?

KEGHEAD [*disgustedly*]: No.

BROOKS: Thought I heard my name called. Any calls through yet?

KEGHEAD [*sourly*]: Yes, we've had the lot but we're stoppin' here for a game of cut-throat bridge.

[BROOKS *lies down.*]

Heard his name called! Thinks he's bloody Joan of Arc.

[*Weariness descends on them again. The lights fade out. After a second the lights go up. They are all sitting in the same position.* KEGHEAD *is asleep.* ROD *is smoking.* KEN CARSON *has joined the group. Outside the moon has waned.*]

JACK: Got the time?

ROD: Ten minutes to two.

JACK: Ta.

ROD: Pretty late tonight, aren't they?

JACK: There's only one line. Larrimah musta took it first.

ROD: How many calls would they have?

JACK: 'Bout sixty.

ROD: Gee.

JACK: Oh, they ought to be through soon.

[*In the distance the sound of a distant train whistle.*]

BROOKS [*sitting up*]: Someone call me?

ROD: No.

BROOKS: Any calls yet?

ROD: No.

BROOKS: Oh well. [*Lies down again.*]

ROD: A man'll be too tired to remember what he wanted to say by the time we get them.

[*The phone buzzes suddenly.* KEGHEAD *stirs.* BROOKS *stirs.*]

JACK: Larra . . . say again . . . Larra . . . Oh yes sir . . . no, it hasn't started yet . . . yes sir, I'll phone you the minute it comes through. [*Hangs up.*] That was Major Murdoch.

[*Exclamations of disgust.*]

KEGHEAD: Wimpy!

ROD: Wonder he isn't doing an inspection of the lines.

KEGHEAD: All right for him. Sitting up in the Officers' Mess waiting for his ruddy call. Probably got down on all the prewar Scotch by now.

ROD: Gee, how I love that man.

KEGHEAD: Of all the . . . oh, I give the game away.

[*A second later the phone buzzes again.*]

JACK: Larra . . . yes . . . [*Then almost shouting*] Larrakeena here . . . Larrakeena.

82

[*Everyone except* OT *is on the alert.*]
Yes . . . can't hear you . . . I say the line's bad tonight . . . Yes
. . . yes . . . [*nods to the boys.*]
   [*They nudge each other.*]
Yes . . . What's first? . . . What's that? . . .
KEGHEAD: Better be Victorian calls first.
ROD: New South Wales—they took first last time.
JACK: Shut up, I can't hear. [*Into phone*] What? . . . Is that you,
   Jean? . . . Yeah . . . Oh, that's better. [*Reducing voice*] Is the
   line bad tonight . . . Oh, have they . . . a bad storm? Oh . . .
   [*Taking out a long board with a paper clipped to it*] Yes . . .
   Perth . . . Yes . . .
KEGHEAD: Perth . . . how is it.
JACK: Mt. Lawley . . . yes . . . number eighteen . . . er . . . 6769
   . . . yes . . . Anyone here calling Perth?
KEGHEAD   Hey, Ot . . . Ot, wake up! . . . Here's your call.
      [*together*]:
ROD   Ot . . . on your feet . . . rise and shine . . .
OT [*sleepily*]: Huh?
KEGHEAD: And get it over quick too. You're the only Perth call
   tonight.
OT: Whassis . . . reveille?
ROD: Your call.
   [OT *is on his feet and outside the door in a second. His voice can
   be heard plainly.*]
OT: 'Ullo . . . 'ulloo . . . 'ullo . . . is that you, sweetheart . . . 'ullo . . .
JACK [*into phone*]: Hold the line . . . You're onto Alice Springs.
OT: 'Ullo Alice darling . . . I mean Daw . . . is that you, Rosebud?
   [*Pause.*] Ullo . . . yes . . . is that you, Dawn? . . . This is Eric.
   [*He has to yell*] Hullo . . . I can't hear you . . . The line's not
   too good . . . [*Long pause.*] What's that love? . . . I didn't quite
   catch that . . .
   [*Everyone pretends to be absorbed in something else.*]
Oh, I'm O.K. What's that? Leave? . . . Oh, you know the old
story . . . yeah . . . I say the SAME OLD STORY . . . Oh,
might be down in October . . . OCTOBER . . . No, I MIGHT
. . . Still love me? . . . I say STILL LOVE ME? . . . Can't you
hear me? . . . Dawn . . . do you still love me? [*trying it very

softly] . . . Well, say something to me then. I can hear YOU . . .
I say . . . SAY SOMETHING TO ME . . . [*Long pause*] YOU
SAY SOMETHING TO ME.

KEGHEAD: Oh Dawn, say something to him. I'm going CRAZY.

JACK [*into phone*]: That's your three minutes.

OT: I got to buzz off now . . . I SAY I GOT TO GO NOW. Give
my love to your mum . . . Hooroo . . . [*With a slight crack in
the voice*] I love you.

[*A pause.* OT *appears in the doorway, sweating. He is conscious
that everyone has heard every word. So is everyone else. They
are elaborately trying to look elsewhere.*]

OT: You can't hear much. [*Gulping*] She never heard a word I said.
Well . . . g'night. [*He goes.*]

JACK [*on phone*]: Yes, hullo . . . Larra . . . Larra . . . Who's next? . . .
Who's next? . . . Yes . . . Victoria.

[BROOKS *and* KEGHEAD *both start up at once.*]

JACK: Yes, St. Kilda . . . [*nodding to* KEGHEAD].

KEGHEAD: You little beauty. [*He is outside the door in a trice.*]

JACK: Hullo . . . Callee is coming to the phone . . . Go ahead . . .

KEGHEAD [*loudly off*]: Molly? Molly? Molly? [*Muttering oaths.*]
Wot's wrong with the bloody thing?

JACK: Watch your language. You're going through three states.

KEGHEAD: Molly? Molly? That you, Moll? [*Suddenly moves*] How
are you, dear? Did you send up the hair restorer? . . . I want
some more biscuits dear . . . Oh, the same as ever . . . NO OF
COURSE I DON'T KNOW WHEN . . . 1950, if I'm lucky . . .
What can I do about it? . . . Of course I've seen him . . . He can't
do anything . . . Well, what you expect ME to do about it? . . .
[*Angrily*] I KNOW! I KNOW! Well, I can't see the minister
up here. Use your sense . . . Well, why don't you? . . . I say
WHY DON'T YOU . . . YOU SEE HIM? . . . WHY DON'T
YOU SEE THE MINISTER ABOUT LEAVE . . . ABOUT
LEAVE . . . NO—LEAVE . . . [*Sinking his voice to a whisper*]
Leave . . . L for Laura, E for Emily, A for apples . . . apples.

JACK: Three minutes.

KEGHEAD: APPLES . . . Hullo . . . hullo, Moll . . . hullo [*Sounds of
exasperation*] How is it. [*He appears at the door.*] How's a man's
luck . . . Wait four hours gettin' the call through because of an

important message . . . and then what happens?

ROD: Did she hear you?

KEGHEAD: Hear me? She's sending me a case of apples! [*He gestures hopelessly and staggers out into the night.*]

JACK: Who's next? . . . Who's . . . ? Hello, Alice . . . yes, finished . . . yes. Who's next? Carlton . . . yes. Any Carlton here?

[KEN FALCON *gets up. Comes to the counter.*]

You Carlton?

[KEN FALCON *nods.*]

Sorry, there's no one answering at that number.

[KEN *doesn't seem to understand. He watches* JACK *hopefully.*]

No one answering. We'll refund that to you . . . Here's your three and six. Here . . . three bob and a zac.

[*He puts the money into* KEN'S *hand.* KEN *nods and moves slowly to the door.* JACK *turns to the others.*]

JACK: It never answers . . . He's been ringin' that number for goin' on two years and they never answered yet.

[*Phone buzzes.*]

Hullo Larra . . . Larra . . . yes . . . Major Murdoch, yes . . . I'll buzz him . . .

[*Lights fade.*]

(*End of Scene*)

ACT TWO

scene 3

Scene: The hut. A Sunday morning. It is now well into September and the dreaded "Wet" is expected weekly. The blazing sun is beating down outside on the red cracked sand. GIG APE, VIC, and OT are turning out their soldiers' boxes, and assortments of all the articles a soldier would have in his box are strewn over the floor and on the beds. OT props up the perennial photo of Dawn where he can see her on the bed.

OT: The little Rosebud, eh. The little rosy snifter. Three weeks from Friday . . . whoo ooooh! [*He kisses the photo.*]

GIG: Dirty perv.

OT: Who's a dirty perv, you dirty perv. Oh, how was the Gig Ape last night at the pitchers . . . Eh Vic, did you hear him?

VIC: Yeah. [*Smiles.*]

OT: Oh, the perv! Gee I laughed.

[ROD *comes in minus his shirt, carrying washing.*]

ROD: Anyone lend me some washing soap?

VIC: You can have this . . . I won't be needing it. [*He throws a bar.*]

ROD: Thanks. [*Glances at* VIC. *Frowns.*]

VIC [*smiles*]: What's up?

ROD: Nothing. Can't believe you're all going on Friday, that's all. I'm going to be a bit lost. The hut full of new faces.

OT [*dancing around waving a singlet*]: The Big Smoke . . . we're going to the Big Smoke. [*Waving a box at* ROD] Have a Milko ball?

ROD: Thanks.

OT: Hey, did you hear the Gig Ape last night? Just as well he's going home?

ROD: No, what happened?

OT: What? Eh, don't tell me youse didn't hear it at the pictures? Did you go to the pictures last night?

ROD: Nup. First pictures for a month and I copped guard.

OT: Oh, wait till I tell you . . . [*He sits on bed roaring with laughter.*]
There's this Rita Hayworth picture on, see . . . wot's it called?
. . . Aw, I forget now . . . "Epilepsy".

VIC: "Ecstasy."

OT: Oho! Gee, wouldn't it be with that skirt? Anyhow there's the
bit where she's makin' up to Fred Astaire.

VIC: Who's making up to Fred Astaire?

OT: This sheila . . . Rita Hayworth, and is she a skirt . . . And she's
in one of them lace dingdongs cut down low on her chest . . .
struth! . . . [*giggles*] and she's making up to Fred Astaire see . . .
on this couch . . . Well, there's a silence you see and suddenly
the Gig Ape calls out from the back: "I can't STAND it."
    [*Everyone roars with laughter.* GIG APE *hits* OT *on the head with a
    tennis ball.* ROD *starts hanging his clothes up on the line.*]

OT: The Gig Ape . . . eh . . . gee, I laughed . . . "I can't stand it,"
he says . . . aw, gee . . .

VIC: Gee, it's hot.

GIG: Hey, are we lucky gettin' out just before the Wet.

VIC: I reckon we'll strike the Wet on the road down.

OT: Rod'll be doin' his first Wet . . . How's that, eh Rod?

ROD: Yes . . . my first Wet . . . Initiated.

VIC: Don't let 'em get you down, boy . . . It's not quite as bad as
they say. Only about ninety degrees humidity.

OT: Yeah . . . it's the humidity. Hey, Gig . . . do you reckon I'd
better wear them shorts down . . . or keep them for arrivin' in
Adelaide?

GIG: Keep 'em, you dope. Those convoy trucks is open all the way
down.

OT [*proudly*]: This pile's all clean . . . These are me clean duds
for meetin' Rosebud at the station.

ROD: Getting married this leave, Ot?

OT: You said it. Just got to talk to Mum first. I'm Mum's only
interest, see. But Mum's a sport. Good old Mum.

GIG [*singing*]: Home to Mum . . . Home to Mum.
    [KEGHEAD *appears in the doorway sweating in full clothes and
    with his hat on.*]

KEGHEAD: How's a bloke's luck . . . coppin' Sunday Orderly
Sergeant again.

GIG: Keghead, Keghead . . .

   [*They all take up the chorus.*]

KEGHEAD: Aw, give it away, will you . . . which is Ken Falcon's bed?

OT: Next to the door there.

KEGHEAD: I got to get a few things out of his box for him.

GIG: Wot's up with him?

KEGHEAD [*busily getting out toothbrush and paste, brush and comb*]: Oh, they're taking him up to Katherine to hospital.

OT: What's he going to hospital?

VIC: What's he got? Dermo?

KEGHEAD [*awkwardly*]: No. They're taking him to the psychiatric ward.

ROD: The psychiatric ward.

OT: What's that?

VIC: Where they take you when you go troppo.

OT: Cripes. Poor old Dean Maitland.

GIG: Is he nuts?

KEGHEAD: Not any more than most of us. [*He picks up things.*] Hey, will one of youse jokers take this box over to the Q Store later and hand his bed in for him . . . He's going to be a long time away. [*He goes out.*]

   [*They are a bit stunned but characteristically don't show it much. VIC and ROD sit down on their beds near each other. After a moment GIG starts to hum the current movie success, "As Time Goes By".*]

OT: How'd it be to go crackers. Would youse know you was nuts or would youse think every other joker was?

GIG: Youse'd think every other joker was troppo but yourself.

OT: Poor old Dean Maitland. [*He starts putting shirts in his kit bag.*] And a week before he was due for leave draft.

GIG: "You must remember this . . . a kiss is still a kiss . . ."

OT: Maybe we orta have talked a bit to the Dean.

   [*Pause.*]

VIC: That's the sort of thing that happens to you if you can't get things off your chest. There must have been a lot on his mind. I never saw him speak the whole time he was here.

ROD: Yeah, I know.

   [SAMMY KUHN *rushes in. He is very obviously Jewish. Wears*

88

thick glasses. Has large clammy red features and carries an exercise book. He speaks in a loud staccato soprano.]

SAMMY: Pardon . . . any of you jokers interested in taking a ticket in a raffle for a bottle of genuine Scotch Whisky?

[*There is a silence. Hostile at that.*]

OT: How much?

SAMMY: Bob a throw.

OT: No thanks.

SAMMY: Anyone interested?

[*Various denials. Everyone becomes absorbed in work.*]

Drawn tonight in the men's mess . . . Anyone care to have a go? No? Thanks, chums . . . [*He goes out.*]

GIG: How is he.

OT: Only arrived last Tuesday. No doubt about him, is there?

GIG: Be running the place next week. Come on over and get the mail?

OT: He won't have sorted her out yet.

GIG: We can get ours though. Come on.

OT: All right . . . just till I fix these sox. [*Picks up sox. Puts them in kit bag. Sees photo, picks it up.*] Friday three weeks you . . . little snifter . . . you watch yourself then. [*Whistles. Puts photo in box. Gives* ROD *the box of Milkos*] Have a Milko, you old bum.

ROD: Thanks.

[*The boys go out.*]

I'll miss Ot. No more gardens . . . no exercises . . . nobody asking me how to spell "fiancee". It's been a good crowd and I wouldn't bet on the type that's coming up here as replacements. If they ever come.

[VIC *looking rather embarrassed hands* ROD *a small parcel.*]

What's this?

VIC: Oh, not much . . . s'pose you'd call it a sort of goodbye present . . .

ROD: Oh . . . thanks. [*He unwraps it. Takes out china shaving mug.*] Oh, I haven't got one either. Thanks, Vic.

VIC: It's been a long time coming up.

ROD: Gee, you shouldn't have. What made you think of a shaving cup?

VIC: I broke yours the first night you came here.

ROD: Oh yes . . . I remember now.

VIC: Did you know it was me?

ROD: I sort of knew.

VIC: Funny you never said.

ROD: Never seemed worthwhile bringing it up. But I'll keep this.

VIC: I'll miss you Rod.

[SGT. BROOKS *appears in the doorway. Hot and on the warpath.*]

BROOKS: Corporal Richards.

VIC: Yes.

BROOKS: Major Murdoch gave instructions these cupboards outside were to be used only for bootbrushes and paste.

VIC: Well?

BROOKS: But they're all empty!

VIC: That's right.

BROOKS: But when I complained about you boys having tins in them last week I didn't mean you to take everything out of them.

VIC: You charged Otford and Kneale with contravening orders and got 'em fined, didn't you?

BROOKS: Major Murdoch did, yes. I instructed you then to clear out all tins and make a report to me.

VIC: Which I did.

BROOKS: After which I expected to find only bootbrushes and bootpaste in these cupboards. Instead of which I find NOTHING.

VIC: What did you expect to find?

BROOKS: I told you . . . bootpaste and bootbrushes, for which the cupboards were made.

VIC: Yeah, well, it's like this . . . The blokes feel that they don't want to be told what they put in those cupboards seeing they made them themselves in their own time.

BROOKS: I don't know about that. All I know is that Major Murdoch came down the lines . . .

VIC: Came snooping down here like usual and had to have something to say about our cupboards like he has to say about everything.

BROOKS: What's this then . . . a jack-up?

VIC: A sort of jack-up. If we can't use the cupboards for our own stuff the way we made 'em . . . we won't use 'em for anything.

BROOKS: Major Murdoch won't like . . .

90

VIC: You can tell Major Wimpy Murdoch from us to go to hell truly.

ROD: That goes for all of us.

BROOKS: I see. I take it you're the ringleader in this, Richards?

VIC: I just happen to be hut corporal now that Andy Edwards has been promoted and moved up to the snake pit with you and the other snakes.

BROOKS [*curtly*]: I see.

VIC: And anyway this is Sunday, so why don't you get off our back for once and pull your big woolly head in?

BROOKS: I'm carrying out my duties, Corporal Richards, whether you like it or not.

VIC: You'll get on.

BROOKS: Better be careful or you'll find yourself on an A4 pretty damn quick.

VIC [*angrily*]: Oh why don't you take a big jump in the lake . . . all this bloody fuss over a few cupboards. That's what's wrong with this place . . . It's bad enough being here with the bloody ants and flies, isn't it, without a few frustrated bastards making it worse by exercising petty authority . . . I've had it. I'm leaving on Friday and I can tell you I'm thankful to see the last of you and your crawling mates. You're a lot of pip-happy crawling runts.

BROOKS: You'll be sorry you said that. [*He moves off.*]

ROD: Good on you, Vic.

VIC: Honest he just gives me 'em, that galah. Cupboards . . . There's blokes getting the guts shot out of them in New Guinea and all he can worry about is cupboards. I'd like to see him and Wimpy faced with a few Japs. Cupboards!

[*Three loud gongs off.*]

ROD: Three for lunch. Better finish the rest after.

VIC: Oh, I'll give you a hand with your washing.

[GIG APE *comes in with* ANDY *and carries letters and parcels.*]

ANDY: Good day, young Rod . . . Good day, young Vic.

ROD and VIC [*together*]: Hullo, Andy.

[*They ignore the fact that* ANDY *is brandishing his new stripes at them.* GIG *hands out letters.*]

GIG: Rod . . . Rod again . . . Stewart—that's the new bloke in the second bed.

[ANDY *takes letter to what was previously* MAC'S *bed*.]

GIG: Parcel for Rod.

ROD: Thanks.

GIG: And two for me . . . Hey, there's one here for Dean Maitland.

VIC: Bit late, isn't it. That must have been the one he's been sweating on the last year.

GIG: I'll take it back to Tommy Evans to repost . . . [*Suddenly*] Eh, can he read now?

VIC: I wonder. [*Getting mess tins*.]

ANDY: Open the one from Darky.

GIG: I am . . . blast you . . . Wait on, can't you? [*Reading and laughing*] "There's a couple of galahs on the way up we met in Adelaide" . . . How is he . . . "The beer is fine . . . and I just met up with a decent sort at Ascot whose name is Mascotte and boy . . ."

[ANDY *and* GIG *shriek with laughter*.]

[OT *comes in the door. He is holding a letter that is open and walking very slowly*.]

GIG: "However you will be glad to know we are all being reposted down South, so they say, if you can trust them cows . . ." Hey, did you hear that, Ot? . . . Darky reckons . . .

[OT'S *expression makes him stop*.]

Anything up?

[OT *sits slowly on the bed. He gives a little smile. Faintly*.]

OT: No. Nothin'.

GIG: We're being reposted . . . All the blokes on leave draft now . . . Darky thinks he'll be going to Bathurst . . . How'd that be after two years in the Territory? Hard to take, eh?

OT [*looking up slowly*]: Remember the girl friend?

GIG: Dawn? Yes?

OT: She got married.

[GIG APE *stares dumbfounded at the letter, his mouth open. The others turn and stop in their tracks*.]

[*Outside comes the sound of two gongs heavily bidding the guests to dine. Commanding notes that echo and die as the lights fade*.]

(*End of Scene*)

ACT TWO

scene 4

Scene: Outside H.Q. ARMCO hut about five days later. It is four o'clock in the afternoon and still blazing hot. The boys are having the afternoon smoko and are sitting in what little shade there is around a stunted tree. They are drinking black coffee. ROD *wears no shirt.* ANDY *wears his plus stripes.* KEGHEAD *sits moodily sipping coffee.*

KEGHEAD: Middle of winter they give you iced lemon drink . . . Middle of summer—hot black coffee. The bastards are mad.

ANDY [*who has been reading Army News*]: Here's a dame bicycled all the way from Geelong to Bendigo in a nightie. Protest.

KEGHEAD: Protest for what?

ANDY: Her husband wouldn't sleep with her.

KEGHEAD: Can't blame the poor bastard . . .

ANDY: Never you mind—she got her divorce.

KEGHEAD: I wonder if Mac cracked his.

ANDY: That bludger wouldn't write to his own mother.

KEGHEAD: Same as all the rest. Up here it's "Oh yes, Keghead, you're my best cobber, I'll write mate . . ." and once they get down to the big smoke, they're on to the nest and you're forgot.

ANDY: It's true. I haven't had a letter for two weeks . . . not from anybody.

KEGHEAD: Gee, this heat . . . [*Wipes his face and neck.*] Couple more weeks and she'll be right on.

ANDY: I'm tipping the end of next week will see the start.

[ROD *comes out on the tail end of this. Carries his mug, and his shirt off.*]

ROD: Not still tipping on leave.

ANDY: The Wet.

KEGHEAD: The filthy rotten stinking Wet.

ANDY: You wait. [*Laughs gleefully*] Oho, you just wait.

ROD: Don't be so ruddy gloating.

ANDY: You typed the Mob 3's yet?

ROD: Yes, just waiting for Wimpy to sign them.

ANDY: The old Wimp. He's just gone down for kit inspection with Vic and the Gig Ape.

OT: They'll be off tonight on the train.

KEGHEAD: Who else is on the draft?

ROD: Kingston from Number One Sub Depot, Sergeant Smokums, young Terry, one of the cooks, and Betty Grable.

KEGHEAD: Betty Grable from the kitchen . . . that greasy cook.

ROD: Yeah. He's replacing Ot.

KEGHEAD: I'm crook on those galahs. Putting me off and putting Betty Grable on and just because the Crab wouldn't let me go.

ROD: You'll be on next month's maybe.

KEGHEAD: I live on maybe's and I've had it.

ROD: Gee I'm sorry for Ot, poor kid.

ANDY: He still coulda went. He coulda went if he'd of wanted to but . . .

ROD: Just won't go home. He said he'd rather someone else went instead.

KEGHEAD: I should have gone. Ot and me come up on the same draft. Gee, I'm crooked on those drongoes. That rotten cook Betty Grable, he's half rotten with dermo too. By gee, if I'm not on the next draft I'm telling you there's going to be the biggest jack-up you ever saw. [*Wipes his face.*]

[SAMMY KUHN *comes out, his red face running with sweat but smiling and blinking behind his spectacles.*]

SAMMY: Any of you jokers like to be in a picnic to the falls on Sunday. We're getting up a truckload.

[*No one says anything.*]

ROD [*after a pause*]: It'd be too hot.

[*Sammy goes.*]

ANDY: The great Gig Ape.

[GIG *walks in. He flops down wearily.*]

ANDY: You passed Wimpy's kit inspection, then.

GIG: I was, yeah, but they copped old Vic. Wimpy come down . . . fat legs wobbling . . . Stand to attention, he says, beside your bed . . . Then he gets down on his knees and opens his box and gets Brooks to go through his kit bag.

94

KEGHEAD: You see . . . you see . . . bastardry all the way along the line . . .

ANDY: He can't do that be rights . . . not according to AMR and O's.

KEGHEAD: He'd crawl into the cot with you if it suited him and that isn't in orders either.

ANDY: Well, go on . . . [*prodding* GIG].

GIG: Someone musta drummed him Vic had extra razor blades . . . He's been saving them up and he had some sent up to him from town. He's got about a hundred saved there . . . Well Wimpy comes across them see . . . Wellllll, WAS it on. You shoulda seen his face.

KEGHEAD: Delight.

ANDY: Lickin' the old chops . . .

GIG: Yeah . . . "Ah Corporal Richards . . . can you explain this?" So Vic tells him the truth.

KEGHEAD: He wouldn't know the truth if it got up and kicked him.

GIG: He listens to it all with the look of a bloody old badger on his face . . . then he just goes on looking . . . through Vic's things and he spots this extra towel . . . THAT does it. He puts Vic on a charge sheet.

KEGHEAD: You see? [*Sighs.*] Oh, the bastardry.

ANDY: Because of a cupboard . . . an empty cupboard.

GIG: Yeah . . . you wait two years to get away from this bastard of a place . . . two years—and then . . .

KEGHEAD: We ought to have a general jack-up.

GIG: I'd be in it if it wasn't that, you know, I was going away tonight.
[ROD *appears in the doorway with a slip of paper.*]

ROD [*in a hushed voice*]: Where's Vic?

GIG: Down in the hut. He's got to unpack everything.

ROD: They can't mean it. They just can't do it to him . . . can they? Can they? [*He looks helplessly at them.*]
[VIC *suddenly appears from the pathway. Everyone looks rather embarrassed.*]

VIC [*calmly*]: Hullo. I suppose you've all heard.

ANDY: Yes, Vic.

KEGHEAD: Gee, the dirty rotten bludgers! . . . Over a towel.

ROD: You're going to fight it, I hope.
[VIC *shakes his head.*]

95

ROD: But Vic, you must . . . You can't let them do this to you. It's absolute victimization . . . just over a petty trifle. It's the frustrated bloody revenge of an egotistical tyrant who thinks because he's got a crown on his shoulders that he's got the right to order your whole life. God . . . why don't you demand to see the Colonel?

VIC: Ever tried that before? Who is the Colonel going to believe? Don't forget an officer's word cannot be doubted . . . because he's a gentleman.

ROD: By Act of Parliament.

VIC: No, take it easy . . . I guess it will work itself out. O.K. I'm not going on the leave draft . . . Well . . . O.K. I know there's blokes up North now who've got more worries on their mind than leave . . . that wake up wondering if it's the last time they'll ever wake up . . . get their guts shot to hell and don't wince about it. I'm safe . . . I sleep at night . . . I watch the sun and the stars . . . It's a pleasant way to rot in the sun sitting on an anthill . . . well, it isn't painful anyway so what the hell. So long, Gig . . . and make sure you don't come back.

[*They shake hands.*]

GIG: So long.

[VIC *turns and goes inside.* BROOKS *appears in the doorway.*]

BROOKS: I told you men the time was 1615 twenty minutes ago . . . That means report back to work . . . What the hell do you think this is? A holiday resort?

[*There is a pause for a second and then it breaks. A cacophony of pent-up insults in true Digger manner.*]

KEGHEAD: Aw, get ripped.

ANDY: You big galah . . . get a great big woolly pup.

KEGHEAD: In your great dinger, you rotten crawling chocko.

ANDY: And bash your charge sheets.

BOTH: Dirty crawling . . .

[*They advance on* BROOKS *who gulps and disappears in the doorway as the lights fade.*]

(*End of Scene*)

ACT TWO

scene 5

Scene: A month later. Night. The hut again. It is a sweltering night in October. SAMMY KUHN, *wearing only brief shorts, is lying on what was previously* GIG APE'S *bed. He is sucking at a bottle of lolly water and wiping the running sweat from his body with a towel. Otherwise the hut is empty. Outside the voices of the swy game are heard.*

VOICES [*off*]: Two bob to swing her . . . Who'll be in it? . . . Two bob in the guts . . . Up and do 'em, spinner.
   [*Pause. Then a chorus of yells.*]
   Heads pay . . . heads pay!
   [ANDY *comes in dripping with sweat. He looks around the gloomy empty hut.* SAMMY *sits up.*]
SAMMY [*gaily*]: Hy, Andy. How are you going Andy, eh?
ANDY: Oh it's you. Where's the boys?
SAMMY: I'm the only one in tonight.
ANDY: I can see that. Where's Ot?
SAMMY: Dunno. He's usually in. [*Holding out a disgustingly wet paper bag*] Like a lolly lush?
ANDY: No. [*Irritably*] Well gees, where is everyone? . . . It's nearly lights out and I can't find the bastards. Is Vic Richards going on the train tonight?
SAMMY: Yeah. So's Keghead, isn't he?
ANDY: Yes. Gee, it's hot.
SAMMY: The Wet's just about on us, I reckon. Have you done a Wet yet?
   [ANDY *regards him with tired disdain. Too tired even to insult him back.*]
SAMMY: Listen.
   [*There is an ominous roll of distant thunder.*]
ANDY: Cripes, the humidity must be over ninety.

[OT *droops in the doorway. He is stripped to the waist. He drops onto his bed without a word.*]

You been over at the swy?

OT: No [*listlessly*].

ANDY: Looks like we'll get it tonight. The Wet, I mean.

OT: Yeah.

ANDY: I hear Vic Richards is moving out tonight.

OT: Yeah.

ANDY: Keghead too. The old faces are thinning out. [*Stretches, then watches* OT.] How's things?

OT: O.K.

ANDY: How's the garden going, Ot?

OT: Give it away.

ANDY: Oh. Ever go over to the swy?

OT: Nup.

[*Thunder.*]

ANDY: Gee, where is everybody? . . . I come over to say goodbye to old Vic.

SAMMY: It was good him getting out of that charge, wasn't it?

ANDY: He threw old Wimpy all right. Strikes me old Wimp will be slower on the bastardry than he used to be . . . I think it's threw a bit of a spanner in his works. Old swine he is.

[VIC *and* ROD *come in.* VIC *is dressed for the road in long KD's. He carries kit bag very full.*]

ANDY: Oh, here he is . . . the big leave man.

VIC: Hullo Andy. [*Pointing to kit bag which he puts on the floor*] This one too Rod.

ROD: Where's your padlock?

VIC: Here.

[*Takes padlock out of his pocket. Gives it to* ROD *who padlocks the kit bag.*]

Gee, I hope I haven't forgot anything.

ANDY: I got a letter here I wondered if you'd post for me in Adelaide.

VIC: Sure.

[ANDY *passes it over.*]

ANDY: Thanks.

VIC [*grinning*]: She's still on, eh?

ANDY: Oho, yes . . . you ain't kiddin'. "Ah Andy," she writes . . .

"oh Andy, I'd like to feel your strong arms around me . . . your handsome lips pressed to mine."

VIC: Struth . . . hasn't she ever seen you?

[*Thunder rolls nearer.*]

ROD: The Wet . . . she come.

VIC: The Wet . . . I go.

ROD: Well . . . I reckon you'd better go and pick up the others . . . Almost time for you to be over at the RTD.

VIC: Yes—well . . . so long, Sammy [*shakes hands*].

SAMMY: Hooray, Vic.

VIC: Ot.

[OT *doesn't stir.*]

ANDY: Why, Ot . . . Vic's goin'.

OT: Eh? OH. [*Sitting up*] Going?

VIC: Yeah, we'll be off soon. So long.

OT: So long. Make sure you don't come back.

VIC: Don't worry. It'll be the islands for me next time . . . the real dinkum war. No more sitting on my pratt among the forgotten legions. [*Pause.*] When are YOU getting out?

OT: Oh, I don't want to go much. I reckon I'll stay on in the old place . . . You get used to it after a while.

VIC [*punching him affectionately*]: Snap out, kiddo.

VOICES [*off*]: Keghead. Keghead . . . the big leave man . . . Where'd you get that hat . . . Going through, Keghead.

[*The object of all this badinage appears in the doorway. He is dressed in full KD's and hat.*]

ANDY: Oh, here he is. The big go-through job.

KEGHEAD: Get ripped.

ROD: Well, you're really off home to Mum.

VIC: Home to Molly at last.

KEGHEAD: Haven't gone yet.

[*They all laugh except* OT.]

SAMMY [*nasally*]: I s'pose you reckon something will happen to stop you. *175445*

KEGHEAD: I wouldn't put it past the bludgers. You wait I'll get a mile down the road and there'll be a ruddy signal to send me back.

[*Laughter. Then thunder rolls nearer.*]

KEGHEAD: Just in time for the Wet. The roads will all be blocked, whad'ye bet me.

VIC: That's right, cheer us up.

KEGHEAD: I knew a bloke up at the river once, been in the friggin' Territory three years. Goes down on leave just this time of year and gets into the Wet . . . in a utility. Crosses the bridge down by Bore 6a just as the river carries the lot away. Drowns!

[*Three gongs sound.*]

ANDY: Three bells.

VOICE [*off*]: All right gentlemen, last spin . . . Who'll be in it? . . . Last spin for the evening.

VIC: Come on, Keg . . . we'd better be on our way.

ANDY: Goodbye Keghead, you old bludger.

KEGHEAD: You galah. [*Shakes hands with* ANDY *and then with* SAMMY.]

SAMMY: See you down South.

KEGHEAD: Bit of an optimist, aren't you?

ROD: How is he? Only been here six weeks.

SAMMY: Right!

VIC: Rod'll soon be the oldest inhabitant here.

ROD: That's going to be tough.

VIC [*touching the side of the hut*]: Well, I've slept my last night here. It's going to seem sort of funny not having the old blokes around . . . the old bull going on at night . . . gee, eh.

KEGHEAD: Oh, get ripped . . . you're like all of them . . . spend three years waitin' to get out of the bloody place and then you start gettin' sentimental over the white ants.

VIC: Who's getting sentimental?

KEGHEAD: Thank heaven we'll never come back to this joint . . . that's one thing certain. No matter where we go . . . they'll never send . . .

[*His words die on his lips.* MAC *is standing in the doorway dressed in full service kit and fatter than ever.*]

Struth!

[*They are all stunned.* MAC *stands aside and waves.* CHRIS *and* OLLIE *sidle in looking dead tired, filthy, and desolate.*]

MAC: How ARE the bastards.

CHRIS: How youse all goin'?

OLLIE: The old place hasn't altered much.

MAC: We just got in on the truck from Larrimah.

ANDY: Well!

VIC: They . . . sent you back?

OLLIE: Yeah, we're the first lot. Darky's with us.

MAC [*spitting*]: The dirty crabby . . .

ANDY: Well, how IS it.

[*The next minute the place is alive with yells. They are all asking questions and bellowing at each other.*]

OMNES: Why did you have to come back? . . . Are they reposting everyone? . . . Thought you'd got new jobs . . . How are the bastards . . . Well, wouldn't it.

KEGHEAD [*sitting on bed*]: I told you. Wot's the use of goin' now?

VIC: You had to come back! After two years' service.

MAC: So much for their dirty promises. Oho, I tell you they had to drag me on the train.

CHRIS: Gee, Ot, you shoulda seen Darky. We had to get Darky rotten with plonk to get him on the train. He went through at Alice but the Provosts picked him up. Gee, he fought.

[DARKY *appears in the doorway. He has a fading black eye and is filthy dirty.*]

OMNES: Darky. Well how are you, boy? . . . Welcome back . . .

DARKY [*ominously*]: I'm warnin' youse if I ever do a tap of work for these galahs again they can take me out and bloody well certify me. I'm tellin' you.

ANDY: What's become of Betty Grable and the rest?

MAC: They'll all be back. Hey, who's pinched me bed?

ANDY: Oh get ripped, that isn't your bed.

MAC: Always was my bed and always will be.

OT: How long are you comin' back for, Chris?

CHRIS: You know what they said . . . They reckoned we'd have to come back until the replacements arrive.

[*Howl of anger at this.*]

ANDY: Replacements!

KEGHEAD: You see? Wot can we do? They got you every way.

VIC: I know them. We'll still be waiting for replacements when I get back.

ROD: Vic, you reckon that you . . .

VIC: I'll be back, son. You'd better keep that bed next to yours free for me.

KEGHEAD: I'll go through when I get to Melbourne . . . you see . . . They'll never find me . . .

[BROOKS *puts his head in the door.*]

BROOKS: All leave draft personnel be ready to leave in five minutes. [*To* MAC] You and the personnel just marched in . . . draw your beds from the Q Store in about ten minutes. I'm just going to find the Orderly Officer and get the key. [*He goes out.*]

VIC: Well . . . au revoir.

ANDY: We'll be seein' you again.

ROD: I'll come up to the truck with you.

VIC: So long, everyone . . . keep the ruddy old flag flying.

KEGHEAD: What did I tell you? A man might just as well cut his ruddy throat.

DARKY [*muttering*]: I tell you . . . they might have got me back but so help me they'll never get any work out of me again.

MAC [*laughs*]: Oh, shut your trap. They all say that. [*Slapping* OT] Well, the old Ot.

OT [*with the first show of life*]: Have you any of those Perth papers you promised?

MAC [*searching in bag*]: Think I'd forget me old cobber. How's the garden going?

OT: Oh, she died. Reckon I'll dig her up again though next Autumn when the Wet's over.

DARKY: Never get a bloody stroke of work out of me.

CHRIS: Oh come on, Darky. He's rotten. Take his arm, Ollie.

[OLLIE *and* CHRIS *start dragging* DARKY *out.*]

DARKY: They'll be sorry.

OT: Hey, come down after and tell us all the GG.

CHRIS: Hey, is the old Wimpy still here?

OT: Still here? There's bigger and better bastardry.

[*They laugh and drag out the protesting* DARKY.]

VIC [*to* KEGHEAD *who is slumped in despair on the bed*]: Hey, come on— we'll miss the truck.

KEGHEAD: No use goin' now if a man's got to come back . . . no use goin' . . .

VIC: Come on. [*He pulls* KEGHEAD *to his feet.*]

KEGHEAD: Aw, what a wonderful leave it's going to be . . . We'll all have something nice to look forward to now. [*To* ANDY] Keep me place at the table.

VIC: So long, Andy. So long, Mac. Be seeing you.

MAC: Be seeing you, sonny boy.

[VIC *and* ROD *go out.*]

KEGHEAD: About January you should expect me back. Right in the middle of the Wet.

[*Heavy thunder echoes round the camp.*]

See what I mean? What can a man do? [*He goes out.*]

[*There is silence for a moment. Then thunder.*]

ANDY: They never come back, eh? Where have I heard that one? Well at least you seen the Big Smoke. What's it like?

MAC: Bloody lovely. I'm engaged.

ANDY: Engaged? [*Roars with laughter.*]

MAC: What's so funny about that? She's a decent sort . . . name's Glory. We're goin' to get hitched after the war when me divorce is through.

ANDY [*roars with laughter*]: You old perv.

MAC: Aw, shut up, you dirty little sawn-off runt. And get off me hat . . . That's me new hat you're sitting on.

ANDY: I wasn't sitting on your hat.

MAC: Think I'm blind, do you?

ANDY: You big fat loafer . . . don't come back here trying any of your raw prawn stuff.

MAC: Aw . . . [*Suddenly sees* ANDY'S *stripes*] So you're a Sergeant, eh? Crawled to Wimpy like the dirty little galah you are.

ANDY: Eh, that'll be enough of that. A bit of respect from you.

MAC: Respect! I'll give you respect, you little worm. Got any lolly water?

ANDY: Yeah, come over to the snake pit. I got a bottle there hung up in a wet sock.

MAC: Just don't try any of this standover business, see. [*Puts his arm round* ANDY] You filthy rotten little . . .

ANDY: I'll soon put you in your place.

MAC: Yeah? Just try . . . [*As they go out*] Just try.

[*An enormously loud crack of thunder resounds overhead. Two bells follow.*]

SAMMY: The boongs reckons that's the sound of the gods getting wild.

OT: Gee, they got enough to be angry about. The bloody Wet's on us. [*He is deep in the papers that* MAC *has brought him.*] Oh wacko, there's a whole page of new exercises . . . Eh, what's this mean? . . . "Reduce your girth." What's your girth?

SAMMY: What do you think it is?

OT: Struth.

[ROD *comes in slowly.*]

ROD: They've gone. [*He goes to his bed*] Strike it's hot. [*He takes out a pair of badly holed socks and starts threading a needle.*] Oh well . . . a woman's work is never done, they say.

SAMMY: The joker that said that never come to the Territory.

[*Little spots of rain hammer on the tin roof. They all glance up.*] Here it comes.

ROD: The big Wet. Four long months of it now . . . We're certainly going to be sick of rain by the time Vic and Keghead get home . . . [*He stops and laughs.*] I mean get back.

OT: Breathe in and then double.

[*Thunder—the rain increases.*]

ROD: Home, eh? I'm beginning to look on the bloody place as home. [*Bites off the thread.*] I'm going troppo.

[OT *suddenly stands on his head.*]

New exercise. [*He notes* OT's *change of manner with approval.*]

[*The rain increases.* OT *suddenly drops down again.*]

OT: Gee, I'll have to work that one up . . . They got fourteen new bicep-improving exercises in this one . . . A bloke might try and get some form up and get in the football team next winter. Might get a trip out of it. Darky went up to Darwin one year as forward.

[*The rain is now pouring down.*]

VOICES [*off*]: Frig the rain . . . belt the rain . . . you beaut. Here it comes . . . the great big Wet . . . etc.

OT: I'm going to round up a few heavyweights for the ring next season. We got all the Wet to get it ready.

SAMMY: I'd be in it.

OT [*disparagingly*]: I thought you would be.

SAMMY: I'd help you get it up I mean . . . [*pause*] if you want.

OT: I'll have to ask Chris and Ollie.

[*One bell sounds through the rain.* OT *pulls the net down and is in bed in a second.*]

Will you put the lamp out, Rod?

ROD: I'll leave it for Mac. He'll be back in a minute. He's just gone over to the snake pit with Andy.

OT: Oho, the old bed . . . she's not bad . . . [*Pause.*] Layin' down and listenin' to the rain . . . she's not bad.

[SAMMY *pulls his net down.*]

SAMMY: Maybe they WILL send those replacements . . . like Chris reckons.

ROD [*laughs*]: You wait and see a year from now.

[*He starts darning his sox lying on the bed. He turns the lamp a little higher. Only a faint gleam comes from it. Lightning flickers outside. The rain pours down.*]

[*In the distance the lonely shrill whistle of a train in the night comes through the rain.*]

VOICES [*shouting from everywhere*]: Here they come! . . . Here come the replacements! . . . Here they come!

[*The train whistle repeats and dies away in the night. Nothing is heard but the steady downpour. After a pause one voice is heard.*]

VOICE [*loud and shrill*]: Get me out of here!

[ROD *smiles. He looks up at the roof thoughtfully. Then he sighs, wipes the sweat from his face with a soiled handkerchief, and puts the first sock down. Takes up the second one.*]

[*The rain increases in volume filling the night with a lonely roaring sound of falling water.*]

[*The lights fade out very slowly.*]

(*The End*)

RAY MATHEW

we find the bunyip

characters of the play
in order of appearance
and original cast

After a try-out at the Pioneer Hall, Wollongong, New South Wales, on 14 August 1955, the play was produced on 29 August 1955 at the Independent Theatre, Sydney, with the following cast in order of speaking:

MRS. POCKS:	Kathleen Skehan
MRS. WILLIAMS:	Marie McKern
DENISE:	Patricia Smith
BLANCHE:	Jill Bloomfield
SNOW:	Peter Barclay
JACK:	Daryl Gunter
BERT:	Richard Letts
GEORGE:	William Callander
TONY:	Brian Paine
ARTHUR:	Warwick Russell
PADDY:	John Meaney

The kitchen of the hotel, one of the town's two hotels. The town in the west of New South Wales, Australia. The time, spring, Saturday night and the morning after.

The play was produced by Geoffrey Thomas and designed by Valerie Baxter for the Theatre for Playwrights.

author's note

This script is not a play: a play is a script, fully produced, before an audience. Being only a script, it is certainly not gospel: lines are meant to be spoken one on top of the other, repeated, hurried over, acted. The producer must work for laughs through dialogue (as well as through characteristic business). He should make a feature of the dialogue's apparent boredoms; its repetitions, catchlines, and monotonies. The play probably needs a static style of production giving each gesture significance, but the dialogue needs to be treated dynamically. The producer might divide it into blocks and work to a climax and/or anticlimax within each division, but no matter how he patterns it he must bear in mind that each character is in a world of his own and only sometimes is acting to, with, or at the others, and at other times is acting in a realm of his own feelings. Consequently, much of the talk cannot be patterned between persons, and there is likewise no reason why all of it should be distinguishable to the audience: the producer must select, even further than the author, whatever of either word or action is to be significant during the give and take of the dialogue and its purely mechanical action.

This is to say that the author has tried to achieve a true comedy and that the production must make the same effort. In the trying, however, do not be afraid of achieving pretentiousness: the play, as it happens, is pretentious. And it cannot hold an audience unless played at its own level. There must be no farcing of the characters, no Dad and Dave, although Denise might be played as a New Australian. Unless the audience feels all the time that the generalizations made by the characters apply not only to their situations but to ours, then the play must flop. It will seem merely a repetitious, banal, and dull portrait of nothing happening in a country hotel.

There is no attempt in the script to be disrespectful or antagonistic to any religion or sect. The author has, simply, observed a few individuals: the production must emphasize this fact.

Despite the quantity of liquor that flows over the boards, the real attitude of the play is one of moderation if not of strict temperance. It will be understood by any one who grasps the play's philosophy (if that is the right word) that life may need no stimulation, and that "something is to be blamed" if it does. I enclose this note and an earnest appeal to the audience, the cast, and the producer for temperance (particularly to the producer and to the cast), not because I think any intelligent playgoer could imagine the play was a plea for more happy drunkards, but because I think that some playgoers might. It takes all sorts to make a theatre. And I wish to be clearly innocent of any part in anyone's downfall.

111

notes on the characters

MRS. POCKS THE PROPRIETOR'S WIFE (LIL). Older than 50. Smokes incessantly. Wears an apron. Is neither fat nor thin.

MRS. WILLIAMS THE WIDOW (BILLIE). Older than 40. With tinted blonde hair.

DENISE THE DAMSEL. With dark hair.

BLANCHE THE BARMAID. The daughter of the house. Is small.

SNOW THE SWAIN. The suitor. A big, young man. With hair either very dark or very fair. He drawls.

JACK THE AMOROUS.

BERT THE MUSICIAN (MR. HORNER). With a piano accordion (concertina, flute, fiddle, or other portable).

GEORGE THE PROPRIETOR, THE PUBLICAN (MR. POCKS). Is of huge size.

TONY THE TALKER. The Dago. His parents were Italian.

ARTHUR THE GINK. Speaks slowly. Is not bright. Is a gink.

PADDY THE DRUNKARD.

112

ACT ONE

The hotel kitchen about seven forty-five one hot Saturday night. A large table. A smaller one. A dresser. A sink. A garbage-can. Chairs. A stove.

PADDY is sitting on a box in the corner, with his head down. DENISE is working at the table altering a summer-frock. MRS. POCKS and MRS. WILLIAMS are at one end of the large table. They are playing rummy.

MRS. POCKS [*with each card*]: Beast! Bully! Beast! The beast of a bully! Great big bully! Makes me sick! Three of a kind! [*She puts down her last three cards, and wins.*]

MRS. WILLIAMS: Oh, you are lucky, Mrs. Pocks! Oh, you are lucky! I can't get anything. I just can't get anything. But I never do. No luck at all.

MRS. POCKS: Lucky at cards, unlucky at—everything else. [*She deals.*] The cow! The fat, disgusting old cow! Shut up, Paddy!
   [PADDY *has not moved a finger.*]
I don't know why I get so worked up. I shouldn't get upset. It's not worth it. He's not worth it. I get so upset, it makes me shake.

MRS. WILLIAMS: You should go away for a holiday. It's making you ill—

MRS. POCKS: Then, he'd know it. Then, he'd know it. When he had to get himself a cook, and a housemaid, and a barmaid, and a slushy—just to do the work I do for him. Then, he'd know it. He might wake up to himself, then. He'd have to do a bit himself. He'd have to mind his tongue. I work from morning till night— He wouldn't get a cook or a maid to do that. Then, he'd just have to watch his step. Oh, I'd like to see—

MRS. WILLIAMS: Out! Rummy! [*She puts down all her cards and laughs.*]

MRS. POCKS: Well, talk about tinny! Sitting there like that! No wonder you were so quiet. Some people are so tinny, they must wear tin pants.

113

MRS. WILLIAMS [*giggling*]: Oh, Mrs. Pocks, I hardly ever win.

[MRS. POCKS *sniffs*. MRS. WILLIAMS *deals*.]

You really shouldn't get upset, you know. It isn't good for you.

MRS. POCKS: Of course I shouldn't. But I do. I do.

MRS. WILLIAMS: Yes.

[*A pause for play*.]

Men aren't worth it, Mrs. Pocks. None of them are. My husband was as good as you'd find *anywhere* but—

MRS. POCKS: That's not saying much.

MRS. WILLIAMS: Oh, I must be *fair*. He was a good man to me. But I know what men are like, all the same.

MRS. POCKS: All they're good for is talk.

MRS. WILLIAMS: And growling.

MRS. POCKS: They're good fetchers. "Fetch me this and fetch me that." [*She laughs at her own joke*.]

MRS. WILLIAMS: And when they've got drink in them!

[DENISE *has been working without much interest in the talk. She has heard it all before*.]

DENISE: They're like animals.

MRS. WILLIAMS: Yes!

MRS. POCKS: Shut up, Paddy!

[PADDY *has given little sign of life*.]

And George shouldn't drink. He can't hold it. He knows that. He can't take it. He's been told—

MRS. WILLIAMS: Time and again! But it's no use talking to them.

MRS. POCKS: The old cow does just as he likes.

MRS. WILLIAMS: They always do. Just as they like. And we women are supposed to put up with it.

MRS. POCKS: Like an animal, he is, Denise. He'll just stagger in here, flop in that chair, and sit there—till it makes him sick. Then I'll have to clean it up.

MRS. WILLIAMS: When I was in business in Gundagai, I was boarding at a hotel there. It wasn't like this one, Mrs. Pocks; you wouldn't believe what some hotels are like. You wouldn't believe it. One night a man came into my room. Yes. And it was only early, too. He just came in the door. And his eyes were glassy, just glassy. I was terrified. I don't mind telling you I was *terrified*. It was a Thursday night, too. I just screamed and screamed.

MRS. POCKS: Well?

MRS. WILLIAMS: Oh, he went away.

DENISE: You were lucky, Mrs. Williams.

MRS. POCKS: You want to lock your door.

MRS. WILLIAMS: I always do. I always do. But it was so early, you'd never have dreamed— You can't be too careful in a hotel. Now, can you? Even in yours, Mrs. Pocks. I always lock the door. And, of a Saturday night, I push the pedestal against it. You can't be too careful in a hotel. And, now, with these "noises" of a night—

MRS. POCKS: I'm not frightened of any man. A man can't hurt you anyway, Billie; you ought to know that: you're a widow.

MRS. WILLIAMS: Mrs. Pocks!

MRS. POCKS: And if a man's drunk he can't do anything; he just hasn't got it in him. Eh? [*She laughs.*] Oh, shut up, Paddy! You're not a man. You're a drunk.

[PADDY *may have moved an eyelash.*]

MRS. WILLIAMS: Disgusting.

[*Paddy tries to stand. Mrs. Pocks pushes him down.*]

MRS. POCKS: Sit down!

[*She and Mrs. Williams go on playing cards.*]

This is a long game. Sit down in that corner, Paddy, and stay there! If you start singing and swearing, I'll put you out.

MRS. WILLIAMS: I don't know how you can be like that to them, Mrs. Pocks. Just the look of them makes me feel *ill*, just sick inside. Though, of course, Paddy's different: we're used to him. He's just like the furniture. [*She giggles.*] But, drunk! What pleasure do they find in it?

MRS. POCKS: In one end and out the other.

MRS. WILLIAMS: Why do they do it? You'd *think* they'd have more sense.

MRS. POCKS: If I didn't know they haven't.

MRS. WILLIAMS: They want to forget. That's it. They want to forget how to think. They just don't want to have more sense; they don't want any.

MRS. POCKS: And they won't get any.

DENISE: They're looking for a cheap thrill, that's all. That's all they've got in life.

MRS. POCKS: And some of the women are worse than the men.

MRS. WILLIAMS: Oh, Mrs. Pocks . . .

MRS. POCKS: Mrs. Mackenzie does her beans in the parlour, every night.

MRS. WILLIAMS: Mrs. Pocks! Not really . . .

MRS. POCKS: I wouldn't say it if it wasn't true.

MRS. WILLIAMS: No. And the baby's pram is always outside the door. [*She tuts.*] Of course, Mrs. Pocks, there's nothing wrong with a drink.

MRS. POCKS: A drink's all right.

MRS. WILLIAMS: Yes. There's nothing wrong with a drink.

DENISE: I wouldn't touch it.

MRS. POCKS [*to* DENISE]: One's all right. It's good for your health.

MRS. WILLIAMS: I do like a shandy, or a stout, or an ale, or a—

MRS. POCKS: Go on. You sound like a drunkard.

MRS. WILLIAMS: Mrs. Pocks, what an awful thing to say! I wish you wouldn't say things like that. Even as a joke. A woman—a woman living alone, in a hotel, in a town like this, has to be very careful. Very careful, indeed.

MRS. POCKS: A widow's got the best kind of husband.

MRS. WILLIAMS: Don't say that, Mrs. Pocks. It hurts me. Albie was very good to me. I must never forget that. With all his faults, Albie was very good to me. And I suppose there are worse husbands than your George.

MRS. POCKS: Where? [*A pause.*] He was nothing when I married him. I brought him everything. He was just a rouseabout. *My* family was one of the oldest in the district. The Cunninghams used to talk to us. And look at me now. Look at him now! He owns this place. He needn't want for anything. And look how I've worked for him. He'd still be shearing if it wasn't for me. And he doesn't even say a civil word.

DENISE: You oughtn't to do so much for him.

MRS. WILLIAMS: You spoil him, Mrs. Pocks. He takes you for granted. Rummy!

MRS. POCKS: Well! [*She collects the cards and deals disgustedly.*] There you go again!

MRS. WILLIAMS: Half your luck, Mrs. Pocks. You usually win every hand.

[MRS. POCKS *sniffs*.]

He takes you for granted, you know. [*She points to a newspaper on the table*.] You've got to keep them guessing. Keep yourself fresh. Why don't you have a new hair-do? Why don't you have a phoney? [*She giggles*.] What a silly mistake!

MRS. POCKS: George wouldn't notice if I was wearing snakes and nothing else—as long as I served the drinks all right, and it didn't cost him anything extra. I wore this in the bar this morning and he said, first thing: "That's too good to be doing the floors in." And it is, too, curse him! I've ruined it. Are you going to read all night? [*She takes up her hand*.] You won't get any good out of the papers.

MRS. WILLIAMS: We ought to send to the papers about the bunyip.

DENISE: No one's interested in an old woman's tale.

MRS. WILLIAMS: Well, I don't know, Denise; we've all heard the noises. Young and old have heard them. You've heard them.

MRS. POCKS [*with her mind on the game*]: Could be a bunyip. Shut up, Paddy! It's your play.

[MRS. WILLIAMS *goes on arranging her cards, slowly and exasperatingly*.]

MRS. WILLIAMS: Although I don't think it is, mind you. It looks . . . Those noises. I can imagine what goes on. [*She tuts*.] The other night, just after, I'm *sure* I heard a woman's voice, a woman's voice—*laughing*. Well, it mightn't mean anything. But you know what the people in this town are like, and it makes you think, doesn't it? [*She begins to play*.]

MRS. POCKS: A lot goes on in this town that no one hears much about.

MRS. WILLIAMS: And they'd just like to have a bunyip to blame it on.

DENISE: It's an awful town.

MRS. POCKS: Damn it, I can't get a thing! I hate this game!

MRS. WILLIAMS: Well, I don't mind if you don't want to play—

MRS. POCKS: Don't be silly, Billie. I'll get something in a minute. [*She picks up three cards, one after the other*.] Damn! Damn! Damn! Ah! You win again! Talk about luck! [*She looks through the pack*.] Just look at that! Have you ever seen anything like it? Everything I wanted! Your deal.

MRS. WILLIAMS: Is it? Are you sure?

MRS. POCKS: Of course I'm sure. You're not going to the pictures, Denise?

[MRS. WILLIAMS *packs the cards.*]

DENISE: I think I've been twice since I came here.

MRS. WILLIAMS: That was with—

DENISE [*quickly*]: *You're* not going?

MRS. WILLIAMS: It's not like us to miss a Saturday night, is it?

MRS. POCKS: It's a rotten old show. I saw it in Sydney. When I had my holiday. *The year before last.* We only have pictures once a week, and then we don't get anything decent. They're years old.

[MRS. WILLIAMS *is dealing.*]

MRS. WILLIAMS: We don't even get the Sunday papers till Monday night. That's as good as years old. What's the use of living in the Atomic Age if you can't get the Sunday papers till Monday night? And we *could* get them. They could send them up in a truck. Consolidated Press could afford that. If the Progress Association would only *do* something, I'm sure we could get them up. Men! I suppose they just sit there and tell one another dirty stories. Oh, I'd love to be at one of their meetings, I'd tell them a—

MRS. POCKS: You wouldn't tell them, Billo, you'd learn a few. [*She laughs.*]

[MRS. WILLIAMS *giggles.*]

MRS. WILLIAMS: I don't know so much about that!

[BLANCHE *has entered, with* SNOW *behind her. She goes to the sink.*]

BLANCHE: Who's telling dirty stories?

SNOW: That all you got to do with your time, Lil?

MRS. POCKS: Don't you Lil me! [*She goes on playing, but she does not watch her cards.*] Here she is! Madam Muck! Don't know how you can look me in the face—

BLANCHE: Well, you should have been more careful. George told you—

MRS. POCKS: Could at least stick up for your mother, for your own mother. Even a dog'll do that.

SNOW: It's over now—

BLANCHE: Why don't you call me a bitch and be done with it. You'll be the bitch's mother.

MRS. WILLIAMS: Oh Blanche, you shouldn't—

BLANCHE: No?

MRS. POCKS [*to* PADDY, *who has not moved*]: Shut up, Paddy! and keep your eyes to yourself! My mother would have knocked me down if I'd talked to her like that.

SNOW: Aw, take it easy, Lil.

MRS. POCKS: Don't Lil me. [*She goes on playing.*] You, you big hulking brute! [*To* SNOW] Hanging round the hotel for what you can get! Why don't you marry her and—

SNOW: We want to get married, Lil—

BLANCHE: He doesn't get anything he shouldn't.

MRS. POCKS: He gets a damned lot of free meals.

[MRS. WILLIAMS *picks up a card that* MRS. POCKS *has discarded.*]

MRS. WILLIAMS: You knew I wanted those.

[*Annoyed,* MRS. POCKS *puts her hand down. She turns to* SNOW.]

SNOW [*quickly, for him*]: Now, ma—

MRS. POCKS: Don't you call me ma!

MRS. WILLIAMS [*delighted*]: Now, Mrs. Pocks, you mustn't get upset!

BLANCHE: Pocks by name, and pox by nature.

MRS. POCKS: And it's your name too.

BLANCHE: Well, it won't be much longer! I don't know why I stick it. I must be mad. I'm just a slave around the place. Do this! Do that! You'd never get another girl to stick it. And George knows it, too! All that I do! And all that I have to put up with! Serving in that stinking bar all day—

MRS. POCKS: It's where the money comes from.

BLANCHE: Who wants the money!

MRS. WILLIAMS: Hoity-toity!

MRS. POCKS: Well, what do you want?

BLANCHE [*miserably*]: I . . . I want . . . I . . .

[*Silence.*]

SNOW: Well, ma, we want to get married.

MRS. POCKS [*sniffing*]: Hm! Don't you call me ma! Hm! I know what George'll say about that. I know what George has said about that already.

BLANCHE: Snow doesn't want to marry George. He wants to marry me.

MRS. WILLIAMS: Fathers are all the same, Blanche. No one is good enough for their daughters. My father used to say—

BLANCHE: I don't care about fathers. I want to live my own life. George this, and George that! All day long! All day long, in that filthy bar full of boozers. Swilling themselves sick. The smell of them makes me sick. All day long . . . Just because my father owns the place. I'm fed up with it all. Shut up, Paddy! I'm fed up with it all. I'm fed up with it all.

[*Enter* JACK, *a boarder. He is half dressed to go out.*]

JACK: Always the same happy family, always!

MRS. POCKS: You keep your mouth shut.

BLANCHE: Shut up.

JACK: Water for a shave! Water! I must look my best. Saturday night. [*He takes a clean cup and fills it with hot water.*]

BLANCHE: Why can't we get married? Why can't we?

[*Silence.*]

JACK: Isn't anyone going to the pictures? They won't put them on if there aren't enough there.

MRS. WILLIAMS: Well, you won't miss much, Jack. It's not a good programme.

JACK: Oh, I don't care what the pictures are like, Billie. I'm taking my girl. Hey diggety-dig! [*He exults and does a little dance.*]

BLANCHE: Why can't we?

MRS. POCKS [*slowly, patiently*]: You know why you can't, and it's no use talking.

BLANCHE: No use talking . . .

MRS. WILLIAMS [*being tactful*]: And it's so hot, Jack. It's too hot to sit in that box. On a night like this.

BLANCHE: It's just because he's a tyke.

[*Silence.*]

MRS. POCKS [*tired*]: You're too young. You don't know what you want. You don't know what's good for you. You don't know anything. I was married when I was twenty-three. That was too young. I was a young fool—

JACK: And now you're an old one.

MRS. POCKS: Well, I know what's what. And Snowy hasn't got anything.

SNOW: That's true enough, Lil. Only my charm. But Blanche is

120

old enough to—

BLANCHE: I'm old enough to know what I want.

MRS. POCKS: All right. All right, if it's so cut and dried, if everything's fixed, you go and ask George. Just you ask George, that's all. You know what happened last time.

BLANCHE: We've been going together so long it's a joke.

MRS. POCKS: Well, as long as you're laughing.

BLANCHE: You make me sick. [*She sits down, head in arms, arms on table.*]

[SNOW *is behind her. He holds her shoulders. A pause.*]

JACK: Er—er—Isn't anyone going to the pictures?

MRS. WILLIAMS: It's too hot, Jack. It's too hot to sit in a box like that on a night like this.

JACK: On a night like this! [*He goes to the window.*] Yes. It'll be a good night. Full moon. Not a cloud. And the dark at the pictures . . . Hell, Billie, haven't you got any life in you? They're only on once a week.

MRS. POCKS: That's enough of that language.

MRS. WILLIAMS: Oh, you are naughty, Jack!

JACK: Just wanted the old girl to have a bite.

MRS. POCKS: I'll old girl you!

MRS. WILLIAMS: If I could only wear something cool, I'd go. [*She giggles.*] Would you think I was too shameless if I bought a sun-dress. We've got such beauties in at the store. But they're a little bit daring for my age, Jack. Do you think I should? What would people say? They look so—*gay*.

DENISE: You want to please yourself.

JACK: Wacko, boy! Mrs. Williams in a sun-suit, the night of the full moon, and me on the prowl! Lock your door, Mrs. Williams! Lock your door tonight—or a bunyip'll get you! See you later. [*He howls like a wolf and goes out.*]

MRS. POCKS: Not if I see you first!

MRS. WILLIAMS [*laughing*]: He's terrible, he really is terrible!
[*Mrs. Pocks takes up her cards.*]

MRS. POCKS: It was my go.
[*Mrs. Williams takes up her hand, unenthusiastically. They play.*]

MRS. WILLIAMS: It will be a lovely night.

MRS. POCKS [*snorting*]: You'd look fine in a sun-dress.

MRS. WILLIAMS: Do you really think so?

MRS. POCKS: You'd look awful.

DENISE: I don't like the look of them myself.

MRS. POCKS: All right if you've got the figure.

DENISE: Well, then. I haven't got the figure.

MRS. WILLIAMS: You don't like them, Denise?

DENISE: No.

MRS. WILLIAMS: Oh.

[*A pause for play.*]

MRS. POCKS: Sit still, Paddy!

[*Silence.*]

[*She picks up a wrong card.*] Damn it!

[*A pause for play.*]

MRS. WILLIAMS [*suddenly*]: We do look a happy family, sitting here. With such glum looks. You'd never know it was a Saturday night.

[*Silence.*]

MRS. POCKS: Damn! I can't get a thing. I'd be better playing patience than playing with you.

MRS. WILLIAMS: All right, then. All right. I've plenty of work to do. Perhaps you would be better playing patience—

MRS. POCKS: Now, Billie, there's no need to—

[MRS. WILLIAMS *has put her cards down, faces up.*]

MRS. WILLIAMS: I'll just run upstairs and get the invoices. Oh, I've got to get them done, anyway. Do you know, they sent me a whole host of new stuff that I didn't order. Heaven knows how we'll get rid of it. We'll have to keep it for Christmas, I suppose, and wrap it up in fancy paper. You can sell anything—

MRS. POCKS: Oh, just finish the game—

MRS. WILLIAMS: No, Mrs. Pocks. I'll just *run* upstairs and get the invoices. [*She shows no sign of running. She moves to go.*] Oh dear, and I've been on the go all day. I get so tired. And this is *really* Saturday night. Sometimes I wonder if it's worth going on. I suppose it is. [*She goes out slowly.*]

MRS. POCKS: You get paid for it. [*She plays patience.*]

[*Quiet.*]

SNOW: Lil.

MRS. POCKS [*absorbed*]: Yes?

SNOW: Lil. Lil. What about putting in a good word for us? You could swing George—

MRS. POCKS [*still intent*]: No one takes notice of me.

SNOW: Aw, Lil—

MRS. POCKS: You're all right, Snow—

SNOW [*pleased*]: Oh, thanks, Lil.

MRS. POCKS: You're all right, but George doesn't like you.

SNOW [*sincerely*]: Why doesn't he, Lil? Why doesn't he think I'm all right, if you do?

BLANCHE: Because George is an old—

MRS. POCKS [*almost at the same time*]: Because George is an old— [*She silences Blanche with a glance.*] Because George is George.

SNOW: Yeah. I suppose so.

BLANCHE [*deliberately*]: He's a cranky, unreasonable, old cow.

MRS. POCKS: That's no way to talk about your father.

BLANCHE: I'll talk about him the way I find him. I find him a cranky, unreasonable, old cow. Don't I, Snow?

SNOW: Yeah. Yeah, you do, hon.

DENISE: Where are the big scissors, Mrs. Pocks?

MRS. POCKS: In the drawer.

[*DENISE goes and gets them.*]

DENISE: Thanks.

[*A pause.*]

SNOW: Come for a walk, hon?

[*MRS. WILLIAMS returns with her invoices.*]

BLANCHE: No.

SNOW: Come on, it'll do you good.

[*MRS. WILLIAMS sits down and giggles.*]

MRS. WILLIAMS: Well, we *old* dames are going to have company, are we? That'll be a change.

SNOW: Looks like it, Mrs. Williams. If you can put up with us.

MRS. WILLIAMS: Oh, I can put up with anything.

MRS. POCKS: Anything?

MRS. WILLIAMS [*giggling*]: Well—almost anything. Anyway, I'll be working; I wouldn't even notice if we were in a pigsty.

SNOW: Do you want to play cards?

[*MRS. POCKS looks up eagerly.*]

BLANCHE: No.

[*MRS. POCKS sniffs.*]

SNOW: Then, come for a walk.

BLANCHE: What's made you so energetic all of a sudden? Think you might find the bunyip? Go for a walk yourself!

SNOW: You couldn't catch the bunyip by yourself.

BLANCHE: It's too hot.

SNOW: Yeah, it is hot.

MRS. WILLIAMS: These days make my head throb. Just throb. It's the glare. It's not just the sun. The sun's all right. That's good for you. It's the glare.

DENISE: It's not good for your eyes.

MRS. WILLIAMS: I won't be able to keep up tennis much longer, now that the real heat's coming. Oh, it was hot last year though. When I was at Gundagai. You could have fried an egg—

SNOW: Yeah?

MRS. WILLIAMS: Yes. It was so hot.

SNOW: Must have been hot.

MRS. WILLIAMS: It was so hot I even bought a two-piece swim-suit. [*She giggles.*]

SNOW: Yeah?

BLANCHE: Where could you swim? Where could you swim? Where could you go? In a filthy old dam, in a hole in the ground.

MRS. WILLIAMS: We had beautiful baths there. Here! [*She sniffs, then giggles.*] I think you'll be seeing me swim in the bath. *You* won't be seeing me, Snow. I know what you're thinking.

SNOW: Aw, no, I wasn't. I wasn't thinking anything—

BLANCHE: Nobody expects you to!

MRS. POCKS [*laughing*]: Good on you, Blanche!

SNOW: Now, hon, I was only—

[*An accordion sounds off-stage.*]

MRS. WILLIAMS: That sounds like Bert.

MRS. POCKS: Hope to heaven *George* isn't with him! He's drunk enough, and I couldn't stand George just now. Stay there, Paddy! [PADDY *has raised his head.* BERT *comes in. He carries his accordion. He stands at the door. He is not sober.*]

SNOW: Hiya, Bert.

MRS. WILLIAMS: Hallo, Mr. Horner. Are you going to play us a tune? [MRS. POCKS *plays patience doggedly.*]

MRS. POCKS: So you're back in town.

124

MRS. WILLIAMS: We'd all love a tune. It'd do us good. It's just what we need. We'd all *love* a tune.

BERT: 'Lo, everyone. I'm glad to be back. I'm glad. Hallo, everyone. Hallo.

MRS. WILLIAMS: I don't think you can beat the old accordion. When I was a girl—

MRS. POCKS: Any of your cheque left?

BERT: You and George'll get the rest of it. But I don't mind. I'm glad.

MRS. POCKS: Well, it won't go into my pocket, I can tell you that.

BERT: I'm glad. I don't care. I'm glad. I was looking for George.

MRS. POCKS: And he isn't in my pocket either.

MRS. WILLIAMS [*giggling*]: And I'm sure he isn't in mine. Oh, I feel so—gay, tonight. And there's no reason. I've got all this work. But I do. I feel so—reckless, utterly abandoned.

MRS. POCKS: You'd think you'd been on the plonk.

MRS. WILLIAMS: Now, Mrs. Pocks, you know that I never—

MRS. POCKS: All right. You haven't.

DENISE: Play us a tune, Bert, before you go.

MRS. POCKS: You'd better not. George might hear it. It might upset him.

MRS. WILLIAMS [*with very little sarcasm, if any*]: That'd be terrible, wouldn't it?

MRS. POCKS [*taking it as sarcasm*]: Yes, it would.

BLANCHE: Yes. [*She turns to* BERT] Yes, play us a tune, Bert. Oh, go on, Bert.

BERT: I was looking for my old mate, George.

BLANCHE: Play us a tune and then look for him. He won't die before you find him. He's coming in here soon.

SNOW: Yeah, play us a tune, Bert.

BERT [*smiling*]: Well—I haven't practised, you know.

BLANCHE: We don't care. You don't have to practise. We just want a tune.

MRS. POCKS: Blanche.

MRS. WILLIAMS: Go on, Mr. Horner. Play us a tune. To the devil with George!

MRS. POCKS: Billie!

MRS. WILLIAMS: I don't care. I don't care. I'm tired of sitting here, looking at work. To hell with George! Play us a tune.

MRS. POCKS: Well!

MRS. WILLIAMS: I said *hell*.

BERT: What'll I play? Name your tune. What'll I play?

MRS. POCKS [*bitterly*]: "The Merry Widow."

DENISE: "White Horse Inn."

BERT: I don't know any new tunes. I know all the old ones though. They're the best.

MRS. WILLIAMS: Do you know "Daisie"?

BERT [*with a charming drunk-smile*]: Daisie who?

BLANCHE: Play any tune, can't you. Play any tune. We don't care what it is. Just any tune.

BERT: Listen to this one. [*He plays "It's a Sin to Tell a Lie".*]
　　[MRS. WILLIAMS *half-sings.* MRS. POCKS *makes humming noises over her cards.* BLANCHE *sings a little.* DENISE *hums under breath as she works.*]

BLANCHE: Dance with me, Snow. Dance with me.

SNOW: Aw, hon—

BLANCHE: Ask me to dance. Go on. Ask me to dance. Ask me.

SNOW: Can I have the honour?

BLANCHE: You have to say "May I have the honour?"

SNOW: May I have the honour?
　　[*A pause.*]

BLANCHE [*smiling*]: Yes.
　　[*They dance slowly.*]
This isn't here. We're in Sydney, Snow. We're at Romano's, or Prince's. I'm wearing a ballerina frock, with tulle and sequins—high heel shoes like stilts. You're in a navy-blue double-breasted with a red stripe in it. You're wearing the tie I gave you for Christmas. The one you've only worn once. We're dancing. Everyone's looking at us. Everyone's watching us dance. [*She looks to* MRS. POCKS *and her cards.*] Fortune-teller! You! Yes, you, woman! Tell us our fortunes.

MRS. POCKS: Seventeen kids, five with red hair. I told you not to put the milk in your tea first. [*She laughs coarsely.*]
　　[*Blanche stops unhappily. But Bert starts the tune again and Snow takes her dancing.*]

MRS. WILLIAMS [*looking up*]: They're a lovely couple. *I*'d love to be dancing.

MRS. POCKS: They don't look too bad.

MRS. WILLIAMS: It makes you feel young again, as though anything could happen. Never grow old, Blanche. Be young while you can. [*She has called out, quite loudly.*]

   [*They all look at her.*]

I'm sorry, Mrs. Pocks. I didn't realize. I was just thinking—

MRS. POCKS: I suppose they'll be married some time or another.

BLANCHE: Sometime or other we'll be stuck in our graves, a hole in the ground. Stuck in a hole. Stuck in this one. Stuck in that one. Sometime or other!

MRS. WILLIAMS: Oh, Blanche, dear—

SNOW: That's what I tell you . . . Sometime or other. Keep dancing. Keep dancing. Can I—May I have the honour? Don't stop, Bert. You're playing at Prince's.

   [*They dance and he whispers to her.*]

MRS. WILLIAMS: When I was on my honeymoon, we danced and danced. We didn't have a penny. But there's no one happier than a bride. They always make me cry. We danced and danced . . . [*She is near tears.*]

MRS. POCKS: Sh! Sh! I might get this out.

MRS. WILLIAMS [*disappointed*]: Oh! Oh, and there's—all this work. [*She bends over it.*]

   [*Snow talks to Blanche very softly. Her words are not so caring about the others.*]

SNOW: You're only young once.

BLANCHE: All those swine in the bar . . .

SNOW: What can you lose?

BLANCHE: The drudge round the place . . .

SNOW: You'll wake up one day. It'll be too late. What did Mrs. Williams say?

BLANCHE: I don't know.

SNOW: You heard what she said.

GEORGE [*off*]: Lil! Lil!

MRS. POCKS: What's wrong with him, now? The old cow? I don't know why I worry. Only time I nearly get it out . . . Bellowing like a bull . . . [*She has talked herself off.*]

SNOW: You're only young once.

BLANCHE [*making an excuse*]: My feet are aching.

SNOW: You'll be sorry one day.

[*They stop dancing.*]

BLANCHE: No. I want to keep dancing. Keep playing, Bert.

SNOW [*as they dance*]: It'll be a bright moon.

BLANCHE: Wishes don't come true.

SNOW: Who's to blame if mine doesn't? My wish doesn't come true. You know why it doesn't.

[*She stops dancing.*]

BLANCHE: Play something lively.

BERT: I can play anything, anything at all. I'm glad. Just name a tune.

MRS. WILLIAMS: Oh, Mr. Horner, you must know "Daisie".

BERT: "Daisie"? Course I know "Daisie". Know every tune ever written. "Daisie" . . . [*He plays a bright tune. It is not "Daisie".*]

[MRS. WILLIAMS *and* DENISE *laugh. They go on working.* MRS. WILLIAMS *struggles to keep working.* SNOW *smiles. He and* BLANCHE *dance again.*]

MRS. POCKS [*off*]: It'd be different if you knew what you were saying. You're too stupid to know what you've done. I didn't leave it open. You did. Don't mutter at me! You know what the doctor said. And now, now you're as drunk as a boot, you old cow, you're as full as a boot . . .

[GEORGE *enters with difficulty. His eyes are half-closed. His face is flushed.* MRS. POCKS *is behind him, pushing and scolding. The dancing and the music stop.*]

MRS. POCKS: Next thing I know, you'll fall down dead. The doctor told you! And that'll be my fault, too. Then you'll stop calling me names! You're not even listening.

GEORGE [*looking unsteadily at* SNOW]: Is he still here?

BLANCHE: It was last Saturday you saw him.

SNOW: How are you, George?

[GEORGE *looks at him expressively and grunts.*]

GEORGE: Get us a cup of tea.

[MRS. POCKS *goes and makes it.*]

MRS. POCKS: Expect me to wait on you hand and foot. And I do it too. Anyone'd think I was your mother. Nothing's too good . . .

MRS. WILLIAMS: Good night, Mr. Pocks.

[GEORGE *grunts to her and sits down.*]

GEORGE: Bert! [*He tries to rise again.*] Good day, Bert.

BERT: Good day, George. It's my old mate, George. I'm glad. Good day, George.

BLANCHE: Play us a tune, Bert. Go on.

GEORGE: I'm tired. [*He moans to himself.*]

BLANCHE: Play some more, Bert.

BERT: I can't, girlie. George is tired. Poor George is tired. Poor old George. I'd hate to be tired.

BLANCHE: Damn poor old George!

MRS. POCKS [*to* BLANCHE]: That's no way for you to speak. [*To the others*] "Poor old George"! He's drunk. He's drunk.

MRS. WILLIAMS: Perhaps just one or two too many—

MRS. POCKS: Damn poor old George!

MRS. WILLIAMS: Oh, Mrs. Pocks, don't damn him when he's in that state.

[*She giggles and notices that* DENISE *has been gathering her things since* GEORGE *entered drunk.*]

Oh, don't go, Denise. I'll have to go if you go. And I've got all this work to do. And I can't work in my room. I haven't got a table. And—and you haven't nearly finished the dress. It's going to be lovely . . .

[DENISE *stays. A pause while* GEORGE *sips tea.*]

BLANCHE [*appealing*]: Bert . . .

[*But Bert looks sad.*]

You can't even have a bit of music. Poor old George. Poor old George. Poor old George the bu—

MRS. POCKS: Blanche!

GEORGE: I'll knock you down.

MRS. WILLIAMS: Oh, dear.

GEORGE [*to* SNOW]: And I'll knock you down too. [*He tries to stand.*]

BLANCHE: You'll need some help. Come on, Snow. [*She turns to go out.*]

GEORGE [*with difficulty*]: Where are you going with that bloke?

BLANCHE: Wherever I like. We're going for a walk.

GEORGE: No daughter of mine—

BLANCHE: You said that last week.

GEORGE: You shut your mouth or—

SNOW: Now, then, George.

MRS. POCKS: You keep out of this.

MRS. WILLIAMS: Play something, Bert. Play something happy.

GEORGE [to SNOW]: It's your fault. You turn her against me. [Tearfully] You tell her to stand up to me.

SNOW: No, George . . .

MRS. POCKS [to BLANCHE]: That's no way to talk to your father.

BLANCHE [deliberately]: The drunken—

MRS. POCKS: Blanche!

BERT: I won't play. I won't play anything. Poor old George. Poor old Blanche. Poor old Mrs. Pocks . . .

BLANCHE: Then don't play! Do as George says! Why shouldn't we go for a walk?

GEORGE: A no-good rouseabout . . .

MRS. POCKS: Tell her he's a tyke.

MRS. WILLIAMS: Now then, Mrs. Pocks, you know perfectly well that—

SNOW: George, you know religion doesn't make any difference. We're all only human, George.

DENISE: Speak for yourself, Snow.

SNOW: It's different for women. Women and religion go together. I've known Blanche since she left school and—

MRS. POCKS: And you've been eating here every Saturday since.

MRS. WILLIAMS: And had the same argument.

BLANCHE: You won't even listen.

GEORGE: You'd be better, my lady, if you gave more attention to your job.

BLANCHE: My job! More attention to my job! That's just what I wanted to hear. My job! Slushing around all day. Fourteen hours a day of drunks. Six days a week. Nobody else'd stay. Anybody else'd get another job.

MRS. POCKS: There's nothing stopping you.

[A long pause.]

BLANCHE: You and George wanted to get married when you were only my age.

MRS. POCKS: Yes.

[A pause.]

BLANCHE: There's nothing wrong with Snow. You can't say anything against him—except that he eats such a lot. But he's a big man. There's nothing wrong with Snow. [*To* GEORGE] You're just a great bully. You're just a great bully. Just a big, fat, drunken bully.

GEORGE: Cut it out, Blanche. [*He gives a sort of muffled groan of anger.*]

MRS. POCKS: Blanche!

BLANCHE [*loudly and clearly*]: Just a great, fat, drunken bully.
　　[TONY *enters.*]

TONY: Always the same happy family, always. I love this kitchen. [*He sits down temporarily.*]
　　[GEORGE *grunts recognition of him.* BLANCHE *sits down sulkily.* BERT *remains absorbed in his thoughts.*]
It's so homely. It reminds me of Wagner.

MRS. WILLIAMS: Good night, Tony. Are we to have your company too, tonight?

MRS. POCKS: He's too mean to pay for a seat. He'll go in at interval.

TONY: On a night like tonight, I won't go in at all. I'm too mean to waste it. The moon's as big as an onion already; I'd rather sit home and cry. Good night, Denise.

DENISE: Good night.

TONY: May I sit near *you* and cry, Billie? It's cold.

MRS. WILLIAMS: But it's a hot night.

TONY: Is it?

SNOW: Yeah.

TONY: Yes. Yes, so it is. Yes, it's a *fine* night. A fine night for bunyips, or lovers—poor lost lovers, or any strange things. Ah, Mrs. Williams, if only I had the go in me to be up to asking you to come out this fine night of the moon. The wattle'll be heavy and white in the moonlight. The trees will be—

MRS. WILLIAMS: No wattle for me, Tony. It gives me the sneezes.
　　[TONY *sneezes.*]

TONY: The sneezes! Well, it was a nice idea. [*He turns to* MRS. POCKS.]
　　[*She is playing patience again.*]
Well, you old witch! Are you still telling fortunes?

MRS. POCKS: Don't you call me that or—

TONY: I'll say it once too often! How about a hand, old witch?

MRS. POCKS: Whenever I look like getting it out . . . Talk about useless . . . [*She is already dealing.*] And keep your mind on the game.

> [*They play in silence.* DENISE *and* MRS. WILLIAMS *work.* GEORGE *is sunk over his tea.* BERT *is leaning miserably against a wall.* BLANCHE *is unhappy at the table.* SNOW *watches the game.* PADDY *says nothing.* TONY *wins.*]

TONY: Got you!

MRS. POCKS: But you don't play right. You're too careless.

TONY: It's my deal. [*He deals.*]

> [*It is a very quick game. He wins. She is disgusted. She deals.*]
> Mrs. Williams, how can you sit there with your beautiful head bent over the table and your beautiful eyes that should be looking at me poring over accounts? Let the firm go broke! What good's the firm? Time for the firm tomorrow—or the next day. Mine! [*He has won again.*]

> [MRS. POCKS *groans.* TONY *deals.*]

MRS. POCKS: You talk too much, that's what it is.

TONY: I was quiet all the first game.

MRS. WILLIAMS [*laughing*]: My eyes *are* looking at you, Tony. And I should be working. You come in here, with all your talk . . . You should be talking to some of the young ones who've got time for your nonsense; I know what men are. All men are the same.

BLANCHE: They all want to work you, to have their own way.

GEORGE: Hm.

MRS. WILLIAMS: Two months after the wedding, a man's interested in nothing but his stomach.

MRS. POCKS: And twenty years after, they're interested in nothing but drink.

TONY: I haven't had a wedding. I'm interested in nothing but cards —at the moment. Rummy—again!

MRS. POCKS: It's the way you deal.

TONY: Well, you deal this time. Don't rub the spots off.

MRS. POCKS: None of your cheek. I'm old enough to be your—

TONY: Grandmother.

> [*They play.*]
> Sitting here, Mrs. Williams. When you could be outside. With

the moon in your hair. Your hair shining like a black mirror.
[MRS. WILLIAMS *pats her tinted hair*.]

MRS. WILLIAMS: My hair's blonde.
[TONY *looks at* DENISE *and her dark hair*.]

TONY: So it is. I meant Mrs. Pock's hair.
[MRS. WILLIAMS *glances at* DENISE.]
It's an awful thing to board at a hotel where there's a woman like
Mrs. Pocks on show, but not available for hire.

MRS. POCKS: That's enough of that.

TONY: Yeah? Admit it's a low neck. Go on, admit it.

MRS. POCKS: You keep your eyes off my neck.

TONY: They are off your neck. [*He picks up a card and displays a
winning hand*.] That's the one I need.

MRS. POCKS: Never seen such luck.

TONY: Lucky at cards ... My deal. [*He deals*.] What are you making,
Denise?

DENISE: You can see for yourself. [*She holds it up*.]

TONY: I've seen.

DENISE: Always polite.

TONY: What a hand! Hallo, Gink.
[THE GINK *comes in. He stands at the door. He wears a black
armband. No one speaks for a moment*. MRS. WILLIAMS *looks
sympathetic. The cards go on*.]

GINK: Hallo, Tony. Hi, everyone. Good night, Mrs. Williams.

MRS. WILLIAMS: How are you, Arthur? You must bear up, you
know. We all have to pass on, sometime or other.

GINK: Yeah?
[*A pause*.]
Would you like a ticket in a raffle? [*He holds out a ticket-book*.]
[*No one rushes forward*.]
They're only sixpence. I haven't sold many.

MRS. WILLIAMS: My purse is upstairs, Arthur.

MRS. POCKS: Always money for something.

TONY: Here, give me two.

MRS. POCKS: You must be in love.

TONY: Generous Joe, they call me.

GINK: But your name's Tony, Tony. Tony the Dago, they call you.

MRS. WILLIAMS: Arthur, you shouldn't—

133

TONY: Fame! [*He picks up a card.*] That one's handy.

DENISE [*bitterly*]: Tony the Talker!

[MRS. POCKS *picks up the card that* TONY *discarded.*]

MRS. POCKS: And that one'll do me.

GINK: Go on, Mrs. Pocks. You have one, too. [*He displays the book.*]

MRS. POCKS: Don't worry me, Gink. Can't you see I'm busy?

SNOW: I'll have one, Gink. And one for Blanche, too. [*He gives him the money.*]

[THE GINK *has some confusion with the change.*]

BLANCHE: I'm not lucky. I can't even win an argument.

TONY: My trouble exactly—one leads to another.

[GEORGE *lifts his head from the table.*]

GEORGE: Ought to be ashamed of himself.

MRS. POCKS: Eh?

GEORGE: Ought to be ashamed of yourself. You ought to be ashamed of yourself, you ought.

GINK: Aw, George . . .

BLANCHE: What's the Gink done?

GEORGE: He ought to be ashamed of himself . . . *It's to bury his father* . . . It's to bury his father . . . [GEORGE *has collapsed again.*]

BERT [*profoundly*]: To bury his father.

GINK: The raffle's to bury my father.

GEORGE: Ought to be ashamed of himself.

MRS. WILLIAMS: Oh, Arthur!

GINK: He's got to be buried.

BERT: Bury his father.

GEORGE: Never heard anything like it . . . I never heard anything like it . . .

GINK: I'll give him the sixpences back, George, if you think I ought to. I'll give them to him back. [*He holds them out.*]

SNOW: Aw, he's got to be buried, Gink.

GINK: Yeah. [*He still holds them out.*]

SNOW: You'd better keep it.

GEORGE: It's disgraceful . . . Disgraceful . . . A disgraceful— disgrace.

BLANCHE: You're a one to talk.

TONY: There's a moral here, somewhere.

MRS. WILLIAMS [*like Joan of Arc*]: I'll go and get my purse. We all have to help. Just look at poor Arthur. Just look at him.

[*They all look.* THE GINK *wilts.*]

You can see how he's worried, how he's struggled. We all have to help. We must do what we can. *I'*ll buy one, Arthur.

MRS. POCKS: Stop fussing around, Billo. Get one out of this. Get one for me too. [*She fumbles money from her pocket and throws it on the table.*]

GINK: Gee, thanks, Mrs. Pocks. Thanks, Mrs. Williams. Which number do you want?

MRS. POCKS: Sh!

MRS. WILLIAMS: Well, I— Well, Arthur, I— Oh, it doesn't— Well, I did have forty-four once in a chocolate-wheel, and it was only two off a prize.

GINK [*looking*]: Forty-four's gone. Gee, I'm sorry, Mrs. Williams. Have seven. You can have seven. Seven's a lucky number.

MRS. WILLIAMS: Oh, thank you, Arthur. Do you really think so? Any number will do for Mrs. Pocks. She's busy. [*She pays him.*]

[*He gives her the tickets. He stands looking at her. She smiles at him. They stand there. It becomes embarrassing. She sits down. He stares at her. A long pause.* MRS. WILLIAMS *is fluttery.*]

MRS. POCKS: Have you grown yet?

GINK: Eh? Oh. Oh, I'd better go now. I suppose I'd better go now. [*He looks at* PADDY.]

BLANCHE: It's no good waiting. He's drunk.

MRS. POCKS: Shut up, Paddy!

GINK: Oh. Oh, he's drunk, is he?

SNOW: Yeah.

TONY: And you waited, Gink. You waited, because you thought he was asleep and was bound to wake up sometime or other, and was sure to want a raffle-ticket. How long would you have waited, Gink?

GINK: Eh? Oh . . .

TONY: I said if he was asleep he was sure to wake up and buy a ticket.

MRS. POCKS [*to* TONY *and* THE GINK]: Concentrate, can't you?

GINK: Oh— yeah. Well—I'll be going. I suppose I'd better be going. A bloke ought to be lucky with the picture crowd. You'd think people who go to the pictures would buy a ticket. I'd better be going.

MRS. WILLIAMS: Good night, Arthur. Best of luck. And—and keep pulling. Keep pulling. We're behind you.

GINK: Yeah. [*He goes out, dazed.*]

MRS. WILLIAMS: It must be terrible for him . . . But his father has to be buried. Do you know, I admire him for it. I admire a man who's got—guts.

TONY: Mrs. Williams!

MRS. WILLIAMS: Go on with the game.

MRS. POCKS: Yes, go on with the game. Interruptions all the time. [*She looks at her cards. She holds up her hand to* DENISE.] Have you ever seen a hand like it?

DENISE [*smiling*]: No.

[*A short pause.*]

SNOW: Come on, hon. Let's go out.

BLANCHE: What's the use? What's the use when you've got to come back? Play us a tune, Bert. Play us a tune.

BERT: No. No, I'm sad. I'm sad. We're all sad. Too sad. We all want something. When we all want something, what's the good of a tune? A tune's too sad.

BLANCHE: I'm not sad. I want to dance.

SNOW: Let's go for a walk.

TONY: I want a tune, too. To soothe the savage breast. It *is* a low neck, Mrs. Pocks. But your breast is calm, as far as I can see.

MRS. POCKS: You'll go too far—

TONY: Not in public, Mrs. Pocks. Go on, Bert, play us a tune.

BERT: No. No. It's all so sad. I'm going to cry, it's so sad.

MRS. POCKS: Sit still, Paddy.

[PADDY *makes a movement.*]

MRS. WILLIAMS: Oh, don't cry, Mr. Horner. Don't actually weep.

BLANCHE: And Paddy's here every week. Drunk and stupid. Drunk and stupid.

MRS. POCKS [*exasperated with the card she has drawn*]: At least he's quiet! I can't keep my mind on the game. Shut up, Paddy! [*Silence.* TONY *wins. She cries out. She deals. A few seconds' silent play.* MRS. POCKS *snatches at a card that* TONY *discards.*] Ah! Got you!

TONY: Rummy! [*He puts down his cards.*]

[MRS. POCKS *throws hers down.*]

MRS. POCKS: Damn!

[MRS. WILLIAMS, DENISE, SNOW *and* TONY *laugh at her. She gathers the cards together again. From outside comes a noise of curlews, but different from curlews.*]

MRS. WILLIAMS: There it is!

MRS. POCKS [*after a moment*]: It's curlews.

TONY: It's the bunyip.

[*They are all quiet again. They again hear the sound.*]

MRS. WILLIAMS: There it is again! Isn't it exciting?

TONY: Just think . . . Out there—somewhere out there—the bunyip.

[*They all listen. There is no sound.* GEORGE *grunts.*]

MRS. POCKS: It's your deal.

MRS. WILLIAMS: Nature's wonderful when you look at it.

TONY: But we haven't looked at it. No one has ever looked at it. The bunyip. Some poor, frightened animal—out there in the dark, in the moonlight—and no one has ever looked at it. [*He deals out the hand.*]

MRS. WILLIAMS: It'd give us a fright if we did.

SNOW: It must be small, or someone'd have seen it.

TONY: No one has seen it, has ever seen it . . .

SNOW: The moon'll be up.

BLANCHE: What difference does that make?

TONY: No one's seen it. Yet it's there . . . I win.

MRS. POCKS: Damn you!

TONY [*still in a dream-thinking tone*]: Please, no.

[*She shuffles and deals again.*]

[*He tries to shake himself back to what is real and present.*] Don't you ever get tired of this?

[MRS. POCKS *merely sniffs.*]

DENISE: Of course, there's no such thing.

TONY: No one's seen such a thing.

SNOW: There might be. You never know what there might be.

TONY: No one's seen such a thing. But we know it's there. Don't we, Mrs. Williams?

MRS. WILLIAMS [*inspired and with faith*]: Yes. *We* know it's there. It's wonderful, isn't it? Isn't it wonderful?

MRS. POCKS [*with her mind on the game*]: What's wonderful about it?

MRS. WILLIAMS: It's wonderful! I don't know . . . [*She giggles.*] It's just wonderful.

BLANCHE: Mournful damn noise every night.

DENISE: It sounds frightening when everything is still.

TONY: It sounds alive; that's frightening. Old Johnny Mulligan says it's a ghost . . .

MRS. WILLIAMS: I went to a spiritualist-house, a seeonce once—

TONY: *It*'s alive, at any rate.

GEORGE [*looking up*]: Curlew.

TONY: Alive . . . And it's spring. It's probably mating.

MRS. WILLIAMS [*giggling*]: Don't be vulgar.

TONY: Mrs. Williams, mating is a perfectly natural—

MRS. WILLIAMS [*archly*]: Oh, Tony!

MRS. POCKS: Billie's a widow.

SNOW: Come on, Blanche. Don't sit there till you're crazy.

MRS. WILLIAMS [*another inspiration*]: Let's *all* go for a walk!

[*They all look at her, surprised.* MRS. POCKS *glares with distaste over her cards.* TONY *leaps up, but he still plays.*]

TONY: Let's all find the bunyip!

MRS. WILLIAMS: Well, we could go for a walk.

TONY: And we might find it—[*He becomes excited, by the idea.*]

MRS. WILLIAMS: We'd be the first—

TONY: It'd be in the papers—

MRS. WILLIAMS: On the wireless, Mrs. Pocks—

SNOW: They'd put it over the A.B.C.

[*This brings them back to reality. There is a pause that leaves Mrs. Williams standing.*]

TONY [*softly*]: It's a lovely night for a walk . . . [*To* DENISE] To look for the bunyip . . . It's a lovely night . . .

BLANCHE: It's too hot.

MRS. POCKS: Shut up, Paddy.

TONY: There's a breeze, now. It'll get cooler. We may never get another chance . . . Night of the full moon . . . Bunyip . . .

SNOW [*to* BLANCHE]: We mightn't ever get another chance.

MRS. WILLIAMS: Oh, come on, Mrs. Pocks! You don't want to just sit here and mope.

TONY: Mope, mope, mo-poke.

MRS. WILLIAMS: You don't want to sit here. [*She looks at* GEORGE.] *People* will take you for granted. Come on, Mrs. Pocks! Come and blow the cobwebs off. It's a lovely night. It's a perfectly heavenly night. It's the night of our lives . . . Damn cards! Yes, damn them!

MRS. POCKS [*impressed*]: What about this game?

TONY: And damn the game! Damn the game!

MRS. WILLIAMS [*with him*]: Damn the game! [*She picks up the pack and throws it in the air.*]

MRS. POCKS: You'll pick them up!

TONY: Good on you, Billie! Damn the game! [*He pulls the cards from* MRS. POCKS' *hand and throws them.*]

MRS. POCKS: You'll pick up every one of them.

[*She goes to collect them but* TONY *seizes her.*]

TONY: Tomorrow, tomorrow! The bunyip, tonight! Let's find the bunyip! A bunyip for Poxie, a bunyip for Poxie, a bunyip for Poxie . . . [*He twirls her round to the tune.*] Let's make it tonight.

MRS. WILLIAMS [*excited*]: A bunyip for Poxie!

MRS. POCKS: Stop it, you fool . . . He's off his head.

MRS. WILLIAMS: I'll have to get my shoes—

TONY: This is a night for slippers, this is the time to be mad. You may never get another chance, may never—

SNOW [*to* BLANCHE]: You're only young once.

TONY: Wear your slippers, Billie. I'll fill them with champagne— if there's any champagne.

DENISE: You are being silly, Tony.

MRS. POCKS: Let—me—go!

[TONY *pinions her tightly.*]

TONY [*whispering like Charles Boyer*]: Oh, you are adorable when you struggle so, my little pigeon-face . . .

MRS. WILLIAMS: Yes, we're only young once. I'm only young once.

MRS. POCKS [*struggling to breathe*]: You were only young once!

[SNOW *has pulled* BLANCHE *to her feet.*]

BLANCHE [*to* SNOW]: It's stupid. It won't change anything.

MRS. POCKS: It's perfectly ridiculous!

MRS. WILLIAMS: It's marvellous! And it's perfectly, perfectly ridiculous. It's making me cry.

BERT: The world's so sad. Everyone wants something . . . [*He mumbles on.*]

TONY: Come on, Mrs. Pocks. Just whisper, yes . . .

MRS. POCKS [*shocked*]: Tony!

TONY: The time's running out . . . You and me, in the moonlight . . . Just think of that . . . The night of the moon . . . Just you and me . . .

MRS. POCKS: Keep your hands still!

[SNOW *has been pleading low and urgently to* BLANCHE.]

SNOW: Come on, Blanche. Tony's right. The time's running out. This is the night . . .

MRS. POCKS [*to* MRS. WILLIAMS]: You'll be sorry tomorrow—

MRS. WILLIAMS [*pulling at her*]: Damn tomorrow! Damn tomorrow! Come as you are!

[*There is a lot of noise. They are talking over one another, mumbling.*]

TONY: We'll be dead tomorrow. The grave'll shut over us, then we'll know nothing. [*To* MRS. POCKS, *in her ear, with passion*] At least, let me live tonight.

SNOW: The grave'll shut over you, then you'll know nothing . . .

BLANCHE: Stuck in a hole. [*She rises.*] Snow and I are going. I don't want to be dead.

TONY: Then we're all going then! Then we're all going to go!

DENISE: I'm not going.

TONY [*deflated*]: Oh.

[*His sudden fall quiets everyone.*]

DENISE [*answering the silence*]: I want to finish this.

[*A brief pause.*]

SNOW: Well, we're going. [*He looks imploringly at* BLANCHE.]

MRS. WILLIAMS: Yes. We're going.

BLANCHE: We are going.

MRS. POCKS: You're not going by yourselves! Traipsing round the bush with that thing. [*She glares at* SNOW].

MRS. WILLIAMS [*knowing her*]: Oh, Mrs. Pocks! You do want to go!

GEORGE: We'll all go. [*He rises and staggers.*]

TONY: Good on you, George! You've got the spirit in you.

[MRS. POCKS *grunts.*]

Blessed be George! You're a real sport, George. You'll find the bunyip.

140

MRS. WILLIAMS: It's a night for finding bunyips. Do come, George. It'll do you good.

MRS. POCKS [*to* GEORGE]: You'll know it in the morning.

GEORGE: It'll be in the papers. *George Pocks. George Pocks.* Come on, Bert. Come on, Bert.

BERT [*restored to life and vigour*]: Yes, George, yes . . . We'll make us all happy . . . And I'll play you a tune. I'll play us a tune.

GEORGE: We'll all be *so* happy. [*To* MRS. POCKS, *pugnaciously*] And I'll feel a lot better.

MRS. WILLIAMS. Yes. Play us a tune, Mr. Horner. Play us a march. We'll all go together.

MRS. POCKS: Never heard anything so stupid . . . Well, come on, if you're coming.

TONY: We're off for the bunyip!

[*He shepherds them into formation.*]

MRS. WILLIAMS: The night of the moon!

[PADDY *stands up, belligerently.*]

PADDY: No, I won't shut up. I won't shut up! We're all going. You're going. I'm going. We're *all* going. We'll make us all happy, happy . . . We'll be young once . . . Grave will close over, over . . . Tomorrow's morning, morning . . . [*Singing*] "The Moon shines bright on my old—"

MRS. POCKS: Paddy! Paddy—

PADDY: Let's get that bunyip. That's all I want. And, cripes, I'll get it! [*He assumes a fisticuffs pose.*] Off to the bunyip! Off for the bunyip!

TONY: Off! Off!

MRS. POCKS: Have supper ready when we get back, Denise. That's a good girl.

TONY: Avaunt! Avaunt! To the bunyip! The bunyip!

MRS. WILLIAMS: Onwards! Onwards! The bunyip!

[BERT *bursts into* "Pack Up Your Troubles". *Someone sings.* TONY *and* MRS. WILLIAMS *are shouting.* MRS. POCKS *is protesting.* PADDY *is leading.*]

PADDY [*as they go*]: Let's get that bunyip. Let's get that bunyip. That's all I want . . . etc.

TONY [*bowing them to the door*]: After you! After you!

[*They sweep out.* TONY *remains. The sound dies.*]

141

TONY: They're gone.

DENISE: Aren't you going?

TONY: No. [*He switches off the light.*]

> [*The moonlight enters. It is very bright.*]
>
> [*After a moment's pause,* DENISE *leans over her work, as though she could still see.*]

No. I don't want the bunyip. What are bunyips to me? [*He goes to the window.*] The night's changed from dark to purple-blue; it looks as though it had just been washed. The stars look like powder; they've lost their points . . . If you don't talk to me, they have no point. [*He pauses.*] The moon's a penny. I'd give you the moon for your thoughts. [*He looks at her.*] The moon's a dead-man's mask, white as a dead-man's face; I could tell you a story about the moon . . . [*He pauses.*] Aren't you keen on stories?

DENISE: Would you put on the light? I'm busy.

TONY: So am I. Shall I tell you what I'm busy at? I'm thinking. And that's not good for me. It confuses me. It upsets me. I don't like it . . . I'm wondering. And that's not good for me either. It hurts me, and doesn't seem to get me anywhere. I'm wondering why my best friends won't tell me . . . You tell me. Go on, you tell me—that I've got B.O.

DENISE: I don't think that's funny.

TONY: Neither do I. You used to think I was funny.

DENISE: Used-to's a long time ago.

TONY: Used-to ought to be tomorrow, ought to be today.

DENISE: It isn't though.

TONY: Oh! Oh, Denise . . . Denise . . . [*He puts out his arms to her*].

DENISE: Oh, Tony . . . Tony. Why *do* you keep talking?

TONY: I'm Tony the Talker, that's me.

DENISE: It's all over. It's all over, do you hear? I won't have anything to— You should never have— That disgusting— I don't want to talk about it. I don't want to think about it. It's over.

TONY: So you're—you're finished. You're—disgusted, because I won't let it drop. What about it? [*He puts his arms around her.*] Because I'm human, you're disgusted . . .

> [*Her arms stiffen.*]

There you go! A man can't come near you. What's wrong with you anyway? Aren't you alive or something? And you put me in the wrong all the time. You put me in the wrong, because I'm living and breathing and want to encourage it. I mustn't touch you. But you'd let me write sonnets about you. That'd be all right! You're living in the wrong age, Denise. Those days are over. When are you going to wake up?

[PADDY *returns. He is exhausted. He goes to his seat.*]

DENISE [*at* PADDY'S *approach*]: Be quiet! Tony, someone's—

TONY [*after* PADDY *has settled*]: What's wrong with you anyway? You're not natural. You're cold. You said you loved me.

DENISE: Will you be quiet? Will you be quiet? There's someone here.

TONY: Someone? It's Paddy. It's only Paddy. Right, mate?

PADDY: Only Paddy . . . [*He relapses into his stupor.*] Only Paddy . . .

DENISE: Be quiet, then! Do you think I want all my life discussed in front of a thing like that?

TONY: A thing like that. He's human, isn't he? He's got a name. Or don't you believe in humans? I think that's what's wrong. You don't believe in humans.

DENISE: I don't want to talk about it.

TONY: I do. It isn't as if we'd done anything. You're no little Emily. *A thing like that.* That's it. You're not human. I'm a thing like me, or a thing like that. That's how you think of me. How do you think of yourself?

DENISE: You're behaving like a—

TONY: Yes. Yes, I am. And you said you loved me. [*He pauses.*] And you said you loved me . . .

DENISE: Well, if I did, I did. I must have thought so. I must have meant it—then. That was then.

TONY: Under the pepper-trees. With your face all dark in the shadow, your hair all light . . . Your eyes were closed. When I kissed you I knew that your eyes were closed. While I was kissing you I was knowing that your eyes were closed . . . And you said you loved me. But you kept your eyes closed. And you kept running away. Running away from me. Running away from love. Oh, I don't want to flatter myself, but it's true. You're running away from love. Love! You don't know what love means. You're frightened of what it might mean. You're frightened all the time. And you pretend to be so prim and so proper. You are so prim and so proper and so sure of yourself, but it's a fraud—like the bunyip. You're frightened. You're frightened.

DENISE: Tony. Tony. Don't be horrible to me . . .

TONY: Horrible?

DENISE: Yes. You're not very fair. You're only thinking of yourself.

TONY: Nobody else thinks of me. Do you ever think of me?

DENISE: Yes.

TONY: You hardly talk to me. You give me the cold shoulder. And you said that you loved me.

DENISE: Yes. Oh you are cruel. You're full of self-pity.

TONY: Yes. Yes. I suppose I am. I suppose it is self-pity. It wouldn't sound *manly* to say I was full of pity for all lost lovers this night of the full moon. I suppose it is self-pity.

DENISE: It sounds very like it.

TONY: You're incredibly hard.

DENISE: I wish you'd stop analysing me. You behave like a school-teacher. Except when you're under the pepper-trees.

TONY: And that's why you hate me.

DENISE: I don't hate you.

TONY: Thank you! You'd like me to be a schoolteacher all the time —someone in a collar and tie, terribly respectable and dignified, never doing unimaginable things like kissing under the pepper-trees. I stop being a teacher at half-past three. [*Changing his tone*] Denise. Let me kiss you. [*A pause.*] Are you afraid to let me kiss you? He doesn't notice. He's too happy to notice. He's drunk, and doesn't notice anything. Denise, let me kiss you.

DENISE: Don't be silly.

[*He kisses her.*]

TONY: That was a twenty-years-married peck. This—[*He kisses her.*]

DENISE [*breaking it*]: No. Tony. Tony.

[*He lets go.*]

I'm sorry.

TONY: You're afraid. You'll always be afraid.

DENISE [*a sudden flare of temper*]: Well, I can't help it! I don't want to be!

TONY: I'm not blaming you.

DENISE: No? I don't know why I let you upset me.

TONY: Perhaps you like me a little—but not as a lover. I was never much of a lover—the schoolteacher special.

DENISE: It's not because you're a teacher or—

TONY: Thank you.

DENISE: If you're going to be stupid . . .

TONY [*gently, putting his arms around her*]: Oh, Denise, Denise . . . We're not here, not in this kitchen, not with Paddy, not with the papers to read or that dress to finish. We're out in the bush. We're looking for the bunyip. It's a spring night. The moon's full. The air's full of moonlight. The air's so light, it makes you skip. And the wattle's—white in the moonlight. We're standing in the shadow of the pine-trees, and we're fearing no evil . . .
[*He bends to her and she moves away.*]
The wattle doesn't make you sneeze, so that's something, but we're still a long way from the bunyip. Oh, Denise, it's dark under the trees—

DENISE [*most soberly*]: Tony.

TONY: We're a long way from the bunyip. We're a long way from the bunyip, we are. [*He puts on the light.*]
[*She looks at him, and then bends over her work. A pause.*]

PADDY [*half-singing, half-mumbling*]: "Change and decay in all around I see . . ."

TONY: Change and decay, Paddy, change and decay . . . We're a long way from the bunyip . . . And you *know* there's nothing else. You do know there's nothing else, don't you?

DENISE: I want to finish this. I wish you wouldn't talk.

TONY: I'll be a long time silent when I'm dead.

DENISE: Why don't you go to bed?

TONY: That rhymes! [*With meaning*] I'd like to go to bed.

DENISE: Don't talk that way.

TONY: Well, then, I'm not ready for bed. I'm not tired. I don't feel like shutting my eyes. I don't want time to run away while I'm not looking at it. Perhaps, I'll read. Read! Some people like to go to bed with a book.

DENISE: Tony!

TONY: Why don't you go to bed?

DENISE: I'm working. I'm trying to work.

TONY: The moon's working. The night's working. Working towards

145

something . . . What are you working towards?

DENISE: I said I'd get supper. I want this finished for church in the morning . . . What are you talking about?

TONY: *I* said I'd read.

PADDY [*out of the blue*]: Reading's a great thing. A man wants to read. That's what a man wants. The world'll be marvellous when every man can read—no trouble at all. That's what they said. The world'll be marvellous—

TONY: It's still true, very probably. The world will be marvellous, when we can all read.

PADDY: No trouble at all when everyone reads—

DENISE: Oh, be quiet, Paddy! We've had enough talk.

TONY: Yes. Here, Paddy. Listen to this. [*He begins to read the first page of the Sydney Morning Herald.*]

[PADDY *listens. He nods affirmation, now and then.* DENISE, *after a moment, goes on with her work.* TONY *reads on.*]

(*End of Act One*)

ACT TWO

Before the curtain rises we hear PADDY *singing "Change and decay . . ."*
and TONY'S *voice as it drones through the births, engagements, silver*
and golden wedding columns, etc. PADDY *finishes once. There is a pause.*
He begins again. He finishes. There is a pause. He begins again. He
finishes. There is another pause. He begins again.

DENISE: Stop singing it! Stop singing it!

[*The curtain rises.* DENISE *is staring angrily at* PADDY. TONY,
who is seated at the table with the paper in front of him, watches
her.]

DENISE: That's the hundredth time you've sung it.

[PADDY *stares at her for a moment. Then he begins again.*]

DENISE: That's the hundredth time he's sung it.

TONY: Hundredth and first—if your first estimate was correct.

DENISE: I hate it.

TONY: I like it.

DENISE: I hate you.

TONY: I like you.

[*Suddenly, with surprised indignation,* PADDY *realizes what has*
been said.]

PADDY: It's a good song. My mother taught it to me. She said it
was a good song. She knew a good song when she heard one. She
made me learn it for church. I was a choirboy. I sang like an
angel. She taught it to me. She knew a good song. Dead and gone.
Dead and gone, she is. Dead and gone.

TONY: She certainly knew a good song, Paddy.

PADDY: Yes. [*After a moment's thought, he sits down, grieved.*]

DENISE: You encourage him, because you know I hate it.

TONY: He doesn't need any encouragement. I'm the one who needs
encouragement. I've read this next column a dozen times. I could
read it to you—only it doesn't make pleasant reading. [*A pause.*]
Listen! [*He pretends to read.*]

In memory of my wife, Lizzie,
Who walked and talked till she grew dizzy
Now at last that she is dead—

DENISE: Stop being silly!

TONY: Now at last that she is dead
I can sleep at night in bed.

DENISE: I don't appreciate your subtle humour.

TONY [*reading*]: "Roberts:—In loving memory of our dear husband
and father John Alfred who passed away December third, 1950:
We think of him in silence,
And often speak his name,
But all that's left to answer
Is his photo in a frame."

DENISE: You're still very silly.

TONY: No, that one's true. Inept, but sincere. [*He points to it.*]
Listen to this one. "Millingdon:—In loving memory of my dear
mother and our dear sister Anne Margaret Millingdon who was
called home November thirteenth, 1941:
Please God take this message
To mother and our sister up above.
Tell her how we miss her
And give to her our love.
Could we but kiss her loving face
And see again her—"

DENISE: No. Tony. Tony, no! Tony . . .

TONY: Or this—
"Many a lonely day,
Often a silent tear—"

DENISE [*crying*]: Tony . . .

TONY: Many a lonely day, Often a silent tear . . . Denise, I love you.
I think I love you, Denise. I think I must love you; I've never
been so cruel before.

DENISE: Tony . . .

[*They are coming together but, suddenly,* PADDY *stands and
begins singing "Change and Decay".*
Oh, Tony, Tony . . . leave me alone. [*With broken feeling*] Leave
me alone.

TONY [*hurt*]: All right.

DENISE: I don't want you to— I don't— I don't want you . . .

TONY: No. Darling— Darling! There, I've called you it. Darling, darling, darling Denise . . .

DENISE: I don't want you to touch me at all. I don't want you to touch me . . . Leave me alone, just leave me alone. [*She turns away and sits down.*]

TONY: No, you don't want me. I don't know how I ever thought . . . It must be the way I look in the mirror. I don't want to flatter myself but I used to think—

[*He talks to cover her tears.*]

And if I do say so who shouldn't, I— Are you all right, now?

DENISE: Yes. Thank you. It's just that I—I'm tired. And Paddy.

TONY: Give it a rest, Paddy.

[PADDY *is not singing, just standing.*]

PADDY: Rest? Oh. Oh, right you are, mate. Right you are if you say you are . . . [*He sits down again and looks asleep.*]

DENISE: Thank you. You ought to go to bed, now.

TONY: That's logic: you're tired; I ought to go to bed. We've discussed my going to bed.

DENISE: Yes.

[*A pause.*]

TONY: Denise?

DENISE: No, Tony. No. Don't start again.

TONY: It's just that—I can't just stop. I know I'm a nuisance. I can't just stop. I've never been this bad before. Admit it: I've never been this bad before. Denise, do you—

DENISE: There's someone coming!

[*He springs away from her.* MRS. POCKS *and* MRS. WILLIAMS *enter.* MRS. WILLIAMS *is limping.* MRS. POCKS *stands looking at* TONY *for a moment.*]

MRS. POCKS: There's the cow. There's a cow, if ever I saw a cow. And Paddy.

TONY: Good night, Mrs. Pocks? Nice night, Mrs. Pocks? Pleasant walk, Mrs. Pocks? Got any bunyips?

MRS. WILLIAMS [*reproachfully*]: Oh, Tony!

TONY: I am sorry; things kept me here.

MRS. WILLIAMS: Oh.

[*She and* MRS. POCKS *give* DENISE *a glance.*]

149

Oh.

TONY: Exactly. Oh!

MRS. WILLIAMS: Well, Tony, at least you could help us to a chair.

TONY: Sorry. Here. Take a chair. Take two. Take three. They belong to the hotel, I don't mind.

MRS. WILLIAMS: Oh, it's no joke. We walked and walked. I'm dead, nearly dead. And my ankle! I wouldn't be surprised if I'd broken my ankle. We walked for miles, and miles, and—miles.

[MRS. POCKS *has been trying to get a word in. She looks bitterly at* TONY.]

MRS. POCKS: Looking for the bunyip, we were. Looking for the bunyip! It just suited you. We played right into your hand. We'll know a thing or two, next time. Shut up, Paddy! There'll be no next time.

DENISE: The kettle's boiling.

MRS. WILLIAMS: I need a cup of tea. But I'm so tired I—

MRS. POCKS: Make us one like a good girl, will you?

[*Denise makes tea.*]

TONY: We kept the kettle boiling for you.

MRS. POCKS: I'll bet you did! Us all out and you doing a line with Denise!

[*There is a pause.* MRS. WILLIAMS *looks at* DENISE.]

TONY: Paddy was here too.

MRS. POCKS: Yes. All the loafers dropped out.

MRS. WILLIAMS [*archly*]: Paddy's no chaperone, you know.

PADDY: Reading's a great thing, you know. When we can all read—

MRS. POCKS: Shut up, Paddy. I'm in no mood to put up with anything.

MRS. WILLIAMS: We are very tired.

MRS. POCKS: Walked me off my legs, she did. My calves are all aching.

MRS. WILLIAMS: Oh, it wasn't that far. But the road was so rough—ruts and holes . . .

TONY: You stuck to the road!

MRS. POCKS: Of course, we stuck to the road.

TONY: Then you didn't find the bunyip.

MRS. POCKS: Of course, we didn't find the bunyip.

MRS. WILLIAMS: The noise did sound a lot closer—but it was in the bush.

MRS. POCKS: We'd have looked a fine sight, snaking round the bush in the middle of the night.

DENISE: Here's the tea.

[*They murmur thanks as they sugar it. They use cups but no saucers.*]

TONY: You must have looked a fine sight anyway; snaking down the road in the middle of the—

MRS. POCKS: Just a pair of old fools.

MRS. WILLIAMS [*almost at the same time*]: Just a pair of fools.

TONY: Snaking down the road! And, all the time, you knew it was in the bush.

MRS. POCKS: Well, we weren't going into the bush.

MRS. WILLIAMS: And we were *enjoying* the walk. It was *lovely*—for a while. The road was like a ribbon. And the moon was so big. You've never seen anything like it, Denise. Everything looked different, somehow.

TONY: You've never seen anything like it, Denise.

MRS. POCKS: Yes, *she* was enjoying it. Just a little bit further, she kept saying, just a little bit further . . . And look at her, now.

MRS. WILLIAMS: Well, I tripped. And we only went as far as the cemetery. I've walked miles—

TONY: You can't go much further than that, can you?

MRS. WILLIAMS: Why, I've walked miles further, in my time. When I was working on the coast—

MRS. POCKS: Well, you won't go far, if you always walk the way you did tonight.

MRS. WILLIAMS: But I tripped, Mrs. Pocks; I tripped. I don't always trip. You don't always trip when you're looking for bunyips, do you, Tony?

TONY: Well—I do.

MRS. WILLIAMS [*not listening*]: And it was lovely and fresh. It was so lovely and fresh—at first. And so cool to be out. Oh, it was glorious! If only I hadn't hurt my ankle!

MRS. POCKS: You should have seen her. Practically dancing. And singing out all the time—just a little further, Mrs. Pocks, just a little further. And look at her, now. Look at me, now.

TONY: I am looking, Mrs. Pocks. It's a sobering sight.

MRS. WILLIAMS: Tony, you don't know what you missed. It really was glorious—if only I hadn't hurt my ankle.

DENISE: It does look a bit swollen.

MRS. WILLIAMS: A *bit* swollen! It looks—

TONY: But it's given you a colour. You look younger.

MRS. POCKS [*snorting*]: Hm!

TONY: And so do you. You're both as red as roses. It's put new life into you.

MRS. WILLIAMS: I suppose it has done us good. I suppose it's done us the world of good, if only we knew it.

TONY: The world of good.

MRS. POCKS: I notice you didn't come.

TONY: I've got enough life in me. And I'm—white as a rose. I don't need a world of good done to me. Besides I was tired.

MRS. POCKS: You do nothing to make you tired. If you had my life! Standing in front of a crowd of kids all day! Yes, that'd make *you* tired!

TONY: And it does. Besides, I was playing tennis today.

MRS. WILLIAMS: Oh dear, I hope my ankle doesn't interfere—I was enjoying tennis so much . . . And the match next week . . .

MRS. POCKS: It'll be hot next week.

MRS. WILLIAMS: Oh, Mrs. Pocks, when I was at Gundagai we played till—

MRS. POCKS: And they won't miss you in the match.

MRS. WILLIAMS: Oh, I know I'm not a good player. But I do enjoy myself, and I always say that's the main—

MRS. POCKS: Aren't the others back yet?

TONY: What others? Are there more of you?

MRS. WILLIAMS: I thought they must all be in bed.

TONY: All in together, girls, This cold weather, girls.

　　[MRS. WILLIAMS *giggles*.]

MRS. POCKS [*not to be diverted*]: What's the time?

TONY: Later than you think. It's late. I can't afford a watch.

DENISE [*looking at the kitchen clock*]: The clock doesn't go.

MRS. WILLIAMS [*laughing*]: Neither does Tony.

MRS. POCKS: You mean he doesn't stop.

MRS. WILLIAMS: I mean he doesn't go. Looking for bunyips.

　　[*A pause. They look at her.*]

MRS. POCKS: Ought to get a new clock, if George isn't too mean to let me buy one. This thing's never been any damned good. It used to go once, if you put it upside down.

[TONY *puts it upside down. They look at it.*]

TONY [*righting it*]: I fixed it last night.

MRS. WILLIAMS: But it doesn't go—oh! [*she giggles.*] We've got some very nice ones in now, Mrs. Pocks, but they're a little bit dear—

TONY: Time's always dear, my dear—very dear.

MRS. WILLIAMS: But it's not really when you think about it. And compared with everything else. Prices nowadays. Everything's gone up.

MRS. POCKS: I'll have a look at them Monday, and see what George says.

MRS. WILLIAMS: You ought to have a clock in the kitchen.

MRS. POCKS: Isn't Blanche home yet?

[*A pause.*]

DENISE: No.

MRS. POCKS: They ought to be in before now.

TONY: Perhaps they went to the pictures.

MRS. WILLIAMS: Oh, the pictures are out. All the lights are out. We looked as we came up the hill. There's no one about. It must be terribly late. And there's mass in the morning.

TONY [*looking at Denise*]: Yes. [*Changing his tone*] Anyway, even Jack's not in yet.

MRS. POCKS: Well, you can guess what he's up to. And I can guess what they're up to. I'll tell that lady a thing or two . . .

DENISE: Tony. I want to say something to you.

[*A pause.*]

TONY: Disappear, characters! Or shall we go walking? She wants to say something to me! Say something to *me*! Shall we go walking?

MRS. POCKS: You might find the bunyip.

MRS. WILLIAMS: It's glorious out.

DENISE: No. No, it doesn't matter. It can wait till morning, some other time, when I've thought about it . . . I've got a headache.

TONY: Missed again! Lost, still lost . . .

MRS. WILLIAMS: Have a cup of tea, dear. There's nothing like a cup of tea.

153

[MRS. POCKS *gives* DENISE *a cup of tea.*]

MRS. POCKS: Here, drink this. You don't look too hot.

TONY: I hadn't noticed. No, she doesn't look too hot.

MRS. WILLIAMS: A cup of tea will pick you up. There's nothing like a cup of tea, is there?

TONY: No, Mrs. Williams, there's nothing like a cup of tea.

MRS. WILLIAMS: That's just what I always say: there's nothing like a cup of tea. Why don't you have one, Tony?

TONY: I? Me? I never drink tea. [*Smiling*] Oh, don't be upset, Billie! I didn't really mean it. Who am I to put Bushell's out of business? [*He hands her a cup.*] Pour us one like a dear girl, and let joy be unconfined.

[*She pours him tea and he takes it.*]

A cup of tea. A whole cup of tea. What more can life offer me? What more does life offer me? [*He sips his tea.*] It's hot. The *tea's* hot. Oh. Oh. A hot cup of tea after *not* going to the pictures! Surely my cup of life is overflowing!

MRS. WILLIAMS: You'll spill it on my skirt. Oh!

[*He spills some tea on her skirt.*]

Oh dear! This is a new one from the store . . . Did you have milk in it?

TONY: Sorry, Mrs. Williams, I didn't— No.

MRS. WILLIAMS: Then it won't stain.

TONY: Good! Let us be without stain. I'm glad.

MRS. WILLIAMS: So am I, young man.

MRS. POCKS: Just what you'd expect.

TONY: I am really sorry. But I was enjoying it so much. I wanted to share it with others, share something of my feelings about it. My whole life has moved towards this night, to this fulfilment . . .

MRS. POCKS: Who gave you the booze?

MRS. WILLIAMS: Oh, Tony, have you been drinking too?

TONY: Why? Have you?

MRS. WILLIAMS: Don't be silly.

TONY: No, of course not. Don't be silly. Don't be silly. Don't be bloody silly.

MRS. WILLIAMS: Tony! I'm surprised at you.

MRS. POCKS: Just listen to that language! Is that how you talk to the children?

TONY: I feel awful.

MRS. POCKS: You have been drinking.

TONY: I wish I had. That'd be something. I'd feel I was getting somewhere.

DENISE: Tony, you're being very silly.

TONY: Damned silly. Damned silly.

MRS. WILLIAMS: Why, Tony, I—

DENISE: I wish you wouldn't go on like this.

MRS. WILLIAMS: Oh!

[*She and* MRS. POCKS *exchange a glance. They look closely at both* TONY *and* DENISE. *A pause.*]

MRS. WILLIAMS: It's a lovely night out. A lovely night to go walking with someone. Why don't you go for a walk?

[DENISE *tenses but says nothing.*]

It's a lovely night for a walk. The moon's like a—like a—

TONY: Like an emerald, like a silver penny, like a milky mirror, like a moon . . .

MRS. WILLIAMS: Like a round of green cheese. My mother used to say the moon was green cheese—

[BLANCHE *and* SNOW *enter.*]

BLANCHE: My mother talks a lot too.

TONY: Hi.

MRS. POCKS: Where have you been?

SNOW: Hallo.

BLANCHE: Out. Where have you been?

MRS. POCKS: What a time to come in!

SNOW: Er—what is the time, Lil?

MRS. POCKS: How should I know! Don't Lil me!

BLANCHE: Well, what are you shooting your mouth off for, if you don't even know the time?

MRS. POCKS: We thought you were coming with us.

BLANCHE: So did we.

SNOW: Well, we went with you.

MRS. POCKS: We've been back for hours. Where have you been?

BLANCHE: Fat lot you care! Can anyone have this tea?

MRS. WILLIAMS: It'll need some hot water.

DENISE: There's some on the stove.

MRS. POCKS: You should have more sense, you big hulking— Keeping her out all hours!

BLANCHE: He's not a big hulk.

SNOW: Pick on someone your own size, Lil. [*He tries to pass it off as a joke.*]

MRS. POCKS: I'll pick on whoever I like.

SNOW: Whoever you don't like.

[MRS. WILLIAMS *almost laughs, but dares not.* SNOW *goes on with great content.*]

I'm too tired to fight with you.

MRS. POCKS: What do you think George will say? Has George gone to bed? Isn't George back yet? Where's George? We thought George was coming back.

MRS. WILLIAMS: He should have been back by now.

MRS. POCKS: He might have hurt himself . . . He'll be furious . . .

[*Suddenly* BLANCHE *bursts into tears.*]

Serves him right . . . His back'll play up now! He's not supposed to take exercise . . . What's wrong with you?

SNOW [*awkwardly, with his hand on* BLANCHE'S *shoulder*]: We had a fight.

MRS. POCKS: Hm! Well, you'll get no sympathy from me.

[*A pause. Disturbed,* MRS. POCKS *watches* BLANCHE.]

MRS. WILLIAMS: Don't cry, Blanche. It's all over now.

TONY: No sense in crying if it's all over now.

DENISE: Your tea's getting cold, Blanche.

BLANCHE: We made it up.

TONY: That's why she's crying.

DENISE: Shut up, Tony! You talk too much.

TONY: Men aren't allowed to cry.

SNOW: No. [*He laughs suddenly, then stops.*]

[*A pause.*]

BLANCHE: Don't take any notice of me. [*A pause.*] You make me sick, all staring at me. You look like fish with your mouths open.

MRS. WILLIAMS [*laughing nervously*]: Well, I—

[*She stops and there is quiet.*]

I'm sure it's going to be a terrible summer—

[TONY *laughs at her tact.*]

SNOW, DENISE, MRS. POCKS: Yes, it's going to—

[*There is another pause.*]

SNOW: Come on, and we'll put some hot water in the teapot.

[*He and* BLANCHE *go to the stove.*]

MRS. WILLIAMS [*whispering urgently*]: Oh, Mrs. Pocks, you shouldn't
. . . You were young once yourself, you know . . .

MRS. POCKS: Young!

MRS. WILLIAMS: Well, it's different when you're young. And you
really shouldn't . . .

[*She and* MRS. POCKS *go on whispering.*]

TONY [*softly*]: Why don't you wake up to yourself, why don't you?

DENISE: I've got a headache. I told you I've got a headache . . .

TONY: If you'd only try . . . only let yourself go . . . only . . . [*He
whispers to her for a moment.*]

[*They are sitting near each other, he intent on her and she looking
down at her sewing.*]

SNOW: Don't cry, hon. Don't cry, hon.

[*He holds* BLANCHE *while she fills the teapot.*]

It doesn't always hurt . . . Only the first time . . . I didn't want to
hurt you, hon . . . Only the first time . . . I can't bear to see you
cry . . . Don't cry, don't cry . . . Doesn't hurt now . . .

BLANCHE: You mustn't go away tonight, you mustn't go away.
You've got to stay here. Snow, you've got to stay here . . . Say
that you will, say that you will—

SNOW: Hon— Come and have your tea.

[*He takes her back to the table and sits her down.*]

You know I can't.

BLANCHE [*quite loudly*]: Snow!

[*The others look round,* TONY *last of all.*]

MRS. POCKS: Well?

BLANCHE [*pleading*]: Snow.

SNOW: I can't.

[*She begins to cry softly.*]

SNOW: You know I can't.

MRS. POCKS: He can't do anything. He's as big as he's useless. What
does she want you to do?

TONY [*deliberately changing the subject*]: I wonder if George is all
right.

MRS. POCKS: We'd hear him bellowing if he wasn't.

MRS. WILLIAMS: Like a bull.

[*She giggles, but a glance from* MRS. POCKS *stops her.*]

MRS. POCKS: Hm!

MRS. WILLIAMS [*changing the subject*]: Have you finished the dress?

DENISE [*working at it*]: No. I've done the tucks. I have to fix the hem. It's nearly finished.

TONY: It's a life's work, Mrs. Williams; a life-time job. Plenty of security; it's a life-sentence. There's plenty of security; you're never out of a job, you've never got nothing to do, you've never got nothing. You've never got nothing . . .

[SNOW *has been whispering to* BLANCHE. *She is still crying.*]

SNOW [*interrupting*]: We're going to get married.

[*Silence.*]

TONY: I talk too much.

[*Silence.*]

BLANCHE: Snow, we—

[*A pause.*]

SNOW: It's all right. [*More loudly.*] We're going to get married. Blanche and me, I mean.

[*There is silence.*]

TONY: Congratulations.

SNOW: Thanks, Tone . . .

[*Silence.*]

MRS. POCKS [*quite calmly*]: When she's old enough to know her own mind . . .

[*A pause.*]

TONY: We'd all be terribly old if we were that old.

SNOW: We're going to get married—soon.

[*Silence.*]

MRS. WILLIAMS: I think I'd better go off to bed . . . My ankle . . . [*Her chair is trapped behind* MRS. POCKS'S. *Her ineffectual efforts cannot free it.*]

BLANCHE: I'm old enough for anything.

TONY: No one's old enough to be married.

BLANCHE: I'm old enough. Snow and I are going to be married soon.

MRS. POCKS: You'll do as you're told.

BLANCHE: I'll do as I like.

MRS. POCKS: You'll do what you're told, you just see if you don't.

SNOW: Aw, Lil—

MRS. POCKS: Don't Lil me! You put her up to it. Standing up to me, and defying me. You just wait and see what George says. George'll tell you.

TONY: If George gets back.

MRS. POCKS: What do you mean?

MRS. WILLIAMS: Oh, Tony, what a dreadful thing to say!

MRS. POCKS: He hasn't been back . . . Has he, Denise?

DENISE: He hasn't been in here.

TONY: I just thought, with the bunyip and all, we've got other things to worry about—before weddings.

MRS. POCKS: You talk too much. And you shut up too, Paddy.
[*A pause.*]

TONY: Do you think we ought to go and look for him?

MRS. WILLIAMS: Do you really think we ought to, Tony?

MRS. POCKS: Would you come too?

TONY: Well—

MRS. POCKS [*triumphantly*]: Yes! [*To* BLANCHE *and* SNOW] You just wait till George gets here.

TONY: I tried, Snow.

MRS. POCKS: And he'll be in a fine temper as it is.

MRS. WILLIAMS: I suppose he's lost his way . . . I've never seen him go outside the hotel before.

MRS. POCKS: His back'll give him hell—hell.

MRS. WILLIAMS: He might have hurt his ankle too.

BLANCHE: He'll be all aches and pains, and letting us know it.

MRS. POCKS: He's sure to be tired. You just dare tell him. You just dare stand in front of your father and tell him, stand in front of him and tell him . . . I'd like to see it. You just go on and do it.

BLANCHE: Oh why won't you help us, Lil? Why won't you help us? I'm nineteen.

MRS. POCKS: Nothing to do with me. You just tell him.

BLANCHE: I'm nineteen. You said that was the reason. Snow and I could both work at first—

MRS. POCKS: That'd suit him.

BLANCHE: And he'd help me with the housework—

MRS. POCKS: Generous Joe!

BLANCHE: You said that was the reason.

MRS. POCKS: There are lots of reasons. You're Church of England.

MRS. WILLIAMS: Now, Mrs. Pocks, you mustn't be bigoted—

TONY: We're only human. Isn't that right, Snow?

SNOW: Yeah . . .

MRS. POCKS: Oh, he'd say anything.

BLANCHE: You're always picking on him. You won't let him say anything. He's not stupid. Not stupid like you. He knows he's alive . . . He says we're going to get married, that's all he says.

MRS. POCKS: You both say too much.

TONY: We talk too much. We all talk too much. Compare us with the ants.

MRS. POCKS: Yes, you talk too much. [*To* BLANCHE] You and Snow! You and Snow! Oh, I know what he's like! He listens to your growling and your grumbling, he calls you pretty names, he gives you ideas—

BLANCHE: Someone has to talk. Someone has to have ideas. Sitting here at night while you play cards! The world could end and we'd never hear about it. Sitting here at night! Pictures once a week! George ordering us around! Why don't you talk about it and think about it—

MRS. POCKS: Talking doesn't do any good.

MRS. WILLIAMS: It only upsets you, Blanche.

DENISE: You're tired, Blanche. Why don't you go to bed?

TONY: Your universal remedy. Mine, too.

BLANCHE: No. Talking doesn't do any good. Snow and I are going to get married.

[*A pause.*]

MRS. WILLIAMS: Now, why don't you go to bed, dear? And have a good rest. You'll feel better in the morning. Everything'll seem different. You can talk about it calmly . . . [*Her voice trails off.*]

BLANCHE: Talking doesn't do any good.

MRS. POCKS [*beginning softly*]: Ridiculous idea . . . Getting married! What do you think it is? Why don't you use your brains? I got married. Just look at me. I got married. And who's he? What's he? Just a rouseabout. Work here and there. A bit of shearing. Drink the cheque.

SNOW: I know I'm not much . . .

BLANCHE: Snow's been saving.

SNOW: But I don't drink much now. You know that.

MRS. POCKS: I know what you think. You think it'll all be fine. You won't have to work in the pub. You can live in a house, and he'll come home of a night. It'll all be lovey-dovey.

BLANCHE: It's not much to want.

TONY: Modesty doesn't help.

BLANCHE: Shut up!

MRS. POCKS: Shut up! I know what you think. You think you can do what you like, that you can pick and choose. But it won't last. You think he's a fine young chap with big round arms. But just look at him. Just look at him. He isn't what you think he is.

BLANCHE: I've looked at him. I'm looking at you. Why don't you help us? You're my mother—

MRS. POCKS: What'll he be like in a few years?

MRS. WILLIAMS: We all get older.

MRS. POCKS: Wait till he's being nice to other girls.

SNOW: Lil, I—

MRS. POCKS: Wait till he's got lumbago. Wait till you've got to wait on him hand and foot. Wait till he's stupid with drink and ugly and then see what you're stuck with. Just wait and see. Wait and see.

BLANCHE [*tenderly*]: Mum . . . [*She goes to* MRS. POCKS.]

SNOW: Oh, Lil, you know me—

BLANCHE: Mum, it won't be like that; we don't want it to be like that; we won't grow old like that. It'll be different. I only want it to be different; it's not much to want.

MRS. POCKS: Don't fuss around me! You shut up, Paddy! Make me another cup of tea.

BLANCHE: I'll get some hot water—

MRS. POCKS: Make a fresh pot, you lazy little devil!

BLANCHE [*snapping back*]: Make it yourself!

DENISE: I'll make it. I want a cup of tea.

TONY: Then, there's something you want.

MRS. WILLIAMS: No, dear, you finish your dress. If only I could get past . . .

[MRS. POCKS *lets her past. She makes a fresh pot of tea.* BLANCHE *and* MRS. POCKS *went on during the exchange about tea.*]

BLANCHE: And don't start calling me names again. Just when I'm thinking you're not so bad—

MRS. POCKS: Not so bad! My own daughter! Do you think I care what you think? My own daughter. You and your Romeo! Think I'm not so bad. Who asked you what you think?

MRS. WILLIAMS: Now, Mrs. Pocks—

MRS. POCKS: And you keep your long nose out!

MRS. WILLIAMS: Oh, Mrs. Pocks! I—I—I'll go to bed.

BLANCHE: I'll go, too.

MRS. POCKS: I didn't mean it, you old fool; I'm upset. [*To* BLANCHE] You'll stay here till George comes, then you can tell him yourself what you think.

[MRS. WILLIAMS *goes on making the tea, sympathetically.*]

BLANCHE: I'll do what I like.

TONY: Those fatal words!

SNOW: Lil—

MRS. POCKS: Don't you Lil me!

BLANCHE [*to* TONY]: Your tongue's too long.

TONY: My tragedy. Cut it off! Cut it off! [*He pokes out his tongue.*]

MRS. WILLIAMS: Don't joke about it, Tony. It might come true—

MRS. POCKS: If we had any sense we would.

DENISE: Why do you take any notice of him?

TONY: Why do *you* take any notice of him?

DENISE: I don't. I don't encourage him at all.

BLANCHE: It's no good, Denise. That won't shut him up. Once Lil and him get wound up, you can't stop them; they go all night—

MRS. POCKS: That's a nice way to talk.

MRS. WILLIAMS: Blanche, you shouldn't—

BLANCHE: I'll do what I—

MRS. WILLIAMS: She is your mother.

MRS. POCKS: And don't you forget it.

BLANCHE: I wish I could—just for a while. We shouldn't have relations. We should be on our own.

MRS. POCKS: If I'd spoken to my mother like that—

SNOW: You've got us all wrong, Lil—

[JACK *enters. The voices stop for a moment, then burst out again.*]

BLANCHE: Fine sort of a mother! Won't even listen—

MRS. POCKS: I've fed and clothed you—

JACK: Always the same happy family.

BLANCHE: Thank you.

162

MRS. POCKS: And you ought to be grateful—
JACK: That's why I like living here.
SNOW: Calm down, Lil—
    [MRS. POCKS *just looks at him.*]
BLANCHE: You'll drive me to anything.
MRS. POCKS: Spoilt you were. Spoilt from the first.
BLANCHE: A fine sort of a life . . . Sitting here playing cards . . .
MRS. POCKS: I sent you away to school—
BLANCHE: A fine sort of a life . . . Serving the drunks . . . Spoilt!
MRS. WILLIAMS: Now, Blanche, dear . . .
BLANCHE: Don't dear me!
MRS. POCKS: Oh, you mustn't speak to her!
MRS. WILLIAMS: Hoity-toity! But, Blanche, you shouldn't . . .
JACK [*bravely*]: Any tea going?
    [MRS. WILLIAMS *offers some to him.*]
MRS. POCKS: It's a fine time for you to be coming in, too!
JACK: Yes, ma.
MRS. POCKS: Don't ma me!
BLANCHE: Oh, what's the use of talking? Talk, talk, talk . . .
TONY: Give me some tea. Ah, it does your kind heart good to see me drinking it, Billie!
    [MRS. WILLIAMS *pours him some tea.*]
MRS. POCKS: There's no profit in boarders!
TONY [*as the tea is poured*]: Tell me—what's a marriage, Mrs. Pocks, dear lady? There must be marriages . . . I ask for myself—leaving these two out of the question. What is a marriage? A man and a woman? Is that what a marriage is? Then marriage could be so simple . . .
MRS. POCKS: I don't want to talk about it.
TONY: Blanche thinks marriage is different—
BLANCHE: No!
TONY: Then what do you think about it?
BLANCHE: Nothing.
JACK: This tea's good.
DENISE: Mrs. Williams made it.
JACK: She'd make someone a good wife.
TONY: Denise doesn't think about marriage at all. How did you go tonight, Jack?

JACK: No good. A girl like a wall. We just looked at the moon. It's a bright moon, you wouldn't know it.

TONY: No, I wouldn't know it.

JACK: And what have you been up to?

TONY [*reflectively*]: . . . "a girl like a wall" . . .

JACK: What have you crowd been doing with yourselves?

MRS. POCKS [*bitterly*]: Ask Tony.

MRS. WILLIAMS: We tried to find the bunyip.

JACK: Any luck?

TONY: Mrs. Williams. You've been married. You tell me.

MRS. WILLIAMS: Married . . . Oh! Oh . . . Being married, it's . . . Well, I don't know.

TONY: You don't know.

MRS. WILLIAMS: Though I will say, Blanche, it's not glamorous; it's not like the pictures at all . . . It's just hard work, plain old hard work. Children and cooking . . . You've got to look after men as if they're children. Look at your father. I'm sorry, Mrs. Pocks, but you know it's true; you wait on him hand and— It's just plain old hard work, Blanche. There's nothing else in it for women.

TONY: It depresses me.

BLANCHE: Well, don't tell me: I've got eyes. I know what I'm doing.

TONY: It depresses me . . . A girl like a wall?

JACK: Well, a wall with niches.

TONY: Oh! Oh. Well—it seems, Blanche and Snow, though I give you my blessing, that marriage is rather more complicated than I thought.

BLANCHE: We're going to get married. We're going to get married, soon. Aren't we, Snow?

SNOW: Yeah.

BLANCHE: No matter what you say. And Snow can stay here, tonight.

MRS. WILLIAMS: Stay here?

MRS. POCKS: The town will like that!

BLANCHE: The town'll have to like it. There's a spare bed on the verandah.

MRS. POCKS: I sleep on the verandah.

BLANCHE: Snow can pull it down the other end.

TONY [*to* MRS. POCKS]: Frightened you can't control yourself?

MRS. POCKS: What do you think George will say about it?

BLANCHE: George sleeps inside.

MRS. POCKS: Well, I—I never—never—I never heard the like of it.

BLANCHE: Well, you've heard, now.

MRS. WILLIAMS: Yes, we've heard, now.

DENISE: Blanche, don't you think you—

BLANCHE: No, I don't think. I don't think. I'm tired of thinking.

TONY: Stop talking for me, Blanche.

SNOW: If it's all right, Lil?

JACK: Of course it is; you're only a boy.

MRS. POCKS [*sarcastically*]: If you're sure it'll be all right with George. If he doesn't mind who I sleep with.

BLANCHE: It's a big verandah.

MRS. WILLIAMS: He's a big boy. [*She giggles, stops.*]
 [*Silence.*]

BLANCHE: Well?

MRS. POCKS: Well! Well! I won't sleep there. He'd better have your bed. You can sleep out near me, on the verandah.

BLANCHE: I— All right.

MRS. POCKS: But I don't know what George will say.

PADDY [*roaring into song*]: "What shall we do with the drunken sailor?" [*He sings.*]

MRS. POCKS: Shut up, Paddy! I said shut up, Paddy.

JACK: Can it, Paddy; can it.

MRS. WILLIAMS: Can't somebody stop him?

DENISE: He's been like that all evening.
 [*They are all speaking together. They repeat what they say to one another.*]

TONY [*shouting over them all*]: Let him sing if he wants to!
 [*Stunned silence, even from* PADDY. *Then they all begin again, repeating their lines.*]

MRS. POCKS [*over the top of them*]: Shut up, Paddy! You ought to have more sense. What do you think George will say? I ought to put you out—

JACK: Where is George?
 [PADDY *stops. They all wonder where* GEORGE *is.*]

He didn't go bunyiping, too!

MRS. WILLIAMS [*giggling*]: We don't know where he is.

TONY: He's still finding bunyips.

JACK: Do you mean he's out walking!

MRS. POCKS [*yelling as* PADDY *gets ready to start again*]: Cut it out, Paddy. Cut it out.

BLANCHE [*sarcastically*]: What do you think George will say?

MRS. POCKS [*loudly*, to PADDY]: Yes, what do you think George will say?

GEORGE [*off*]: What about George? What about George, eh?

MRS. POCKS: He's drunk.

GEORGE [*off*]: George is a jolly good fellow.

MRS. WILLIAMS: Oh dear, and the doctor said—

BLANCHE: Where did he get it?

MRS. POCKS: How should I know? You had the keys.

BLANCHE: You've got them.

MRS. POCKS: I haven't.

GEORGE [*off. With emphasis*]: George is a jolly good fellow.

TONY: Apparently, George has the keys.

GEORGE [*off*]: What about George?

TONY: The question of the hour: what about George?

[MRS. POCKS *moves to go to him*.]

MRS. POCKS: George! George!

[GEORGE *and* BERT *enter. They have been drinking*.]

GEORGE: Here's George. Here's George. A jolly good fellow.

JACK: Glad to meet you.

TONY: What's in a name?

GEORGE: Here's George. George and his old friend, his old mate, his old cobber . . . Good old Bert . . .

[BERT *smiles sheepishly*.]

BLANCHE: You silly old fool! You'll be sorry tomorrow.

MRS. POCKS: And you won't get any sympathy from me.

MRS. WILLIAMS: Well, at least, he looks pleased with himself. He's happy enough, now. Aren't you, George?

BLANCHE: Lil's the one that's got to look after him while he's "happy".

MRS. POCKS: He'll be sorry in the morning.

TONY: All be sorry in the morning. I'll be sorry tomorrow.

166

JACK: Tomorrow never comes.

TONY: Right.

GEORGE: I don't care about tomorrow ... Care about tonight. Good night. Goodnight, everybody. Good night. Good night. Good night ... [*He sinks into a chair, his head in his arms on the table.*] [*Now that* GEORGE *has let him go,* BERT *begins to sing.*]

BERT: "I don't want to set the world on fire—"

GEORGE: Sing "Yarrawonga". Sing "Back to Yarrawonga".

BERT [*continuing*]: "I just want to start—"

GEORGE: "Back to Yarrawonga".

BERT [*continuing*]: "A flame in your heart—"

[GEORGE *sinks down again.*]

MRS. WILLIAMS: He's really drunk.

BERT: "Just want to start a flame in your heart . . ." [*He quiets himself.*]

MRS. WILLIAMS: He's really drunk. He'll be as cranky as anything soon.

BLANCHE: He's stinking.

MRS. POCKS: That's no way to talk! He'll be like a bear with a sore head.

[DENISE *gathers her things together.*]

DENISE: I think I'll be off, now. Goodnight, everyone.

MRS. WILLIAMS [*reluctantly*]: Yes. I'd better go, too.

BLANCHE [*bitterly*]: The party's just starting.

BERT [*delighted*]: Is it a party?

GEORGE [*looking up*]: A party? It doesn't look like a party. [*He puzzles over it.*]

[BERT *takes* DENISE'S *arm as she passes him.*]

BERT: Oh, don't go. Oh, don't go. Didn't you hear Blanche? The party's just starting . . .

DENISE: Let me go. Let me go.

BERT: I'm going to play for you. I'm going to play you a tune.

DENISE: Take your hands off me. Take your hands off me, you drunk.

BERT: A tune like you've never heard, a tune to sing with. I know I can play you a tune.

SNOW: Yeah. Play us a tune, Bert.

[*Pleased,* BERT *links his arm with* DENISE'S.]

BERT: Yes, I can play you a tune.

DENISE: Take your *hands—off—me*. Let—*me go. You're drunk.*

BERT: I'll play just for you. I'll play better than I've ever played . . .
[*He pauses to think.*] Drunk?

GEORGE: Drunk.

BERT: Drunk?

DENISE: Yes, you're drunk.

BERT: Not *drunk*. [*He points to* GEORGE.] He's not *drunk*. He's happy.

TONY: Which is to be drunken.

JACK: Expensive way of getting happy. Wish I could afford it.
[GEORGE *rises*.]

GEORGE: Don't go to bed. Don't anybody go to bed. Don't go to
bed. [*He goes to the back window* (*or out the door, off-stage*).] It's
a beautiful night. It's a wonderful night. [*He flings his head out.*]
The moon! The moon . . . [*He is sick.*]

MRS. POCKS: George! [*She goes to him and pats his back.*]
[BLANCHE, JACK, *and* TONY *may go over to help—screening him.*]

GEORGE: The moon!

TONY: It affects me that way, too.

BLANCHE: He makes me sick.

JACK: Not on the floor!

DENISE: They're both disgustingly drunk.

PADDY: Drunk's all right. Drunk's a bit of all right.

MRS. POCKS: Shut up, Paddy. Are you all right, now?
[*They retrieve* GEORGE.]
Silly old cow.

MRS. WILLIAMS: At least, Paddy's different. He just sits and—

TONY [*profoundly*]: We're all drunk, all.

MRS. WILLIAMS [*giggling*]: Oh, do you think so? I do feel so gay!

DENISE: Goodnight.

GEORGE: Don't go. Don't go. Don't go and leave me. I want people.
I want people. I'm lonely. It's lonely here. I'll cry if you leave
me. Don't go and leave. [*He blubbers. He catches hold of* DENISE'S
skirt. He holds it imploringly.]

DENISE: He'll be sick again.

GEORGE: Don't go. Don't go. It's lonely. It's so lonely.

BLANCHE: Don't go, Denise.

GEORGE: No. No. No . . .

BLANCHE: Wait till we get him to bed.

MRS. POCKS: You can sleep in in the morning.

MRS. WILLIAMS: But it's mass in the morning.

GEORGE: No, don't go and leave me . . . Lonely. Lonely, here . . .

DENISE [*after a pause*]: All right. [*She sits down.*]

    [*A pause.*]

MRS. POCKS: Come on, George. Come on. Give me a hand, Tony.

    [TONY *facetiously holds out a limp hand.*]

    You and Jack take him.

JACK: And we pay to stay here!

TONY: No profit in boarders!

    [GEORGE *is a deadweight. They cannot shift him.*]

GEORGE: No. No. Won't go to bed. Don't want to go to bed. It's a beautiful night. It's a beautiful night. It's a beautiful night . . .

    [*Under his own steam, he reaches the window.*]

TONY: He'll be sick if he looks at the moon.

MRS. WILLIAMS: Poor old George.

MRS. POCKS: Stupid old cow! He knows he can't hold it.

JACK: Did you find the bunyip, George? Did you find the bunyip?

GEORGE: It's a beautiful night.

TONY: He found it was a beautiful night.

BLANCHE: He's got a few more surprises coming too. Hasn't he, Snow? He'll hear some news.

TONY: That was news enough: a beautiful night. Do you think George ever looked at the night before? Do you think he knew about beautiful nights? [*He is talking quickly, partly for* DENISE'S *benefit.*]

MRS. POCKS [*glancing at* BLANCHE]: When he was courting.

MRS. WILLIAMS [*laughing*]: Oh, they're all moonlight and roses when they're courting.

MRS. POCKS: I suppose we'd better get him to bed.

GEORGE: Won't go to bed.

MRS. WILLIAMS: Well, George, we can hardly sit up all night holding your hand. [*She giggles at the thought.*]

GEORGE: Where's Bert? Bert! Bert! Where's Bert?

BERT [*very sadly*]: George . . .

BLANCHE [*unpleasantly*]: Your old mate Bert's here.

GEORGE: Bert's here! Hallo, Bert. How are you?

BERT: George . . . George . . . They're unhappy. They're all unhappy.

GEORGE: It's a beautiful night, Bert. It's a beautiful night.

[*A pause.*]

Are you unhappy?

MRS. POCKS: Now, he'll start to cry.

MRS. WILLIAMS: Don't worry about anyone else, George; you stay happy.

BERT: George . . . George . . .

GEORGE: Not happy if Bert's not happy . . .

BERT: Not happy if anyone's not happy . . .

GEORGE: Not happy if Bert's not happy . . . Not happy if Bert's . . .

MRS. POCKS: Oh, you are happy, Bert! Tell him you're happy.

[BERT *points to* DENISE.]

BERT: *She's* not happy. She's *not* happy.

MRS. WILLIAMS: Oh, Denise, tell him you're happy.

BERT: I can't be happy if she's not happy.

BLANCHE: Shut him up, Denise. Shut them both up, for heaven's sake!

SNOW: Aren't you happy?

DENISE: Yes. Yes, of course, I'm happy.

GEORGE: Not happy if Bert's not happy . . .

BERT: Are you really? Are you really happy?

DENISE: Yes. I'm really happy.

JACK: She's happy. I'm happy, we're all happy.

TONY: Decline that.

BERT: I'm glad.

MRS. WILLIAMS: Bert's happy. Now, George?

MRS. POCKS: Well, you stupid old drunk, are you happy?

GEORGE: You happy, Bert?

[BERT *is too happy to speak.*]

Are you really happy, Bert?

[*After a long pause*, BERT *smiles to himself.*]

BERT: Yes. Yes, I'm happy.

GEORGE: Then I'm happy, too.

[*A pause.*]

TONY: We're all so terribly happy that we can't move; I've never seen a wax-works look happier.

MRS. POCKS: Now, you can get him to bed.

GEORGE: No, I'm not going to bed. I'm not going to bed. Am I, Bert? It's a beautiful night . . . It's no good going to bed . . . Only shut your eyes . . . It's no good shutting your eyes. It's a beautiful night . . . Play us a tune, Bert. Play us a tune.

MRS. POCKS: Well, I'm going to bed. You can look after yourself.

GEORGE: It's no good going to bed, it's no good.

BERT: The party's just starting.

GEORGE [*getting the idea*]: A party! That's what we want, a party! It's a beautiful night for a party . . . Isn't it, Bert?

MRS. POCKS: A party! At this hour of the night—

GEORGE: Lil. Get us some beer . . . Free beer for everyone! Free beer . . . That's the way, Bert! That's the way, Bert! Here are the keys, Lil.

JACK: Wacko!

[TONY *looks under the table.*]

MRS. WILLIAMS [*indignantly*]: What are you looking for?

TONY: The Archangel Gabriel.

[MRS. POCKS *picks up the keys.*]

MRS. POCKS: Free beer! Free beds are what you want.

GEORGE: Free beer! Free beer for everyone!

MRS. POCKS [*seeing that he means it*]: You must be off your head.

GEORGE: Free beer for all my friends here. Free beer for everyone.

MRS. POCKS: You're just throwing your money away.

GEORGE: You heard what I said.

MRS. POCKS: *I'm* not going to give it away.

BLANCHE: Do as he says, Lil.

JACK: Yeah, do as he says.

MRS. POCKS: He'll kill me when he's sober.

TONY: Perhaps he'll never be sober.

DENISE: There's been enough to drink already.

GEORGE: Free drinks for everyone! Go on!

MRS. POCKS: I— [*In a very afternoon-tea style*] Would you like a drink, Billie?

MRS. WILLIAMS: Oh, I—I—

MRS. POCKS: Would you like one or wouldn't you?

JACK: Say that you would, Billo.

MRS. WILLIAMS: Well . . . Just a shandy. I do like a shandy.

MRS. POCKS: All right, then. But you know who's to blame. [*To*

BLANCHE] Take that useless bloke of yours and get a couple of bottles.

[BLANCHE *and* SNOW *move to go.*]

And some lemonade.

[BLANCHE *and* SNOW *go.*]

We'll all have a drink. We've earned one. [*To* TONY] I don't know if you've earned one.

TONY: Denise didn't go either.

DENISE: I don't want one, thank you.

MRS. POCKS: Denise was back here making herself useful.

TONY: Oh, you flatter her, you flatter her.

GEORGE: Bert! Bert! Play us a tune, Bert.

JACK: Yes, play us a tune.

MRS. POCKS: We've had enough nonsense—

MRS. WILLIAMS: We could make it a real party—wine, women, and song!

TONY: Mrs. Williams!

JACK: What are you suggesting?

MRS. WILLIAMS: Oh, I didn't mean . . . I only meant . . . Oh, you're pulling my leg!

JACK [*shocked*]: Mrs. Williams!

TONY: But I never touched your leg. I was only looking for Gabriel.

MRS. WILLIAMS: Oh, you're terrible, you're really terrible, Tony. You're both terrible. Aren't they terrible, Denise? Pulling my leg! Next thing, you'll say you were looking for the bunyip.

JACK: Mightn't be a bad story.

MRS. WILLIAMS [*delighted*]: Isn't he—terrible?

MRS. POCKS: He gets terribly on your nerves. They both do.

GEORGE: Bert! Bert! Play us a tune, Bert.

MRS. WILLIAMS: Oh, yes! Do play us a tune. Do let him play us a tune, Mrs. Pocks. Bert—Mr. Horner . . . When I was a girl, we used to have parties. Someone would play the accordion. We all used to dance. We used to dance the stars out. Oh, how we danced! It's not the same now; everything's different. Do play us a tune.

GEORGE: 'd cheer us all up.

JACK: It'd keep us all happy.

MRS. POCKS: That'd be hard!

JACK: Go on, play us a tune. I'm feeling mad.

MRS. WILLIAMS: Do you feel it, too? I feel so—so—so—

TONY: So gay?

MRS. WILLIAMS: Yes. That's just it. There's no other word. I feel so *gay*.

BERT [*quite suddenly*]: What'll I play?

MRS. WILLIAMS: Play "Daisie".

JACK: Play something. Will you dance, Mrs. Williams? Are you game?

GEORGE: "Back to Yarrawonga."

MRS. WILLIAMS: I'd love to dance. I'd love to dance.

GEORGE [*more loudly*]: Play "Back to Yarrawonga".

TONY [*looking at* DENISE]: Play "Lamentations".

BERT: The world's so happy. The world's so happy. Everyone's waiting to sing. Everyone's waiting to sing!

JACK: Then play, man, play!

TONY: We all *want* to sing.

GEORGE: "Back to Yarrawonga." The old ones are best.

MRS. WILLIAMS: I know that song. How does it go?

[BERT *begins to play it.* MRS. WILLIAMS *takes up the tune.* JACK *dances with her. They both sing.* GEORGE *staggers upright and beats time.* MRS. POCKS *begins to hum.* TONY *sings with the others.* DENISE *almost sings.* BLANCHE *and* SNOW *re-enter. They have more than two bottles, and no lemonade.* BLANCHE *laughs at* MRS. POCKS, *then she smiles. She too sings. She and* SNOW *get out some cups for the beer. They are all singing loudly.* DENISE *moves towards the door.* TONY, *on the floor, catches at her hand. She leaves it in his for a moment, half-turns back to him, then quickly goes out.* TONY *then begins to sing very loudly, very determinedly.*]

ALL: "Back to Yarrawonga, To the land of the kangaroo!"

TABLEAU

(*End of Act Two*)

ACT THREE

Before the curtain rises we hear the meal-gong ring. A long pause.
It rings again, furiously. A pause. When the curtain rises MRS. POCKS
is at the sink. She is doing the washing-up from the night before.
GEORGE *is seated at the end of the table near her. He is dazed.* PADDY
sits in his old place but apparently he sees nothing or very little.

MRS. POCKS: Cups. Cups. Beery cups. And not one of them paid for.
I told you you'd be sorry.
[GEORGE *looks sorry.*]
Just look at them. Cups. And more cups. Beery cups. It's all
right for you. You just sit there.
[GEORGE'S *face is eloquent.*]
It's all right for you . . . No, don't offer to help; I wouldn't dream
— The towel's over there. Sorry for yourself, now. Feel terrible,
don't you? You've got no-one to blame but yourself. There!
Feel any better? You've got no-one to blame but yourself. The
doctor told you. I told you . . . The doctor told you a long time
ago. I told you last night. If you will get on it . . . You can't
take it, now. In your condition. Just look at you. [*With relish*]
Just look at you.
[GEORGE *is a picture.*]
Look at the size of you. Anyone'd think you were going to have
a baby. Well, it's not my fault—don't go blaming me. I told you
. . . The doctor told you . . . But you just wouldn't lay off it.
The booze'll kill you in the finish. Hm! You're half-dead, now.
Just look at you. Hold this. [*She puts a cup in his hand.*] You were
happy enough last night. You were happy enough last night.
[*She is getting a tea-towel.*] I said you were happy enough last
night.
[GEORGE *grunts. She looks at him. A pause.*]
GEORGE: Yes.
MRS. POCKS: Yes. Free beer for everyone. Free beer for everyone!
Hm! [*She snaughs—half snorts, half laughs.*] Hold this. [*She gives*

174

him a tea-towel.] You must have been drunk. You must have been really drunk. I've never heard the like of it. I've never heard the like of it, and I've worked in the pub for years. Free beer for everyone. Free beer. And you make yourself sick on it. [*Changing her tone*] Don't just hold them, George. Put them together. Wipe it.

[GEORGE *wipes the cup earnestly and wearily.*]

Morning sickness, eh? Just how do you like it? Men! If they knew what it was like! Not so happy this morning, eh? Just a little bit off colour? Just a little bit sour?

GEORGE: Lil . . . [*A pause while he braces himself for speech.*] Lil . . . Shut up!

MRS. POCKS: It's your conscience you want to shut up. You know you were wrong; you shouldn't have done it. The doctor told you. I told you. You can't take it, now. You just can't take it— not in your condition. Just look at you. I told you. The doctor told you—

[DENISE *enters. She is wearing a house-gown.*]

DENISE: Good morning, Mrs. Pocks.

GEORGE [*grunting*]: Hm!

MRS. POCKS: What's good about it?

DENISE: I just wanted some hot water for my hair.

MRS. POCKS: The kettle's hot.

[DENISE *gets herself a cup of hot water.*]

Did you see any of the others up?

DENISE: I knocked on Mrs. Williams' door.

MRS. POCKS [*sarcastically*]: Will she be fit for mass? [*Annoyed*] Oh, those cows of boarders, they won't get up! [*She goes off and rings the gong.*]

[*George still holds the cup and towel.*]

GEORGE: Nice day.

DENISE: Yes.

[DENISE *goes off as* MRS. POCKS *returns.*]

MRS. POCKS: They can go without if they won't get up. It's the same every Sunday. If they'd all get up, or all stay in . . . It's their coming in dribs and drabs, like Brown's cows . . . You ought to talk to them, George. You ought to tell them.

GEORGE [*with an effort*]: Yes.

MRS. POCKS: That one's wiped enough.

> [*He stops wiping it. She takes it from him and gives him another. She goes on cleaning up.*]

Wipe this one. Disgusting exhibition of yourself. Dancing on the table! Hitching up your trouser leg! Who do you think you are— Betty Grable? [*She laughs at her joke and goes on laughing.*] Free beer for everyone! Free beer! Free. Beer.

> [MRS. WILLIAMS *enters and* MRS. POCKS *stops laughing.* MRS. WILLIAMS *wears a dressing gown and slippers.*]

MRS. WILLIAMS: Here, Mrs. Pocks!

MRS. POCKS: Well, someone's still breathing! You've got a companion, George.

MRS. WILLIAMS [*with a delighted giggle*]: Mrs. Pocks!

MRS. POCKS: A fine night you made of it!

MRS. WILLIAMS: Good morning, George. Now, Mrs. Pocks, I—

MRS. POCKS: Oh, and so did he. Can-can dancing! I'd never have believed my ears. I could hardly believe my own eyes.

MRS. WILLIAMS: Oh, Mrs. Pocks, I didn't—

MRS. POCKS: You did. I saw you.

MRS. WILLIAMS: Perhaps you need glasses or—

MRS. POCKS: I saw you. I saw you. [*Changing her tone*] I never thought you had it in you. At your age.

MRS. WILLIAMS [*giggling with delight*]: Oh—you know—there's life in the old girl yet.

MRS. POCKS: I wish there was some life in the others. They'll be wandering in for something to eat all morning. What'll you have?

MRS. WILLIAMS [*sternly*]: Mrs. Pocks, it's communion.

MRS. POCKS: Oh well, you can make your own toast then.

MRS. WILLIAMS: Nothing, thank you.

> [MRS. POCKS *sits down.*]

MRS. POCKS: Make us a fresh pot of tea, then.

MRS. WILLIAMS: Well—well, I won't have any. I think I'll have— a glass of hot water.

MRS. POCKS [*laughing*]: Oh, that's how it is, is it? Not so lively this morning?

MRS. WILLIAMS: I wish you wouldn't joke about last night, Mrs. Pocks.

MRS. POCKS: I didn't mention last night. Whatever put last night into your head? I was talking about this morning.

MRS. WILLIAMS: Oh—I—I—I don't know. I don't know. But I wish you wouldn't joke about last night.

MRS. POCKS: I'm the only one who can.

MRS. WILLIAMS: You were leading the singing.

MRS. POCKS: I was not.

MRS. WILLIAMS: When we sang "Tipperary".

MRS. POCKS: I was the only one sober.

MRS. WILLIAMS: Oh, Mrs. Pocks . . . How can you?

MRS. POCKS: I didn't touch a drop.

MRS. WILLIAMS: You know, Mrs. Pocks, there's nothing wrong with a drink.

MRS. POCKS: I know there's nothing wrong with a drink, but I didn't have a drink last night. I didn't have a mouthful.

MRS. WILLIAMS: Well, if you've forgotten that, I suppose you've forgotten everything else.

MRS. POCKS: I haven't forgotten anything.

MRS. WILLIAMS: You don't remember playing chasings with Tony in the backyard?

MRS. POCKS: No, I don't.

MRS. WILLIAMS: You don't remember singing "Hark the herald angels sing, Beecham's Pills are just the thing"?

MRS. POCKS: No, I do not.

MRS. WILLIAMS: Then you should have been like me and had only one drink. [*She sips her hot water.*]

[TONY *enters.*]

TONY: That Pocks woman's the one. She drank like a fish.

MRS. POCKS: I'm not taking any of your lip. Didn't you hear the gong go?

TONY: *Good* morning morning morning, you adorable creature—oh! [*He groans and holds his head.*] Oh! Is it morning?

MRS. POCKS: You'll get no sympathy from me. I told you—

TONY: My mother told me, but look at me now.

MRS. POCKS: You certainly look a picture.

MRS. WILLIAMS [*primly*]: Good morning, Tony.

TONY: 'Morning, Scarlet.

[MRS. WILLIAMS *smiles.*]

MRS. POCKS: Neither of you'll get any sympathy from me.

[TONY *shuts his eyes and gropes like a blind man.*]

TONY: That gentle voice! That soothing tone! Surely it's Mrs. Pocks talking. If only I could see her! [*Opening his eyes*] Ah, yes! A pox to be sure . . . Only, send your twin away.

MRS. POCKS [*laughing*]: Well, you can get your own breakfast—

[TONY *pats* GEORGE'S *head which has now collapsed into his arms.*]

TONY: How are you, mate?

MRS. POCKS [*continuing*]: I'm not working all day for the likes of you. The gong went an hour ago—

TONY: Half an hour! Oh, Mrs. Pocks, you're heavenly. Life still goes on. You're heavenly. And it's good to see someone else sober. I like a woman who can hold her liquor. And you are holding an awful lot.

[*She throws the dish-cloth at him. He catches it.*]

Out! What can I have?

MRS. POCKS: What do you want?

TONY: Steak.

MRS. POCKS: There's eggs. If you think I'm going to cook steak—

TONY: Please, I was joking. I spoke in jest.

MRS. POCKS: All right. I'll cook you some eggs then.

TONY: Toast. Dry toast.

MRS. POCKS: Well, I'm certainly not standing round watching toast for you. Watch it yourself!

TONY: Chuck us the breadknife.

[*She chucks it.* TONY *cuts some bread and puts it in the toaster. He is looking out of the window.*]

What a beautiful morning. The sun's come up again. Aren't you surprised. I'd never have thought it. After last night . . . the sun's shining. I can hear the birds singing . . .

MRS. WILLIAMS: It's going to be hot.

TONY: Hear the bunyip last night, Billie?

MRS. WILLIAMS: I slept like a log.

MRS. POCKS: Like a water-logged—but it wasn't water. [*She is highly pleased with her joke.*]

TONY: Well, most of it was.

MRS. POCKS: There's no water in the beer at this pub. The beer here—

TONY: Is marvellous—when it's free. I thought you might have been out after bunyips again, Billie. I heard a noise—about five.

MRS. POCKS: That was George. I had to turn him over then.

MRS. WILLIAMS: Did you sleep with him?

MRS. POCKS: It's all right, Billie, we're married. Anyway, he was dead all night—except when he was sick. He could hardly stand . . . It wasn't safe to leave him.

TONY: Well, it wasn't George then. It sounded like footsteps. Someone— [*He stops.*]

MRS. POCKS: Someone what?

TONY: Someone had to go across the back, I suppose. We all had reason enough.

[MRS. POCKS *looks suspicious.*]

Er—er—the toast is burning.

MRS. POCKS: Watch it yourself.

[*He turns it over.*]

This hotel is run properly; none of the guests have to go across the yard of a night.

TONY: Not while I'm eating, Mrs. Pocks, please.

MRS. POCKS: About five o'clock . . . About five o'clock . . .

[SNOW *enters.*]

SNOW: Hallo. All up?

TONY: No, I always walk in my sleep. Have since childhood.

[BLANCHE *enters. She is wearing shorts and sweater.*]

MRS. WILLIAMS: Really, Tony! Did you? I used to when I was a child, but I haven't done it for years. Fancy you being a sleep-walker, too. Isn't that a coincidence?

TONY [*looking at* BLANCHE *and* MRS. POCKS]: Remarkable.

MRS. POCKS: Where are you going in those clothes?

BLANCHE: Snow and I are going to tennis. Sunday *is* my day off.

MRS. POCKS: Where did you get those shorts?

MRS. WILLIAMS: They look very nice, Blanche.

BLANCHE: I've had them for months. I sent away for them.

MRS. POCKS: You didn't tell me about them.

MRS. WILLIAMS: But, Blanche, we have such a nice line in at the store.

BLANCHE: What's wrong with my shorts?

SNOW: They look good on her.

TONY: Very good.

MRS. POCKS: They're not on very much of her.

MRS. WILLIAMS: Don't be old fashioned, Mrs. Pocks. Everyone's wearing that type of thing now. They're a bit conservative if anything. The ones at the store . . . And I saw a picture of Palm Beach in *Truth* last week—

MRS. POCKS: *Truth*!

BLANCHE: Anyway, there's nothing wrong with them and I'm going to wear them today.

TONY: There's nothing wrong with the legs either, Blanche.

BLANCHE: You keep your eyes where they're welcome.

MRS. POCKS: Well, you've practically got a welcome sign. [*She laughs at her wit.*]

BLANCHE: I want a cup of tea. I don't want any breakfast.

MRS. POCKS: I don't know what George will say.

TONY: Ask him and see.

    [*A pause.*]

BLANCHE: George! [*A pause.*] George!

    [*No answer.* BLANCHE *pours tea for herself and* SNOW. SNOW *cuts some bread and throws it to* TONY *to toast.* GEORGE *suddenly looks up.*]

GEORGE: 'Morning. Good morning. [*His head sinks down again.*]

TONY: Very sensible thing to say, too. It is a good morning.

MRS. POCKS: You talk too much, Tony.

TONY: "Sing me the old sweet songs of yesteryear." [*He holds out some toast*] Have a slice, Mrs. Williams.

MRS. WILLIAMS: No, thank you, Tony; you mustn't tempt me.

TONY: Aw, shucks, Billie . . . Can't a bloke have a go?

MRS. WILLIAMS [*laughing*]: Now, Tony—

BLANCHE: How you can feel funny at this hour of the morning—
    [MRS. WILLIAMS *reaches for the toast.*]

MRS. WILLIAMS: Well, I'll just have half. I feel a little bit faint. It'd be awful if I fainted from *hunger*. I won't have any butter, though.

TONY: I think that's wise. Have some jam?

MRS. WILLIAMS: Thank you. I couldn't have communion anyway, after this tea . . . And it must have been after twelve last night when we—we . . . This is delicious jam, Tony; where did you get it?

TONY: I ought to kick you, Billie.

MRS. POCKS: That's *George's strawberry*! You leave that alone.

MRS. WILLIAMS: I'm sorry, but I only used a scrape.

MRS. POCKS: It's him I'm talking to. He puts his nose into everything.

BLANCHE: Is there anyone in the dining-room yet?

MRS. POCKS: The cows won't get up.

BLANCHE: Well, if they do come down for breakfast, Lil, you'll have to wait on them—

MRS. POCKS: Naturally, I can cook and serve too. Would you like me to—

[GEORGE *suddenly raises his head in answer to* BLANCHE'S *call.*]

GEORGE: Eh?

[*Silence.*]

[*He looks around.*] What did you want, Blanche?

BLANCHE: Nothing.

GEORGE: Don't tell me lies . . . You asked me something . . . I heard you. I distinctly—distinctly—heard—you—

BLANCHE: That was ten minutes ago.

GEORGE: Don't you speak to me like that . . . [*he is very cranky and becomes inarticulate.*] What did you say?

BLANCHE [*significantly*]: It's what I'm going to say—

MRS. POCKS [*quickly*]: She wants to go and play tennis.

TONY: You were young once, George—I suppose.

[BLANCHE *butters some toast.*]

BLANCHE: But he was too fat to play tennis.

[BLANCHE *and* SNOW *eat.*]

MRS. POCKS: George was a fine figure of a man.

MRS. WILLIAMS: You're still a fine figure of a man, aren't you, Mr. Pocks?

TONY [*with a gesture*]: The barber of Seville, a figure O!

BLANCHE: Then he was probably too drunk to play.

MRS. POCKS: What a way to speak! What a way to speak to your father.

BLANCHE: I'll speak just the way I like!

TONY: "Sing me the old sweet songs of—"

[GEORGE *makes an effort to stand.*]

GEORGE: I'll knock her down. Let me at her. I'll knock her down.

MRS. WILLIAMS: Oh dear!

GEORGE [*to* SNOW]: And I'll knock you down, too.

SNOW [*surprised*]: I didn't say anything.

BLANCHE: The way you are you'd need a lot of help.

GEORGE: No daughter of mine . . .

   [MRS. POCKS *catches him as he almost falls.*]

MRS. POCKS: George!

   [*She guides him to the seat and lets him fall into it.*]

GEORGE: No daughter of mine . . . No daughter of mine . . . No daughter
   of mine . . . [*repeating the phrase, his head drops on to the table.*]

MRS. POCKS: Now, you've started him.

BLANCHE [*almost tearful*]: Well, I won't be bullied. I don't want to
   be bullied.

MRS. POCKS: You should just take it all in.

BLANCHE: I won't . . . I won't . . .

MRS. POCKS: You'll do as I tell you—

BLANCHE: I'm finished with—

   [*They are both shouting.* JACK *enters.*]

JACK: Still happy! Still cheerful!

TONY: Still living! Still breathing!

JACK: And you're all actually up—after last night! [*He goes to the
   yard door, breathes and exercises.*] What a beautiful morning!

BLANCHE: Oh you, shut up!

MRS. POCKS [*at the same time*]: Stop chattering!

JACK: 'Morning, George.

   [GEORGE *looks at* JACK *doing knee-bends and he grunts.*]

   Yes, lovely morning. 'Morning all.

MRS. WILLIAMS: Good morning, Jack.

JACK: Sleep well, Billie?

MRS. WILLIAMS: I was so tired. I was so tired I—didn't even lock
   my door.

TONY: Oh, Mrs. Williams!

JACK: Curse the luck! And I didn't even try the handle last night!
   But I'll be panting around tonight—in my tropical pyjamas.
   So watch out, watch out . . . [*He has finished exercising. He has
   taken a cup and filled it with hot water. He makes for the door
   with it.*]

182

MRS. POCKS: What are you doing with that water?

JACK: Shave, lady, shave! Feel. [*He holds his chin out temptingly.*]

MRS. POCKS: You come and have your breakfast first.

JACK: Breakfast! I couldn't look at food. Besides I've got a meet on; I've got a date at tennis.

BLANCHE: Someday that girl'll wake up to you.

JACK [*going*]: It's me charm, it's me fatal beauty.

MRS. POCKS: Why don't you buy a shaving-mug? And bring that cup back.

JACK [*off*]: Tomorrow . . . Tomorrow . . .

BLANCHE: He's got a dozen of them up there.

MRS. WILLIAMS [*still laughing at him*]: He's—he's terrible. Just terrible.

MRS. POCKS: There's no profit in boarders.

[*Silence.*]

TONY: That attempt at tactfulness has hurt us all.

BLANCHE [*without looking up*]: If he's still conscious, you'd better tell him I'm getting married.

MRS. POCKS: Tell him yourself. It's not my job. I've enough to do.

BLANCHE: George!

MRS. WILLIAMS: Oh, Blanche . . .

SNOW: George!

[GEORGE *stirs.*]

GEORGE: Well?

SNOW: Well, George . . . it's like this . . .

BLANCHE: We're going to get married.

MRS. POCKS: They want to get married, George.

MRS. WILLIAMS: You were young once yourself.

[*A pause.*]

GEORGE: Eh? What'd you say?

MRS. POCKS: They want to get married.

TONY: Australia needs babies.

GEORGE: Good idea. Good idea.

BLANCHE [*to clear the misunderstanding*]: I'm the one who's getting married.

GEORGE: Hm! [*A pause. He goes to speak but sinks on the table again.*] [*A pause.*]

MRS. POCKS: There, you see. Now, you're answered.

BLANCHE: What kind of an answer's that?

SNOW: Well, he didn't say no . . .

TONY: Remarkably non-committal.

MRS. POCKS: And he didn't say yes.

[BLANCHE *is preparing to storm. Her mouth opens and shuts.*]

MRS. WILLIAMS [*bravely*]: That toast was delicious.

TONY: Have another half.

MRS. WILLIAMS [*accepting it*]: A sheep as well as a lamb.

TONY: Yes, go on; I won't tell.

MRS. WILLIAMS: Well, I shouldn't . . . [*coyly*]. And my figure doesn't matter to anyone.

BLANCHE: Come on, Snow. I'm fed up.

SNOW: You didn't eat much—

BLANCHE: Don't you start being funny!

MRS. POCKS: So there is something he can do!

MRS. WILLIAMS: You're not coming to church, Snow?

[MRS. POCKS *sniffs.*]

It's a specially late mass, thank goodness. I'd never have been able to get there if— Are you going, Snow?

SNOW [*embarrassed*]: Aw . . . Aw, I'll skip it today.

MRS. WILLIAMS: It's a pity it's only once a month, isn't it?

SNOW: Yeah. Yeah, it is.

BLANCHE: Well, come on. See you later. [*She moves to go.*]

[GEORGE *sits up.*]

GEORGE: Wait on, Blanche. Wait a minute. What did you say? What did she say? Getting married? Getting married? Getting married, to who?

BLANCHE: Oh, you've come to, have you? Snow and me. We're getting married. We're engaged. We're getting married in two months. It's all arranged. In two months. We're getting married. Aren't we, Snow?

SNOW: If you've got no objections, George; we'd like—

MRS. POCKS: Have you ever heard the like, George? I tried to tell them—

GEORGE: Getting married to who?

BLANCHE: Getting married to Snow.

GEORGE: Snow?

BLANCHE: Snow.

GEORGE [*trying to recall him*]: Snow? Snow? Snow?

SNOW: Yeah. Me. [*Sheepishly*] I suppose she likes me.

GEORGE: Lil! She says she's getting married to Snow!

MRS. POCKS: There was no need for her to say anything to you at all. They're not getting married, if I have anything to do with it. I'd rather see her go on the town than—

BLANCHE: And you might yet!

MRS. WILLIAMS: Blanche!

TONY: Well, it's a nice town.

BLANCHE: You'd just about drive anyone to it. There's nothing wrong with Snow. There's nothing wrong with getting married to Snow.

GEORGE [*with an effort at dignity*]: None of my children's going to marry a no-hoper rouseabout. They put his brother in a reform school! And just look at his face! Just look at him.

[*They all look.*]

SNOW: Now, George—

GEORGE: *None* of my children's going to marry a no-hoper rouseabout—

BLANCHE: You've only got me.

MRS. POCKS: Because the other two died. That's why we worry . . . What thanks do we get?

BLANCHE: Oh mum—you shouldn't want thanks all the time. You shouldn't want thanks . . .

MRS. POCKS: That's too much to ask—gratitude.

SNOW: You've looked after Blanche real well . . .

MRS. POCKS [*incensed*]: Thank you.

BLANCHE: And I'm grown up, now.

GEORGE: Neverthe—Neverthe—nonetheless, no daughter of mine's going—

BLANCHE: Don't be a pig-headed old fool, George. Because you'll be sorry if you are—

SNOW: I'm sending away for a ring.

MRS. POCKS: I suppose you'll put it on a lay-by.

[MRS. WILLIAMS *starts to laugh.*]

SNOW: No. I've been saving.

BLANCHE: He's been saving.

GEORGE: No daughter of mine . . .

BLANCHE: Oh why don't you shut up! You're drunk. You're drunk. You don't understand.

GEORGE: I'll knock her down. I'll knock her down. [*He stands swaying.*]

[MRS. WILLIAMS *wags her finger at him.*]

MRS. WILLIAMS: Oh, George, George! You were really *too* gay last night.

[*The wagging of her finger knocks him down again.* DENISE *enters.*]

DENISE: Hallo, Blanche . . . Snow. Sleep well, Mrs. Williams?

[TONY *holds up the bread-loaf.*]

No, thanks. I'll just have a cup of tea. [*She returns the cup she used earlier and gets herself some tea.*]

[*A pause.*]

TONY [*just before* BLANCHE *can speak*]: You're up late.

DENISE [*coldly*]: This is my second trip downstairs.

TONY: Oh. Oh, that's how we are. [*Deliberately rudely*] I had to make a few trips downstairs last night myself.

MRS. WILLIAMS: Don't be vulgar, Tony: it doesn't suit you.

TONY: Oh, Mrs. Williams, you say the nicest things . . .

MRS. POCKS [*to* BLANCHE, *just as she was going to speak*]: Well—are you going?

BLANCHE: Now, you want to get rid of me! I don't feel like tennis.

SNOW: Aw, come on, Blanche.

BLANCHE: I think you're mean. It isn't as if you couldn't afford a wedding . . .

GEORGE: No daughter of mine—

BLANCHE: If he says that again . . .

GEORGE: Have a bit of respect, girl.

MRS. POCKS: Why don't you listen to your father?

MRS. WILLIAMS: Have some more tea, Blanche. [*Bravely*] I'm having another cup. There's nothing like a cup of tea . . .

BLANCHE: No, there's nothing like a cup of tea.

[MRS. WILLIAMS *pours her one.* GEORGE, *hurt, sits quiet again.*]

TONY [*to* DENISE]: Did you sleep well?

DENISE: Yes, thank you.

MRS. POCKS: Pour us a cup, Billie. [*She takes the dish-cloth from* GEORGE *and wipes the cup.*]

[DENISE *returns.*]

Here you are.

TONY [*to* DENISE]: If you slept well, you must have missed the singing.

DENISE: Yes.

BLANCHE [*over her tea*]: I'm fed up. I'm just fed up. It's driving me out of my mind . . .

SNOW: Take it easy, hon; have some more toast . . .

BLANCHE: No.

TONY [*to everyone but* DENISE]: It's going to be a fine day—bright sun, clear sky.

MRS. WILLIAMS: It's going to be hot. Summer's really coming. As long as it's not like last year. Oh, it was terrible then! And the nights! They were *terrible*: you couldn't sleep. And the mozzies were—were—

TONY: Terrible?

MRS. WILLIAMS: They *were* terrible. That was a dreadful summer. It was really terrible. But of course I was at Gundagai then . . .

TONY: It sounded like Gundagai. Or Wagga Wagga. Denise!

DENISE: Yes?

TONY: It'd be cool for walking tonight. Or just now . . .

DENISE: Yes—I suppose it would be . . . but it's getting very hot.

TONY: Yes. Denise!

DENISE: Yes?

TONY: Nothing—I—I— Nothing. Just Tony the Talker talking. Sorry.

[BERT *enters*.]

BERT: Don't be sorry.

[*He waits till most of them are looking at him.*]

Don't be sorry. Don't be sorry about anything. It's a beautiful morning. It's a *beautiful* morning. It's a BEAUTIFUL morning. Isn't it? [*He looks at them all suspiciously.*] But why's everyone up so early?

MRS. POCKS: Early?

TONY: Hiya, Bert!

MRS. POCKS: Ought to be ashamed of yourself wandering in at this hour of the morning. Well, you won't get anything out of me. And just look at the state you've got George in—

BERT: Hallo, George.

187

MRS. POCKS: What are you going to have? Eggs?

BERT: Oh, I don't want food. Hallo, George. I brought my—[*He plays a few bars of "Waltzing Matilda".*]

[*There are mixed reactions to his effort.*]

Isn't everyone happy? Don't you like music? Why do you look sad? [*To* BLANCHE] Why do you look sad?

BLANCHE: I am sad.

[*This answer staggers him.*]

TONY: It's church Sunday, Bert.

BERT: Oh. [*After a thought he plays a little of a hymn.*]

TONY: And, of course, we've just paid our rent.

[BERT *switches to the "Dead March".*]

MRS. POCKS: There's no profit in the board you pay.

BERT: Mrs. Pocks is happy. She's just the same as always. Hallo, Paddy. Are you happy?

MRS. POCKS: Shut up, Paddy! Don't you start him talking.

BLANCHE: Has he been sitting there all the week?

TONY: He has to go outside now and then—like the rest of us—eh, Bert?

MRS. WILLIAMS: Oh, Tony!

BERT: Oh. Oh—yeah, Tony. Yeah! [*He becomes quite enthusiastic.*]

DENISE: Tony's trying to be offensive, Mrs. Williams.

TONY: All right, then: he goes outside now and then like some of the rest of us.

[MRS. POCKS *and* MRS. WILLIAMS *laugh.*]

DENISE: I'm going to get ready, Mrs. Williams.

MRS. WILLIAMS: I suppose I'll have to, too . . .

DENISE: Are you coming now?

TONY [*quite softly*]: Denise. Are you going, now?

MRS. WILLIAMS [*after a pause*]: Come on, Denise. See you later, boys and girls. Be good. Be good.

[DENISE *and* MRS. WILLIAMS *go out.*]

TONY: Give us some music, Bert. Play us a tune. Anything.

MRS. POCKS: Don't you go squeezing that box here. I've had enough of this stupidity—

TONY [*catching her hand, but speaking quite sadly*]: Aw, have some gaiety in you, girl.

MRS. POCKS: And don't you go crawling—[*Changing her tone*] Girl!

Old enough to be your [*as he speaks*] sister!

TONY [*holding out his arms to her*]: Grandma!

[*She laughs. He catches her.*]

MRS. POCKS: Stop it! Stop it now, or I'll—[*She grabs a large spoon.*] I'll dong you.

[*He releases her.*]

Snow, go and ring the gong. Make yourself useful for a change.

SNOW: Righto. [*He goes off.*]

BLANCHE: Why don't you stop picking on Snow?

[MRS. POCKS *snorts. The gong sounds off-stage.* SNOW *returns. A pause.*]

TONY: Go on, Bert. Play us a tune. Cheer us up.

MRS. POCKS: You heard what I said. Play us a tune! On a Sunday morning . . . You ought to be ashamed of yourself after last night—

GEORGE: Yeah, play us a tune, Bert. Why shouldn't Bert play us a tune? We'd all like a tune. Play us a tune, Bert.

BLANCHE: Play "Here Comes the Bride".

[GEORGE *scowls.*]

MRS. POCKS: That's enough of that, Blanche. You're being silly.

BERT: I'll play you a tune. I'll play your old favourite tune. Your old favourite . . . [*He starts "Yarrawonga".*]

[GEORGE *makes a kind of a moan in time.* TONY *sings and waves his tea. Even* PADDY *makes an accompanying noise from his corner.* BLANCHE *hates it.* SNOW *approves.*]

MRS. POCKS: This kitchen's just a damned noise.

TONY: Mind your language; it's Sunday. [*He rejoins the singing, very loudly.*]

[BERT *and* GEORGE *are making a lot of noise.*]

MRS. POCKS: Damn you and your chatter! Damn you! I'd give anything for a bit of peace. Shut up, Tony! Paddy— Damn you! There's no peace and quiet. Damn you!

BERT: Sorry, Mrs. Pocks. Sorry. [*He stops playing.*]

[*The others trail off. There is silence.* MRS. POCKS *is triumphant. Then, looking at her, very deliberately* GEORGE *begins to sing.*]

MRS. POCKS: George! George! George . . .

TONY: Give him a go.

GEORGE: Have some life in you, Lil. [*He goes on singing.*]

[BERT *picks it up*. PADDY *joins in*.]

SNOW: You're only as young as you feel, George.

BLANCHE: Goo-goo.

TONY [*clapping his hands*]: Come on, Lil. Life begins at sixty.

MRS. POCKS: I'm not sixty.

[MRS. WILLIAMS *enters. She claps her hands with delight*.]

MRS. WILLIAMS: Another party? Another party? At this time of day?

[*She is ready for a party. She is dressed for church*.]

TONY: Sing up, Mrs. Williams. Let your head go.

MRS. WILLIAMS: But I've got my hat on. [*She giggles and takes it off*.]

MRS. POCKS: There'll be no free beer today, not while I'm sober.

TONY: Wacko!

MRS. WILLIAMS [*offended*]: I only came in for some change. I don't want any free beer. I only wanted some change. I've only got notes—and I do like some change.

MRS. POCKS: Handy at church.

MRS. WILLIAMS: Yes, I like to have it. You never know. And if you've only got notes, it's so embarrassing . . .

MRS. POCKS: I can't hear what you're saying.

[*The noise is still on*. MRS. POCKS *is finishing the washing and drying*.]

I can't hear a word. [*To* BERT] Oh, get out of here with that thing. Get out of here. Go and sing in the yard. Go over to the park. Give someone else a circus. Go on. Go on. I mean it. Get out of here. And don't let me hear that thing again—

[*She has chased* BERT *to the door*. GEORGE *stands*.]

GEORGE: Lil. You're throwing me out. You're throwing me out.

[BERT *plays mournfully*.]

You're throwing me out.

MRS. POCKS: Yes, throwing you out. You and your old mate. Throwing you out.

[GEORGE *looks at her*. BERT, *seeing how things are, bursts into "Yarrawonga". Singing, the pair march out*.]

SNOW: You don't want to be too hard, Lil . . .

MRS. WILLIAMS [*a little disappointed*]: At least, Paddy's a quiet drunk, usually. [*She sits down*.]

MRS. POCKS: You're always sticking up for him.

MRS. WILLIAMS: *I* am! Why, my dear woman, I haven't any . . .

What a ridiculous thing to suggest. I merely said that Paddy's a quiet drunk.

MRS. POCKS: That's more than can be said for others in this room.

[MRS. WILLIAMS *is offended.* TONY *assumes a hurt expression.* MRS. POCKS *gets the change from the dresser. It is in a tea-pot.*]

Well—isn't it quiet? Now, they've gone I'll probably get a bit of peace and quiet . . . [*her tone is without conviction and a little uneasy*]:

MRS. WILLIAMS: And I suppose you feel like it, after last night.

[MRS. POCKS *opens her mouth to speak but changes her mind.*]

MRS. POCKS: They've gone to bowls, I suppose.

MRS. WILLIAMS: And we know what that means.

BLANCHE: Well, they're happier when they're drunk. They might be happier when they're drunk.

MRS. WILLIAMS [*with disapproval*]: We all might be.

TONY: Last night, at any rate, we all were—with a few notable exceptions.

MRS. WILLIAMS: Tony, I wasn't—

TONY: If we could make it last it'd be all right.

MRS. POCKS: If you knew how it'd take them.

MRS. WILLIAMS: Well, I suppose if "happiness" is all you want, you can buy it in bottles.

MRS. POCKS: You didn't buy it; it was free.

SNOW: Everyone wants to be happy, Mrs. Williams. You can't blame a man for having a drink . . .

MRS. WILLIAMS: Oh, a drink's all right. I like a shandy myself. If it were only one drink though. Or two. Or three, but—

TONY: Or five, or six, or seventeen, you mightn't be able to blame a man for having a drink. [*He laughs at his own exasperation.*]

MRS. WILLIAMS: Oh, Tony—

TONY: You might blame something else though. You might blame something else if a man has seventeen drinks.

MRS. WILLIAMS: There's no excuse for—

BLANCHE: You might as well know, we've got to be married.

[*There is a silence.*]

You might as well know we've got to be married.

[*The pause continues.*]

MRS. WILLIAMS [*reproachfully*]: Oh, Snow . . .

191

SNOW: I—er . . . I—

TONY: Congratulations, Snow.

MRS. POCKS [*to* SNOW]: You ought to—you ought to . . . Standing there like a great gawk . . . Why don't you say something?

SNOW: Gee, Lil . . .

MRS. POCKS: What do you think George will say? What do you think George will do? How long, Blanche?

BLANCHE: Oh, I'm not having a baby.

MRS. WILLIAMS: Oh.

MRS. POCKS: Of all the stupid frights to give a person—

BLANCHE: Not that I know of.

MRS. WILLIAMS: Oh, Blanche!

BLANCHE: But Snow and I are going to get married.

MRS. POCKS: I— Blanche, you shouldn't— Snow . . . What sort of a life can he give you?

SNOW: Aw, Lil, I—

MRS. POCKS: Don't you Lil me, you— In a few years you'll be just like the rest, drinking your cheque, swearing at her of a Saturday night.

BLANCHE: I don't know if I'll have a baby—not right away. But I hope so. I want one. We both want one. Don't we, Snow? Don't we?

SNOW: Eh? Yeah . . .

MRS. POCKS: I— I— [*She hurries out and rings the gong furiously.*]

BLANCHE: Well, what are you staring at?

TONY: Very well bowled.

BLANCHE: And I'm not sorry. I'm not sorry, Mrs. Williams. I'm glad. I'm glad.

MRS. WILLIAMS: But, Blanche, you don't know . . . But it will be so lovely. It'll be the making of you—a baby. Oh, Snow, I'm so happy. I ought to rouse on you, but I can't. It'll be so wonderful — a baby . . .

[*The gong rings again.*]

TONY: The old girl's celebrating.

MRS. WILLIAMS: But what will George say? [*Then, a little delightedly*] Won't he be furious! [*Worried again*] Whatever will George say?

BLANCHE: If only we'd stop saying that, nobody would care what George said.

192

[MRS. POCKS *re-enters.*]

MRS. POCKS: Those cows must be glued to their beds. Well—breakfast's off. They can wait for dinner. Not that it's far off, now—blast them! Sit up, Paddy! You look like something the cat dragged in. And keep your mouth shut, do you hear? You haven't heard anything. No one's heard anything. [*She takes the cards from the drawer and begins to play patience.*]

MRS. WILLIAMS: Of course not, Mrs. Pocks. We wouldn't dream—

MRS. POCKS: We're not even going to talk about it— Blanche. Blanche . . . when?

BLANCHE: Last night.

[MRS. POCKS *sniffs and goes on playing.*]

MRS. POCKS: Oh you're a stupid girl! You've no more sense than a fly. Come and kiss me. Oh, stop fussing! Stop fussing around me! Anyone'd think you were—think you were a child . . . Oh, men! Men! Men! . . . it's all right for them! Isn't it, Snow? You great big good-for-nothing—

MRS. WILLIAMS [*giggling*]: Well, he's turned out good for something.

[MRS. POCKS *gives her a terrible look.*]

Well . . . Hasn't he?

MRS. POCKS: It's all right for them. [*To* TONY] Yes, you can smile. You're the same as the rest of them. They're all alike. They're after one thing. And they'll bill and coo till they get it. Oh, I know what goes on. I'm not blind. And when they get it, what are they like? How do they treat you? They treat you like dirt. You're good to wait on them, and that's all there is to it. Well, stop your crying. It's too late to cry, now. You should have cried then, and he might have left you alone. But I doubt it. [*She looks fiercely at* SNOW.] What are you crying *for*? You're getting married, aren't you? You want to marry him, don't you? Isn't that what you want? Stupid as they make them!

BLANCHE: Snow . . .

MRS. POCKS: Snow! Snow! I wonder he's got the hide to look me in the face after what he's done—

SNOW: I'm not looking you in the face, Lil—

MRS. POCKS: No! That's men all over. And don't call me Lil! You'd better start calling me ma . . . [*She plays cards.*]

SNOW: Gee, thanks, Lil—ma.

[MRS. POCKS *winces but says nothing.* MRS. WILLIAMS *gushes with delight.*]

MRS. WILLIAMS: It might be grandma soon.

TONY: Then we can really offer congratulations?

MRS. WILLIAMS [*tearfully*]: I'm so happy. I'm so happy. I do so love a wedding. But what will George say?

MRS. POCKS: I'll see about George.

BLANCHE: He can say what he likes. I've got to be married.

MRS. POCKS: Well, don't skite about it. And speak with some respect. He *is* your father.

TONY: Really?

[MRS. POCKS *threatens him.*]

Deal us a hand.

[*She packs the cards.*]

MRS. POCKS: Just as I was getting it out—

TONY: You couldn't get out of a paper bag. You'd only just started. Anyway, you were cheating.

MRS. POCKS: I was not! I never cheat at patience.

TONY: You keep that for playing with me, eh?

MRS. WILLIAMS: Then it's all turned out fine. Fine and dandy, as they say. [*She giggles.*] Blanche has found the bunyip.

MRS. POCKS: I'll thank you not to be coarse, Mrs. Williams: it's Sunday.

MRS. WILLIAMS: I didn't mean—

BLANCHE [*to* MRS. POCKS]: Say that you're pleased.

[MRS. POCKS *stops dealing.*]

Say that you don't mind.

MRS. POCKS: Of course I mind. Of course I'm pleased. It's not every day I get a son-in-law.

TONY: You're not so much losing a daughter—

MRS. WILLIAMS: As getting a son. That's what Mr. Williams said to my father.

MRS. POCKS: Come here, Snow. Come here and let me look at you. [*She looks. She sniffs.*] Hm! Size and all, I never would have thought it of you. Give us a kiss. [*She holds out her cheek.*] Come on, I won't eat you.

[*He kisses her.*]

TONY: Any for me?

MRS. POCKS: There's no profit in boarders. Well, are you going to play or aren't you?

[*They play rummy.*]

Are *you* going to sit round here all day or are you going to tennis?

SNOW: Yeah. [*He moves to go.*]

BLANCHE: All right. I'm sorry.

MRS. POCKS: Sorry! Have you ever seen the like of it! The girl doesn't know her own mind. Sorry! [*She picks up a card that* TONY *has thrown away.*] That'll do me. [*A pause.*] Blanche. Blanche . . . Do you think you wouldn't mind the baby—straight off like? You wouldn't mind if it was?

BLANCHE: No. No, I'd be glad.

MRS. POCKS: Hm! Hm! Ought to be ashamed of yourself! In my day— Go on. On your way. On your way.

[BLANCHE *kisses her, but she brushes her away.*]

SNOW: See you later, everyone . . .

[*He and* BLANCHE *exit. A second of silence.*]

MRS. POCKS: You know, she's getting a big girl now. She needs something to keep her occupied or she'll start to mope. I was only young when I was married. And I suppose she could do worse.

MRS. WILLIAMS: Well, we haven't much choice now, have we?

MRS. POCKS: If that's the way you're going to talk, Mrs. Williams—

MRS. WILLIAMS: I didn't mean—

MRS. POCKS: You never mean anything, but you say a lot—

TONY: Rummy!

MRS. POCKS: Blast! [*She throws her cards down.*] Blast you, Tony. You knew I wasn't watching.

TONY: Yes. [*He deals.*]

MRS. WILLIAMS: But you really are pleased, Mrs. Pocks . . . I am. I'm so pleased. If it were my own daughter, I—

MRS. POCKS: Don't be silly. I've never been so annoyed in all my life. Doing a thing like that! That great brute of a fellow! Girls nowadays aren't—

TONY: Watch the game, gran.

MRS. POCKS: Don't you gran me. I'm not a grandmother yet.

MRS. WILLIAMS: You might be soon. Oh, I know I shouldn't have reminded you they had to get married. But I'm so pleased—

MRS. POCKS [*deliberately*]: If they do have a baby—mind you I'm not saying they will, or even that it's likely—but if they do, you don't know a thing about it.

MRS. WILLIAMS: Now, Mrs. Pocks, you know I wouldn't—

MRS. POCKS: When I was a girl—

TONY: No True Confessions on a Sunday, please. [*Reassuringly*] We don't know anything about having babies.

MRS. POCKS: It's what everyone gets married for. Isn't it? Just a little bit early. That's all. It might be just a little bit early.

DENISE [*off*]: Are you ready, Mrs. Williams?

[TONY *reacts.*]

MRS. WILLIAMS: Here, dear.

[DENISE *enters. She is dressed for church, and nothing else. She carries white gloves.*]

DENISE: It's not half past yet. I'll have a cup of tea now.

MRS. WILLIAMS: It's just as well Father Flane has such a long way to come. I'd never be able to manage early mass. I still feel worn out, just worn out. And I'm so comfortable, sitting here. That walk last night, Mrs. Pocks! And my ankle! Thank goodness it's all right now. It's as good as—as—as good as—

TONY: Gold?

MRS. WILLIAMS: It's as good as gold.

TONY: Are you sure it was the walk that knocked you up?

MRS. WILLIAMS: Now, Tony, you know I didn't have more than a taste. Just an eye-wash really. But the walk was glorious! And I'm sure it was good for me.

MRS. POCKS: Good for the bootmaker.

MRS. WILLIAMS: Well, we enjoyed it. We did enjoy it. Oh Tony, there was a stick on the road and we thought it was a snake; we laughed and laughed.

MRS. POCKS: Like a pair of old fools.

MRS. WILLIAMS: There are fools and fools, Mrs. Pocks. And we did enjoy it.

[MRS. POCKS *snorts.*]

Oh, Mrs. Pocks, let's go again tonight. I'm sure you'd enjoy it even more than last night. Let's go again. I'm sure I won't trip this time. And it was glorious. It was simply glorious.

MRS. POCKS: Are you off your head? It was awful.

MRS. WILLIAMS: There's no church for you people tonight, and you'll just be sitting here. Just sitting here with your stuffy old cards. Silly old cards!

MRS. POCKS: You leave them alone.

MRS. WILLIAMS: Oh, I'm not going to throw them—*not just now*. You'll be sitting in here, being taken for granted, and you could be out there. And it was glorious. Admit you did enjoy it. Go on. Admit it. You did enjoy it, at first. Now admit you enjoyed it at first.

TONY [*talking for* DENISE]: The moon will rise earlier tonight. The wattle will be heavy and white in the moonlight. If you look up high you'll see the gum-blossoms.

MRS. WILLIAMS: No wattle for me, thanks. It makes me sneeze.

TONY: Crushed again.

MRS. WILLIAMS: It will be lovely though, Mrs. Pocks. It will be lovely. We must get out and make an effort, then the heat won't get us down. We must make an effort. We might even find the bunyip, this time. You never know.

MRS. POCKS: Like Blanche, eh?

[*She laughs and* MRS. WILLIAMS *giggles.*]

MRS. WILLIAMS: Oh, I never thought . . . I didn't mean . . .

[TONY *wins the hand.*]

MRS. POCKS: It's uncanny the way he does it. [*She deals.*] Oh, well, I'll see how I feel. I suppose it does me good to blow the cobwebs off once in a while. But no making a habit of it, mind!

MRS. WILLIAMS: Oh it's no good, if you make a habit of it.

TONY: How about it, Denise?

DENISE: How about what?

TONY: Last night wasn't the end of the world. Tonight's coming. Interested in walking with an awfully nice fellow? Are you? Are you interested in walking? It'll be cool then.

DENISE: No, thanks, Tony. I have to work on Monday mornings.

MRS. POCKS: Don't you work on the others? [*She laughs.*] It'd knock a few pounds off . . .

MRS. WILLIAMS: Oh, you could go, Denise. We won't be awfully busy tomorrow . . .

TONY: You still need to live. I'm going to make some more toast. Watch this hand, Mrs. Williams; you've got time.

[*He makes more toast.* MRS. WILLIAMS *plays his hand.*]

MRS. POCKS: If Billie had to run down the hill it'd do her good. Knock a few pounds off her.

MRS. WILLIAMS: We can't all have your figure.

[THE GINK *knocks.*]

MRS. POCKS: Yes?

[THE GINK *enters.*]

GINK: Can I come in? Hallo, everyone. Hallo, Mrs. Williams.

[*They hallo back at him.*]

MRS. WILLIAMS: How are you, Arthur?

GINK: Couldn't be better, Mrs. Williams, thanks very much.

MRS. WILLIAMS: I thought you might have been moping about your father . . .

GINK: Oh. Oh, yeah. The raffle went all right.

MRS. WILLIAMS: I'm so glad. Oh, I really am glad. I was worried sick. I'm so happy for you, Gink—oh! Arthur, I mean. I am sorry . . .

GINK: That's all right, Mrs. Williams. I'm used to it. Everyone calls me that . . . Everyone except you . . .

MRS. WILLIAMS: I hope I never—

GINK: Oh, you can call me Gink too.

MRS. WILLIAMS: But I don't think—

GINK: I'd like you to call me Gink.

MRS. WILLIAMS: Oh, Arthur . . . Gink! What a nice compliment.

MRS. POCKS [*triumphantly*]: Rummy! That's one to me! [*Disgustedly*] Aw, you're too easy. Why don't you pay attention?

MRS. WILLIAMS: We'd better be going. Are you ready, Denise?

DENISE: Yes. [*She has cleaned her cup. She draws on her gloves.*] Yes, I am just about ready.

TONY: Denise! . . . Say one for me, will you? Say one for me.

MRS. WILLIAMS: Bye . . . Bye . . . See you again, Arth—Gink. [*She giggles and goes to the door.*]

[DENISE *follows her.*]

DENISE: See you later, Mrs. Pocks.

TONY: Goodbye, *Miss.* Goodbye, *Miss.*

GINK: Ta-ta, Mrs. Williams. Any time you like—

MRS. WILLIAMS [*seeing another meaning*]: Oh, Arthur . . . [*She giggles and goes.*]

198

[DENISE *follows her out.*]

TONY: Have another deal while I get the jam.

[MRS. POCKS *deals.*]

MRS. POCKS: That's the strawberry again.

TONY: Thanks.

MRS. POCKS: There's no money in you cows. You eat all the damn profits.

TONY: But you love us, Mrs. Pocks, you love us. You couldn't live without us.

MRS. POCKS: Your play.

[*They play.*]

GEORGE [*off, in distress*]: Lil! Lil! Lil!

[*There is a burst of bacchanalian music from* BERT'S *accordion. It ends with a fall.*]

MRS. POCKS: That cow! Whenever I get anything— Do you think he's in the cellar? He shouldn't— The doctor told him . . . I'll wring his neck, I will. I'll wring his neck. [*She has talked herself from the room.*]

[TONY *eats moodily.*]

TONY [*chewing*]: What would you do, Gink, if there was nothing to do?

GINK: Nothing.

TONY: Yes.

[*A pause.*]

GINK: You know—that Mrs. Williams—her husband's dead.

TONY: Yes.

GINK: She's real well educated, too.

TONY [*pulling his leg*]: She's had four husbands.

GINK [*in delighted horror and unbelief*]: Go on!

TONY: Buried 'em all.

GINK: She's real well educated.

TONY: Naturally.

GINK: Yes. [*He ruminates.*]

[*Silence.* TONY *finishes his toast.*]

TONY: Well, Gink, you can bury him, now.

GINK: He has to be buried.

TONY: We all have to be sometime, Gink.

GINK [*surprised*]: Yeah.

TONY: Don't worry what anyone says.

GINK: No, Tone . . .

TONY: Who got the prize?

GINK: What prize, Tone?

TONY: For the raffle.

GINK: Oh! Oh, I dunno.

TONY: What was the prize?

GINK: Oh, a— a— a . . . I dunno. I forget. I dunno. Do you have to have a prize?

TONY: No. I suppose not. I don't suppose anyone knows what the prize is, or who gets the prize, or if there is a prize. It's a cheering thought, Gink: nobody knows. It's not just me. You're a great comfort. You're a wonderful optimist.

GINK: Am I, Tony? . . . But you don't need glasses.

TONY: No?

GINK: No. Don't look to me as though you do. You see all right, don't you? You know I'm here?

TONY: Yes. Yes, I know we're here. I see that very clearly.

[MRS. POCKS *returns*.]

MRS. POCKS: They've got some more beer, I couldn't get it off him. He ought to have more sense. The doctor told him. I told him. No wonder Blanche doesn't know her own mind for more than two minutes. He's happy enough—but just wait till afterwards. There's always afterwards. [*She has picked up her cards.*]

[*The game is resumed.* TONY *has stacked the cards.*]

TONY: But we still live, Mrs. Pocks. We still live. Perhaps I do need glasses.

MRS. POCKS: Are you winning? Whenever I get a decent hand something interrupts—

TONY: It was a private joke.

[*They play one more card.*]

Rummy!

MRS. POCKS: Well, talk about quick on the trigger! I've never seen anything like it. I've never seen the like of it. You don't give me a go. Go on, have a deal! Of all the rotten cows! You don't even know how to deal properly.

[*He goes on dealing.*]

I've never seen the like of it!

[PADDY *stands up and bellows.*]

PADDY: "Waltzing Matilda, Waltzing Matilda,
You'll come a-waltzing Matilda with me . . . etc."

MRS. POCKS: Shut up, Paddy! Sit down and shut up!

TONY: Let him sing if he wants to. If he's got something to sing about.

GINK: Yeah.

MRS. POCKS: Shut up, Paddy!

TONY: The Gink wants him to sing. I want him to sing. He wants to sing. Sit down and play.

[*They play.* PADDY *sings.* THE GINK *sits there, smiling.*]

(*The End*)

JACK McKINNEY

the well

a universal folk tale in an australian idiom

characters of the play
in order of appearance

and original cast

The play was first produced on 19 October 1960 at the Twelfth Night Theatre, Brisbane, with the following cast in order of appearance:

GRANDPA:	David Brewster
BERT DILLON:	John Hawcroft
BILLY DILLON:	Antony Tuxworth
SUSIE DILLON:	Gail Ypénazar
MR. DILLON:	John Moorhouse
MRS. GRANT:	Dell Dawe
HERBIE GRANT:	Peter Tuxworth
DICK HARRISON:	Ian Austin
TED GRANT:	Ken Goodwin
MARY GRANT:	Rosemary Campey
CHARLIE DILLON:	Wilfred Camps
PREACHER:	Peter Rogers
POLICEMAN:	John Saltzer

The action takes place on two neighbouring five-acre farms. Poverty-stricken broken-down fences, unpainted weatherboard houses, unlined. Tumbledown sheds. In background, dead ring-barked trees.

The play was produced by Eunice Hanger, and the set was designed and executed by Robert Dick and Kitty Breeden.

author's note

MANNER OF SPEECH

All characters speak elliptically. They leave out the logical connectives of their thought processes; there are long pauses between sentences instead. Their dropping of "h" and "g" is not obvious or pedantic; it is part of a general tendency to take short cuts in their speech. They don't say " If you see him tell him that I have been"; they say "You see him, tell him I been". But their speech is not dictated by laziness only. An instructive sense of euphony also operates. They say "I never seen it", "He never done it" because these slip off the tongue more easily and pleasantly than "I didn't see", "He didn't do". With these people it is speakability, not grammar or logic, that counts.

GENERAL

Though time must of course be given for the laughs, laughs should not be played for. They should be allowed to emerge naturally out of character and action—these people in this particular predicament. Particularly in the first two scenes the comedy should not be over-emphasized, as this will throw the rest of the play out of focus, its purpose being essentially serious: it is intended to be a "serious comedy".

NOTE TO PRODUCER

This is not a story about events; it is a study of people. It is not the story of a feud, but of the tensions and confusions that people become involved in when they set themselves apart from one another. So it is not the story line that matters, but the reactions of these simple folk caught in a situation of their own creating.

205

notes on the characters

GRANDPA. In wheel chair with old grey blanket over his knees. He has no active part in the action of the play; he is just a sort of background chorus of a "said-the-raven-nevermore" kind.

BERT DILLON. Twenty-five. Ragged shirt and shorts, bare-footed.

BILLY DILLON. Twelve. Similarly dressed.

SUSIE DILLON. Ten. Similarly dressed.

MR. DILLON. Fifty. Uncut grey hair, unshaven. Ragged shirt, rolled-up sleeves, ill-fitting trousers roughly held up with a belt. He is vague and uncertain from chronic worry. He occasionally turns on the children, but evidently doesn't mean it and nobody takes it very seriously. He has recently joined a fantastic sect, "The Children of the Lord Resplendent", as some compensation for his general frustration and inadequacy.

MRS. GRANT. "Next door". Forty. Haggard, hair dragged back anyhow. Stockingless, sand-shoes. Her relationship with her husband, Ted, is not antagonistic; it is a sort of weary, habitual, defensive affection. When they have a row, they know, through years of practice, not to let it go too far and get out of hand. Mrs. G. is the more apt at this sort of thing—Ted is inclined to blunder on; she knows how to create a diversion, or to take advantage of any diversion that occurs at the critical moment—this is instinctive rather than calculated, of course.

HERBIE GRANT. Fourteen. Ragged shirt and shorts, bare feet.

DICK HARRISON. Political agitator, rather better dressed than Ted Grant, just as Ted is a bit smarter than "next doors". Dick is also a bit shrewder and more alert than Ted—that's why he's organizing the bean pickers while Ted picks beans.

TED GRANT. Forty. Big, good-natured, but inclined to get angry and bluster when bewildered. Anti-boss politics are his compensation for his inadequacies, as "religion" is for Mr. Dillon.

MARY GRANT. Eighteen. Comely, dressed as indicated.

CHARLIE DILLON. Eighteen. Smarter in appearance than the rest of the Dillon family, a bit better educated, or anyway not so careless in speech. Works in nearby town in a grocery store owned by a member of the Children of the Lord Resplendent Sect.

PREACHER. This is his official title as leader of the Children of the Lord Resplendent Sect.

POLICEMAN.

ACT ONE

scene 1

The Dillons' kitchen. GRANDPA *is seated in his old wheel-chair by the stove.* BERT, BILLY, SUSIE *are seated at cheap pine table. No table-cloth. Tin plates, enamel mugs. Open tin of jam on table. Loaf of bread on table between* BERT *and* BILLY. MR. DILLON *enters by back door. Hangs hat on peg beside door. Takes a few steps forward and looks enquiringly from table to stove.*

BERT [*back to* MR. D. *Might be speaking to anybody*]: On the stove. [MR. D. *takes plate of stew from side of stove. Stops and looks at* GRANDPA'S *plate. Gives him a tit-bit off his own plate (with fingers). Sits at head of table.*]
Get the fence fixed?
[*Pause—there are always long pauses between speeches.*]
MR. D.: Fence? Huh! Ain't a fence. Give's a bit of bread.
GRANDPA: The fence—the fence.
[*Nobody takes any notice of him.*]
BERT [*cleans knife on side of plate, cuts bread, and tosses it to* MR. D.]:
When's *he* gointer do somethin' to it?
MR. D.: Him? Huh! [*About to start eating, looks up.*] You say grace?
BERT: Never thought.
MR. D.: Preacher said it was one of the main things. Haveter say it after, now.
BILLY: Can I have another piece?
MR. D.: Do somethin' to the fence—him? When I take the law on him. That's when.
BERT: Their poddies was through again this mornin'. I put the dog on 'em.
MR. D.: Man ought to take the rifle to them.
BERT: He reckons he sees the dog on 'em he'll shoot it.
MR. D.: The dog?

BERT: Yair.

MR. D.: Better not. Two can play at that game. Who told yer?

BERT [*jerks his head over shoulders to "next door"*]: She told Charlie.

MR. D.: Who?

BERT: Her — the girl.

MR. D.: Told Charlie?

BERT: Yair.

MR. D.: What d'yer mean? Yer don't mean that's on again, do yer?

BERT: Again? Ain't never been off.

MR. D.: Didn't I tell him he had ter cut her out?

BERT: Tell him—yair. But makin's different.

MR. D.: He oughter 'ave more respect for his parents. He knows what we think of *them*.

BERT: It's always been on. Ever since they uster come home in the school bus together.

BILLY: He took her to the pictures, Sat'day.

MR. D.: How d'you know?

BILLY: Seen 'im.

SUSIE: Yes, we both seen 'em.

MR. D.: What, into town?

BILLY: Yair.

MR. D. [*to* BERT]: How'd they go in?

BERT: I dunno. Never seen 'em.

BILLY: Went in the car—Robinson's.

MR. D.: Robinson's. Brought 'em home, too, I s'pose.

BERT: Yair, that's right. He did. I seen the lights. Dropped 'em down at the corner.

MR. D.: Huh! So's we wouldn't know.

BERT: Yair.

MR. D.: There an' back, eh? That'd cost a packet.

BERT: Knock a coupla quid rotten, be what he charged to take Mum in.

MR. D.: No sooner earnin' wages than he's goin' agen his parents . . . How old is she, the girl?

BERT: Her? Same as him, ain't she? Yair, that's right, she is.

MR. D.: Eighteen? [*To himself*] I dunno . . . boys these days . . . his mother in hospital an' all . . . goin' to the pictures . . . sittin' there in the dark. I dunno . . . [*To* BERT] They been goin' out

210

together other times, d'yer think?

BERT: Where's he go when he goes out of a night?

MR. D.: Over playin' draughts with young Smith, don't he?

BILLY: He doesn't sometimes. He goes the other way, out toward the reserve.

MR. D.: The reserve?

BERT: Draughts? It's somethin' more'n draughts he plays, y' ask me.

[MR. D. *glances at children and shakes his head admonishingly at* BERT.]

Why don't you have a go at him about it?

MR. D.: I might get Preacher ter speak to him. He might take more notice. [*To himself*] The way things are now-a-days . . . an' the sort of pictures they see . . . an' sittin' there in the dark . . . The reserve? [*Shakes his head with a troubled air.*] Mum in hospital an' all.

BILLY: Can I have another piece?

[*Nobody takes any notice.* BERT *and* MR. D. *eat steadily, brooding.* BILLY *reaches out for bread.* BERT *reaches out and snatches loaf away from him without looking up.*]

[*Appealing to* MR. D.] I only had two pieces.

SUSIE: I only had one.

MR. D: Give 'em half each, then.

[BERT *wipes knife on edge of plate. Picks up loaf, wipes knife again on cut end, cuts slice, cuts in half. Tosses them half each.* BILLY *tears a handful off his piece and scrapes up last of stew with it. Long pause—they go on eating.*]

Baker been?

GRANDPA: The baker? The baker?

BERT: Yair.

MR. D.: Leave any bread?

BERT: No.

MR. D.: Didn't leave anythin'?

BERT: Yair.

MR. D.: What'd he leave?

BERT: That [*jerks head at piece of paper lying on table between him and* BILLY].

[*They all stop eating and look at paper.*]

[*Pushing paper towards* BILLY] Read it.

[BILLY *picks up paper and looks at writing.* SUSIE *tries to look over his shoulder but he holds the paper away from her.* SUSIE *makes face, and puts out tongue at him.*]

Go on. Read it out.

BILLY [*reads slowly*]: Two white, half brown.

BERT: No. The other side. What *he* wrote.

BILLY [*turns paper and reads slowly*]: No money, [*pause*] no bread.
[SUSIE *giggles.* BERT *makes a vague threatening gesture at her.*]

MR. D. [*to nobody in particular*]: That'll do now. [*To* BILLY] Show's here. [BILLY *passes paper to him. He reads slowly, no particular expression, just examining the fact*] No money, no bread. [*Tosses paper onto table.*] [*To* BERT] You see him?

BERT: No. Left it on the gate post.

MR. D.: Huh! [*Long pause. They eat.*] Seems we'll have ter do a bit of bakin'!

BERT: Pity mum wasn't home.

GRANDPA: When's Jean comin' home?
[*Nobody takes any notice of him.*]

MR. D. [*to* BERT]: She won't be up ter doin' any bakin' when she does come.

BERT: Aw, we'll manage.

MR. D.: Have ter. [*To himself, reflectively*] No money, no bread. Hummm!

BILLY [*during preceding* MR. D./BERT *passage, gets up carrying plate. Goes to back door. Whistles to dog*]: Here, boy, here, boy. Here y'are. [*Scrapes plate to his left side. Watches dog—out of sight—for a moment, then looks to his right. Turns quickly to table.*] Hey! What d'yer know? [*Tosses tin plate into tin dish on washing bench beside stove. Goes back to door and peeps out.*]

BERT [*looks over shoulder at* BILLY—*slight pause*]: Well, what?

BILLY [*turning to table*]: She's comin'.

MR. D.: Who's comin'?

BILLY: Her [*jerks his head toward next door neighbours*].

BERT [*incredulously*]: Next door?

BILLY: Yair.

MR. D. [*incredulously*]: Comin' here?

BILLY [*peeping out*]: Yair. She's gettin' through the fence.

MR. D. [*contemptuously*]: Fence! Huh!

BILLY [*jeeringly*]: She's hung up on the barb wire. Her dress's caught.

[SUSIE *makes to jump from table.* MR. D. *reaching out pushes her down.*]

MR. D.: You stay where y'are. [*To* BILLY] Come back here.

BILLY [*taking last peep*]: She can't get loose. Oh cripes, get an eyeful of that.

MR. D.: You come here, I tell yer.

[BILLY *comes back to table.*]

BERT [*goes to window*]: Yair. She's comin' here all right. She's tryin' ter get through the fence. What's *she* want, I wonder. [*Comes back to table.*]

MR. D.: Mighter seen yer doggin' the poddies.

BERT: No, she never. They went through up the other side of the well.

MR. D.: They can see the well from the house, can't they?

BILLY: No they can't. That patch of lantana blocks it.

MR. D.: How d'you know? You been over there?

BILLY: No.

SUSIE: You have, see?

BILLY: I never.

SUSIE: You did.

BILLY: I never did.

SUSIE: Yer did, yer did.

GRANDPA: What's that, what's that?

MR. D.: That'll do, I tell yers. [*To* BILLY] And if I catch you goin' over there . . .

BILLY: Well, I only went ter get me aeroplane. It flew over there.

SUSIE: There, y'are, see.

BILLY: Well, it's got nothin' ter do with you.

MR. D.: That'll do, I tell yers. [*To* BILLY] Tellin' lies an' all. Preacher hears about that, there'll be trouble. Lyin'. One of the worst things yer can do, haven't yer heard him say?

BERT [*turns round, glances at window. Aside*]: Hey! here she is.

[MRS. G's *head seen passing window.* SUSIE *goes to jump up.* MR. D. *pushes her down. Knock on wall beside door.*]

MRS. GRANT [*off*]: Hey! Yers there?

[MR. D. *and* BERT *look at one another.*]

MR. D. [*to* BERT]: It's her all right. What's *she* want I wonder?

BERT: I dunno.

MRS. G. [*off*]: Yers there?

GRANDPA: What's that. Somebody there?

> [BILLY *and* SUSIE *look at one another. Giggle.* MR. D. *makes vague threatening gesture at them.*]

BERT [*to* MR. D.]: Better go, I s'pose?

MR. D.: S'pose so.

BERT [*gets up, taking piece of bread in his hand and biting it as he goes. Lounges against the door post—to* MRS. G., *off, looking down on her*]: What yer want?

MRS. G. [*off*]: It's me cow.

BERT [*at door—always pauses slightly before speaking*]: Yer cow? What about yer cow?

MRS. G.: She's took a header.

MR. D. [*at table*]: A header?

GRANDPA: What's that? What's that?

BERT: What d'yer mean, a header?

MRS. G. [*moves and can be seen at foot of back steps*]: Down the well.

BERT: Down the *well*?

GRANDPA: What well?

BERT [*looking toward* MR. D.]: Down the well?

MR. D.: The well?

BERT [*to* MRS. G.]: You see her?

MRS. G.: No.

BERT [*to* MRS. G.]: How d'yer know, then?

MRS. G. [*slightly impatiently*]: I seen her.

BERT: You just said yer never.

MRS. G.: I seen her *down* the well.

> [*Fairly long pause—*BERT *looks at* MR. D.]

BERT [*to* MRS. G.]: What of it?

MR. D.: What's she want?

GRANDPA: What's that? What's that?

MRS. G.: Can yers come over?

BERT [*to* MR. D.]: Down the *well*?

MR. D. [*incredulous*]: Funny thing ter me.

MRS. G.: Yair. Can yers come?

BERT [*looks at* MR. D.]: What can *we* do?

MRS. G.: I dunno. Somethin'. Get her out. Rope or somethin'.
  [BERT *looks at* MR. D. *A long pause.*]
GRANDPA: Down a well? What is? Where?
MRS. G.: Pull her up or something. I can't.
MR. D. [*to* BERT]: Where's *he*?
BERT: Who?
MR. D.: Him [*jerks head over right shoulder in direction of next door*].
BERT [*to* MR. D., *aside*]: Her old man? [*partly a question and partly
  "I see what you mean"*] [*To* MRS. G.] Where's yer old man?
MRS. G.: 'E's up Budrim.
  [*Run up and down the scale with repetitions of "Budrim".*]
BERT [*glancing at* MR. D.]: Up Budrim?
MR. D.: Budrim?
MRS. G.: Yair, he's up Budrim.
MR. D. [*to* BERT]: What's he doin' up Budrim?
BERT [*to* MRS. G.]: What's he doin' up Budrim?
MRS. G. [*louder, to* MR. D., *bending forward to see round door*]: 'E's
  pickin' beans.
BERT: Pickin' beans?
MRS. G.: Yair, up Budrim.
BERT [*to* MR. D.]: 'E's pickin' beans, up Budrim.
GRANDPA: Budrim? Budrim?
MR. D.: Budrim?
  [*Long pause.* BERT *looks at* MR. D. MR. D. *looks at* BERT. MRS. G.,
  *seen through door, shifts from one foot to the other, looking up
  at* BERT.]
GRANDPA: What's the matter? What yer say?
MRS. G.: 'Ow's she?
BERT: Aw, not too bad. Gettin' well. 'Ome one of these days.
GRANDPA: What well? What's down the well?
MRS. G.: Kids any bother—her away? Oughter send 'em over. I
  could look after 'em.
MR. D.: What's she say?
BERT: The kids.
  [THE TWO CHILDREN *look from* BERT *to* MR. D.—*giggle.* MR. D.
  makes vague threatening gesture at them.]
  [*To* MRS. G.] It's all right. They're all right.
MR. D.: Course they're all right. Why wouldn't they be all right?

[THE CHILDREN *giggle, and he makes a pseudo-threatening movement at them.*]

MRS. G.: I know. I just thought. It ain't the same—their own mother.

MR. D. [*raising voice and addressing her for first time*]: It's their own father lookin' after them.

MRS. G.: I know. It ain't the same, though. Their own mother. They take more notice.

BERT: They take notice. Never fear.

[THE CHILDREN *giggle—long pause.* BERT *shifts restlessly from one foot to another.* MRS. G. *looks away across at her own place— the direction in which* BERT *and* MR. D. *have nodded—scratches her left calf with heel of her right foot. Looks up at* BERT.]

MRS. G.: Well, yer comin?

[BERT *looks at* MR. D.]

MR. D.: What's that?

BERT: Wants to know if we're goin'.

MR. D.: Can't she see we're having somethin' to eat?

BERT: We're havin' dinner.

MRS. G.: I know. After.

MR. D.: How long she been down?

BERT: How long she been down?

GRANDPA: Down whose well?

MRS. G.: I dunno. Couldn't find her this mornin'. She ain't been milked.

MR. D.: Won't make that much difference—all she gives.

MRS. G.: Went ter pull a bucket a water. Water the cabbages. Bucket wouldn't go down. I takes a look. Real dark down there. Couldn't see at first. There she was: jammed like.

MR. D.: Still kickin?

BERT: Still alive?

MRS. G. [*leaning forward, to* MR. D.]: No.

BERT: Dead?

MRS. G.: No, not kickin'. Just standin' there.

BERT: Still alive?

MRS. G.: Yair. Yer comin'?

MR. D. [*to* BERT]: He's away?

BERT: Yair. Budrim.

[*Long pause.* BERT *looks at* MR. D. MR. D. *looks at* BERT. MRS. G. *looks up at* BERT *pleadingly.*]

GRANDPA: What's that? What yer say?

MR. D.: S'pose we'll have ter.

BERT: Bloomin' awkward—down a well.

MRS. G.: I know. She's our only milker.

MR. D. [*contemptuously*]: Milker! Huh! [BERT *looks at* MR. D.] S'pose we'll have ter. When we're finished.

BERT [*to* MRS. G.]: When we're finished. We'll be over. [*Returns to table.*]

MRS. G.: O.K. Thanks. Yer won't be long? [*Going off.*]

BILLY
SUSIE } [*together. Jumping up*]: We come too?

MR. D.: Yous just stay where y'are, see?

BILLY
SUSIE } : Aw, cripes!

SUSIE: Yer don't wanter get mixin' with them. We're different from the likes o' them.

BILLY: Well, Charlie—

BERT: Never you mind about Charlie.

BILLY: Well, cripes!

MR. D.: That'll do now. You stay here with yer grandad.

GRANDPA: Where yer goin? What's that?

MR. D. [*to* BERT]: Better go, I suppose.

BERT: Yair. Bloomin' awkward, down a well. [BERT *rises.*]

MR. D.: Gotter say grace, remember.

BERT: Yair. Nearly forgot again.

MR. D.: You say it.

BERT: Aw, I can't remember.

MR. D.: Go on. *He* said to. We all had to have a go.

BERT: But I can't remember.

MR. D.: You know. [*Slowly*] Oh Lord—what's it again?

BILLY: Oh Lord we thank you—

MR. D.: Thou.

BILLY: No, thee—

MR. D.: Yair, that's right—thee. [*To* BERT] You go on, you say it. Oh Lord, we thank thee . . .

BERT: Oh Lord, we thank thee—

217

MR. D.: For this, what is it?—your—no, thy bounty.

BERT: Thy bounty.

BILLY: What's bounty anyway?

BERT: Never mind about that. We thank thee for this thy bounty—

MR. D.: It means all this [*waves hands over table*]. All yer tucker, an' that. That's bounty. Yer gotter thank the Lord for all that.

BILLY: Well, the baker never left no bread.

MR. D.: Now you just be quiet.

BILLY: Well, he never.

MR. D.: That's different. This is religion. [*To* BERT] Go on.

BERT [*to* BILLY]: You shut up about the baker. [*Reaches over and pushes his head down into a prayerful attitude.*] For this thy bounty.
[BILLY *reaches out and sneaks piece of bread off* SUSIE'S *plate— she has head bowed and eyes closed—*BERT *without looking up reaches out and takes it from* BILLY.]

SUSIE: He took me piece.

MR. D.: Be quiet, I tell yer.

BILLY [*to* MR. D., *pointing to* BERT]: Well, he's taken it now.
[BERT *is undecided what to do with bread; then puts it in his own mouth.*]

MR. D.: Will yers be quiet? [*To* BERT] Go on.

BERT [*mouth full*]: I can't remember the rest.

MR. D.: Oh, well, that'll do I suppose.

BERT [*rather eagerly—more at home with a cow in the well than with grace*]: Yair. Cow down the well and all.
[*They rise.*]

MR. D. [*to* CHILDREN]: You kids stay with yer grandad. And yer'd better look at yer lessons. Preacher'll be here any day now. [*To* BERT] Yer got the contribution, have yer?

BERT: Yair. Up on the dresser [*jerks head toward dresser*]. Not the lot. Couple more bob wanted.

MR. D.: Might have that be the time he comes. Well, come on then. [*Goes to back door. Takes battered hat from peg beside door. Goes off down steps.*]

GRANDPA: What's that? Where yer goin.?
[BERT, *about to follow* MR. D., *turns back, goes to stove. Takes a piece of wood from wood-box. Opens door of stove (drop-type) with piece of wood. Looks in at fire. Throws piece of wood back in*

wood-box and gets bigger piece. Puts kettle to one side. Closes stove-door with kick from right foot (bare) placing one hand on back of GRANDPA'S *chair to keep balance. Makes a face and rubs right foot against back of left leg. Goes to back door. Takes hat from peg. Follows* MR. D. *down back steps.*]

[CHILDREN *jump up from table to watch them.* MR. D. *and* BERT *can be seen first through back door, going out through back gate; then they turn right toward well.* CHILDREN *leave window and go to back door.* MR. D. *and* BERT *can then be seen through window, going across paddock.* CHILDREN *dive for dresser, pull out packet of mixed fruit and each take a handful. Cram it in their mouths. Giggle.*]

What yer say? Where yer goin'?

(*End of Scene*)

ACT ONE

scene 2

The well on the farm next door. A well with two-handled windlass, a butcher's gallows. Some dead trees. MRS. GRANT, *kneeling down, peering into well, with both hands shading her eyes. Enter* MR. DILLON *and* BERT *in front of gallows.*

MRS. G. [*looking up*]: I can just see her. It's that dark.

MR. D. [*kneeling shading eyes like* MRS. G. *and peering down*]: She in the water?

BERT: Might as well go home, she is.

MRS. G.: No, there's a stagin', sort of. She's on that, I think.

MR. D.: I can just see 'er.

BERT [*shading eyes*]: I can't.

MRS. G.: It's dark at first. Yer get uster it.

MR. D.: Yes, I can see her. Looks all right.

BERT: What depth is there?—water?

MRS. G.: Not much. Six feet or somethin'. Don't make much, in the winter.

BERT [*to* MR. D.]: Can't be on the main stream.

MR. D. [*to* BERT]: A soak I s'pose. I always reckoned he'd never get water here.

BERT [*peering down*]: I can see her. She's on the stagin', she's all right, I think.

MRS. G.: Hope she is. Other one went dry on us. Ted'll be crook we lose her.

MR. D.: Pity he wasn't home himself. Don't see what we can do.

MRS. G.: He's pickin' beans. Up Budrim.

MR. D. [*looking round contemptuously at barren surroundings*]: Enough for him to do at home, I'd say.

MRS. G. [*pleadingly*]: But yer'll have a go, won't yers? Have ter do something. Our only milker.

MR. D. [*to* BERT]: What can *we* do?

MRS. G.: He had ter go bean-pickin', the way things was. We never done no good outer the potatoes. [*Looks vaguely over right shoulder in direction of potato patch.*] You know how it is.

MR. D.: Oh, how do I know? [*To* BERT] What d'yer think?

BERT [*doubtfully*]: If we could get a rope round her. [*Looks up at windlass, across at gallows, taking stock of the situation. Reaches out and shakes upright of windlass to test its strength.*]

MRS. G. [*peering down well*]: If it hadn't been for the stagin'.

MR. D. [*peering down*]: The stagin!

MRS. G.: He put it in when the water dropped back, last winter. He was gointer put in a drive. Get more water.

MR. D. [*contemptuously*]: He was gointer?

MRS. G.: Yairs.

MR. D.: A drive?

MRS. G.: Yairs.

MR. D.: But he never?

MRS. G.: No, he never.

MR. D. [*to* BERT *contemptuously*]: He was gointer put in a drive.

BERT [*to* MR. D.]: Yair. Gointer—but he never. [*Shakes windlass again.*]

[MRS. G. *looks up at windlass.* MR. D. *and* BERT *look up at windlass.*]

MR. D. [*to* BERT]: What yer think?

BERT: What'd she go, cow that size? Four or five hundred? [*Looks up at windlass again*] Not a hope with the windlass. Bloomin' awkward.

MR. D.: Yair. It's awkward.

MRS. G.: *He* was here, I wouldn't mind so much. It's him bein' away.

MR. D.: Yairs. If he was here. But he ain't.

MRS. G.: She had ter pick now to go an' do it.

MR. D.: He had ter pick now to be away, you mean.

MRS. G.: We lost her, I dunno what he'd say. But *I* couldn't help it. I couldn't find her this mornin' when I went ter milk her. I sent the boy out lookin' for her. He ain't back yet, and her here all the time.

[*Long pause. They all look vaguely round as if for inspiration.*]

BERT: Well, what we gointer do?

MR. D. [*looking at windlass*]: Windlass won't hold her.

BERT: Haveter rig a sheerlegs.

MR. D. [*to* MRS. G.]: You got a rope? This won't do [*indicating light half-inch rope on windlass for pulling bucket up*].

MRS. G.: Rope? I dunno, I think so. Might be in the shed [*looks toward house*]. Yair, that's right. A rope. He was gointer use it if he'd put the drive in.

BERT: Yairs, if . . .

MR. D.: That oughter do.

MRS. G.: I'll go an' see. [*Goes off in direction of house.*] Won't be long.

MR. D. [*looking round*]: Bean-pickin'. Cripes. An' look at the way things are. [*Looks at old spring-cart off-stage.*] Look at his cart there out in the open.

BERT: Been a good cart that. [*Goes over and inspects it.*] Wheels still sound, too. Just gointer ruin.

MR. D.: Yair. If there was more work and less politics he mighter got somewhere.

BERT: Yair. And we wouldn't be here pullin' his cow outer the well.

MR. D.: We ain't pulled it out yet, neither. I still don't know how we're gointer do it.

BERT: Why not tell her to send up to Budrim for him?

MR. D.: Oh, we'll have to do something! I s'pose.

BERT: Yair. But what?

MR. D. [*looking at gallows*]: Ain't that a pulley-block on them old gallows?

BERT [*looking*]: Yair, that's right.

MR. D.: What'd he use the gallows for?

BERT: Coupla winters back. You remember. He started killin' his own beef. Tried to sell us some, you remember?

MR. D.: Yair, that's right.

BERT: Police stopped him or somethin'. Butcher put him in, I think. Killin' without a licence. [*Goes over to gallows.*] Here's another block on the ground. This'll do.

MR. D.: Yair. That and the rope.

BERT [*coming back with pulley-block*]: Leaves his gear all over the place.

MR. D. [*goes over to sheet of corrugated iron. Lifts it with his foot*]: Here's a rope under here.

BERT: Any good?

MR. D. [*picking up coil of hemp rope*]: Been lyin' there in the wet, that's all. Ain't hardly been used, I'd say.

BERT: Bloke like him oughtn't to have anythin' good, leaving it lyin' about like that.

MR. D. [*examining the rope*]: Still a good rope, if it was looked after.

BERT: Bet he don't know what he's got and what he ain't got.

[MR. D. *and* BERT *look significantly at each other.*]

MR. D.: I remember now, he bought it at Atkinson's sale. Gave thirty bob for it.

BERT: And then never used it. That's goin' on eighteen months ago. Left around to go rotten.

MR. D.: That'll be the rope she's lookin' for?

BERT: Could be . . . Here she comes now. Hasn't got any rope neither.

MRS. G. [*coming on*]: Couldn't find it. Ain't in the shed. A new rope too, as good as, I remember.

MR. D. [*holding up rope*]: This it?

MRS. G. [*going over*]: Must be I think. Yair, that'll be it. Where was it? It's all right, ain't it? [*Examines rope.*]

MR. D.: Aw, it'll do. That an' the pulley block.

BERT: If we can wind her up someways. [*Looks at windlass.*]

HERBIE [*off*]: Hey, Ma.

[MR. D. *and* BERT *look up.* MRS. G. *stands peering down well.*]
[*Off. Impatiently*] Hey, Ma.

MRS. G. [*half turning*]: Shut up.

MR. D. [*to* MRS. G.]: What about sendin' for him?

MRS. G.: Ted? Up Budrim? But I ain't got no one ter send. He couldn't get back till tomorrow anyway. Can't yers do somethin'? The rope's just about new.

HERBIE [*off. More impatiently*]: Hey, Ma-a-a-a.

MRS. G.: Shut up, I tell yer.

HERBIE [*off*]: Who's goiner milk this cow?

[MR. D., BERT, MRS. G., *look at each other. Pause.*]

MRS. G.: What cow?

HERBIE [*off*]: Our cow, a course.

MRS. G.: Milk her? She's down the well.

HERBIE [*off*]: The well? [*Pause.*] What d'yer mean, down the well?

I got her here in the yard.

[MR. D., BERT, MRS. G. *look at one another, then peer down well, then look at one another again.*]

HERBIE [*coming on*]: What d'yer mean, down the well? I found her on the reserve. The back fence's down.

[MR. D. *kneels down, shades his eyes with hands as before.* BERT *likewise. They look up and stare at one another.*]

MRS. G. [*to* HERBIE]: There's a cow down the well.

HERBIE: Down the well? How'd she get down there? It ain't ours. I got her in the yard.

[MR. D. *and* BERT *peer down again and look up at one another.*] Whose cow is it?

MR. D.
BERT } [*together*]: It's *our* cow.

[*Long pause.*]

MRS. G.: What d'yer mean, it's your cow? [*Peers down well.*]

MR. D.
BERT } [*together*]: It's our cow.

BERT [*peering down*]: It's Daisy. I can tell by the horns.

MRS. G.: Down our well?

[*They all look blankly at one another.*]

How'd she get there?

HERBIE: Come through the fence, I s'pose, like she done before.

MRS. G.: Through the fence?

BERT: The fence?

MR. D.: Oh, the fence!

[*They all look vaguely in direction of dividing fence.*]

MRS. G.: Down our well?

MR. D.: Through the fence—and down the well!

BERT: Down the well!

[*They all peer down the well, then look at one another.*]

MRS. G. [*suddenly realizing implications of this changed situation*]: Well, what about yers gettin' her out of our well?

MR. D.: We'll get her out, don't you worry.

MRS. G.: Yers had better, and pretty quick too.

MR. D.: D'yer think we're gointer leave her there? Cow down a well? Our only milker?

BERT: I'll whip over to Smithy's. Get his truck. Soon pull her out, the pulley-block and the rope.

MRS. G.: Yer'd better too. He comes home and finds her there, there'll be trouble. Cow down our well.

MR. D.: Trouble! I know who'll make the trouble. The fence was fixed, she wouldn't be down the well.

MRS. G.: The fence?

MR. D.: Yair, the fence. I've spoken to him often enough about it—about doin' it up. Yer poddies was through again this mornin'!

MRS. G.: Ah! So that's how one of them got his leg torn? Yer been puttin' the dog on them?

MR. D. [to BERT]: We never put the dog on them, did we?

BERT: No, I never even seen them.

MRS. G.: Yer never seen them, how d'yer know they was in your place?

BERT: Kids seen 'em, that's how.

MRS. G.: *He* reckons he'll shoot that dog, he sees it onter them poddies.

MR. D.: Two can play at that game, he'll soon find out. You keep yer poddies out of our place, that's all.

MRS. G.: And what about our well? That cow dies down there, what we gointer do for water? When Ted hears about it—

MR. D.: Yers oughter have yer well covered. Shouldn't be open like that.

MRS. G.: Course we had ter leave it open. How we gointer pull water outer it, it ain't open?

MR. D.: Open well—kids mighter fallen down it.

MRS. G.: Our kids never come near it.

MR. D.: Not talkin' about your kids, talkin' about ours.

MRS. G.: Your kids been over here, have they? What they doin' here?

MR. D. [hastily]: Course they ain't been over here.

MRS. G.: Yer just said they had.

MR. D.: I never did. They never been over here. What'd they wanter come over here for?

MRS. G.: They never come over, how they gointer fall down the well?

MR. D.: Well, they never been over here, that's all.

MRS. G.: You keep them away from here, then. An' another thing we don't want that Charlie of yours hangin' round, neither.

MR. D. [*indignantly*]: Him hangin' round! Her stringin' him on, yer mean.

MRS. G.: Stringin' him on! You let Ted hear yer say that!

MR. D.: I'll let him hear me, don't you worry.

MRS. G.: She's a good girl, none better. It's him leadin' her astray.

MR. D. [*laugh of scorn*]: Astray! Huh!

MRS. G.: If anythin' happens to that girl of mine . . .

MR. D.: What d'yer mean, if anythin' happens?

MRS. G. [*looking quickly at* BERT]: Never you mind what I mean. You'll have Ted to deal with, anythin' happens. You stop your Charlie hangin' round, that's all. An what about this cow?

MR. D.: Yair. We lose that cow, somebody's gointer pay for it.

MRS. G.: Don't you worry, *he*'ll have somethin' ter say about payin' when he comes home.

BERT [*jerking thumb down well*]: Look the sooner she ain't down there any longer the better.

MR. D.: Yair. You whip over and get Smithy's truck. I'll slip home and get a coupla corn sacks. Have ter make a sling.

BERT [*going off back left*]: And fetch the axe. Haveter rig up a sheer-legs. Haveter knock down a coupla saplin's, three saplin's.

MR. D. [*going off back right*]: Yair, I'll get the axe.

MRS. G. [*hands on hips, looking defiantly after them*]: Don't you go choppin' down our saplings. You chop down yer own saplings. It's your cow.

(*End of Act One*)

ACT TWO

scene 1

Kitchen on Grant's farm. Similar to previous scene—bare table, plain kitchen dresser, plain chairs, stove recess. Window on each side of door. Pair of gumboots beside door. Fishing rod against wall near dresser. Wooden form along one side of table. (Any small details to differentiate set from the one used previously.)

MRS. G. *is stirring saucepan on stove.*

DICK HARRISON [*off*]: Yer there, Ted? [*Comes to back door.*] Hullo Missus. How are you? [*Enters, hanging hat on peg beside door in familiar manner—bicycle clips on trousers.*]

MRS. G. [*looking round*]: That you, Dick?

DICK: Yairs. How are yer? [*Without waiting for reply*] Ted back?

MRS. G.: Yair. Having a shave. [*Calls out*] Hey, Ted.

TED [*through open door of room off*]: That you Dick? [*Comes to door holding safety razor, face lathered on one side.*]

DICK: Meself, entirely. How's things? Got back, eh?

TED: Yairs. Just a while ago. Just doin' a bit of scrub fallin'.

MRS. G.: Didn't he need it, too. Bet he hasn't had a shave since he's been away.

TED: Yair. Hadter have one soon as I got home. Missus goes crook on me. Says I ain't shaved—you know how it is. [*Hand to side of his mouth and a lewd wink at* DICK. *Then looks sideways at* MRS. G.]

DICK [*laughing*]: I got a fair idea.

MRS. G. [*turns to stove*]: Aw, you men.
  [DICK *laughs and sits down at table.*]
  [*To* TED] You go walkin' about shavin' you'll cut yerself, that's what you'll do.

DICK: Better buy 'im an electric razor for his birthday, Missus.

MRS. G. [*wryly*]: Yair, and buy meself a Jaguar the same time.

DICK: That'll be the day.

227

TED: Somebody gave me a Jaguar I'd have ter get the free air on credit. [*Going back into room*] Won't be a minute.

DICK [*laughing as he speaks loudly to* TED, *in room*]: Things ain't that bad are they? How'd yer get on after I seen yer? Did he come good?

TED [*off*]: Yair, after we shoved a gun in his ribs.

DICK: That's the lurk. Bore it into 'em. He paid up, eh?

TED [*comes to door, chin held high, shaving (upstroke) under chin. Speaks from corner of mouth*]: Yair. I was a bit gallied at the last, though. Reckoned he was gointer see the C.P.S. before he paid us. See what the award said. [*Goes back into room.*]

DICK: He was only bluffin'. Anyway, yer got it? For the time we took off for the meetin' too?

TED [*coming on, drying his face on a none too clean towel*]: Yair, the lot. Had ter stand him up though. Told him he never paid up we'd get the others to walk off. They hadn't finished the rest of the beans.

DICK: Beans was still toppin' the market too. He wouldn't wanter miss the good prices.

TED: No, we had him where we wanted him. [*Moves to stove and hangs towel on nail on wall.*]

DICK: Good work. Tactics. That's the lurk. Wait till yer got 'em in a jam. Their pockets—that's where it hurts 'em, lousy cows.

MRS. G.: Hurts us, sometimes, too.

TED [*slaps her affectionately on the backside*]: What's crawlin' on yer, Missus? We never stood up ter the plutocrats, where'd we be today? [*Sits at table.*]

MRS. G. [*glancing round kitchen, shrugs shoulders*]: Me, I wouldn't know.

DICK: Don't sling in yer alley, missus. There's a good time comin'. It's the likes of us'll be runnin' the show, one of these days.

MRS. G. [*resignedly*]: Oh well. Yous two gointer have a cup of tea?

TED [*to* DICK]: Can yer stay?

DICK: Yair. [*To* MRS. G.] Don't mind if I do. May as well have as good a time as we can till the good time comes. [*Realizing that woman isn't entering into the spirit of the thing, tries to jolly her.*] You'll be dressed in silks and satins then, Missus, and servants to wait on the ting ting ting.

MRS. G.: I don't want no servants. Wouldn't know what to say to them.

TED: You'll soon find out when the time comes. [*To* DICK] Won't she? An' what about our psalm singin' friends next door. Where will they come in?

DICK: Them? It's the likes of them stops us from getting anywhere, with their Jesus-loves-us and everythin'll be right in the next world. Always cryin' about their sins.

MRS. G.: Their sins—

DICK: Sins. We'll give 'em somethin' better than sins to think about, won't we Ted?

TED: Too right. We'll—we'll—

DICK: I know what we'll do with them. Stick 'em on the shit-cart. [*Laughs apologetically*] Sorry Missus.

[TED *laughs and looks at* MRS. G.—*she turns to the stove and pretends not to notice.* TED *winks at* DICK.]

TED [*covering up for* DICK]: Well what about this cup a tea, Missus?

MRS. G. [*pours water into teapot*]: Ain't done any bakin'. Didn't expect yer back till tomorrow. And I had a bit of bother yesterday. Tell yer about it after. [*Puts teapot on table. Goes over to dresser for cups and saucers.*]

TED: Bother? What d'yer mean, bother?

MRS. G. [*putting cups and saucers from dresser on table*]: Oh nothin'. [*To* DICK] The milk's hangin' outside in the cool.

DICK [*rising*]: I'll get it. [*Goes out through back door.*]

TED [*to* MRS. G.]: What bother?

MRS. G.: Oh, them [*nodding her head towards next-door neighbours— pouring three cups of tea*].

TED: That psalm-singing mob! We don't want anything to do with them. What they been thinkin' up?

MRS. G.: They never thought it up. Not this time. Just happened.

TED: What?

[DICK *returns.*]

MRS. G. [*to* TED *aside*]: Tell yer after. [*To* DICK] Bread's in the dresser there.

DICK [*putting billy on table*]: Cow's still givin' a bit a juice anyway. [*Goes over to dresser.*]

MRS. G. [*to* DICK *at dresser*]: Jam too. [*Answering his remark*] Yair, but I thought she wasn't gointer.

[DICK *puts jam and bread on table. Glass jar with sugar already on table. Sits down.*]

TED: Why, what happened?

[DICK *and* TED *take noisy gulps of tea.*]

MRS. G.: Oh, nothin', the way it worked out. I thought somethin' was gointer though.

TED [*to* DICK, *impatiently—but don't overdo it at this point. Reserve anger for later*]: Christ! If wimmin ain't mysterious. Bit of trouble, no trouble, coulda been this, coulda been that.

[MRS. G. *goes over to stove, puts piece of wood on fireplace—puts kettle to one side.*]

[*Seeing she isn't going to respond, and so changing subject*] Where's Mary?

[MRS. G. *moves saucepan from side of stove onto fire. Lifts lid, looks in, gives contents a stir. Puts lid back. Puts spoon on top of it. Stands there back to men, hand resting on mantelpiece.*]

Where'd yer say Mary was?

MRS. G. [*over her shoulder*]: She's around. Feedin' fowls or somethin'. Mrs. Johnson didn't want her today. Gone down to Brissie for a couple days.

DICK: Some people have it pretty smooth, don't they?

TED: Yer tellin' me.

MRS. G. [*over her shoulder*]: Had ter go down—see the doctor.

TED [*contemptuously*]: Mrs. J.? Nerves! That's all she's got. What about yer cup a tea? Gettin' cold.

MRS. G. [*without turning, one hand still on mantlepiece, head resting lightly on right arm*]: Have it in a minute.

DICK: She's lucky ter be able ter afford nerves. [*Laughing*] I can't.

TED [*glancing at woman and seeing she's not very responsive tries to jolly her*]: No more can you, can yer, Missus?

[MRS. G. *doesn't answer for a moment.* DICK *glances enquiringly at* TED.]

MRS. G. [*without turning, and in a flat expressionless voice*]: Can I what?

TED [*laughingly*]: Afford ter have nerves.

[MRS. G. *doesn't answer. Her left hand—closest to audience—comes down and clutches corner of apron.*]

[*Looking at* MRS. G.—*blundering on*] Can yer?

[*No answer*—DICK *looks from* TED *to* MRS. G.]

[*General effect of silence and looks is to "spotlight"* MRS. G.]

MRS. G. [*suddenly*]: Yous two can look after yerselves. [*Goes quickly across room to bedroom, face averted from men, showing to audience, on verge of tears. Enters bedroom, shuts door.*]

TED [*looking after her, bewildered*]: Well, for Christ sake!

DICK [*quickly gulping down last of his tea—rising*]: Well, look it was just about the meeting Saturday I wanted ter see yer. Yer'll be there all right?

TED [*absently, still looking at bedroom door*]: Saturday? Yair, that's jake.

DICK [*with slight change of manner and an abrupt business-like rather domineering political organizer kind of voice*]: And be sure and get the others. I seen the blokes at the mill. They'll all be along. [*Goes to back door and reaches for hat*] How yer comin' in?

TED [*turning to him at last*]: Comin' in? Oh, Robinson's car, I s'pose.

DICK [*with air of arranging details*]: That's right. There'll be four of yer.

TED: Three. Arty always goes fishin' Saturday. [*Looks back at bedroom door.*]

DICK: Fishin! With a meetin' on! He better pull up his socks, he wants any jam on his bread. Anyway, that'll be three of yer. Yers can all dub in. Won't cost that much. If things go our way at the meetin', might be able ter pay for the car outer kitty. If we get that motion through. That's the main thing. Oughter have things all our way, if we get a good roll-up. And look, another thing.

TED [*looking at bedroom door, vaguely*]: What's that? [*Not a specific question, just a sort of "were you saying something?"*]

DICK [*glances at bedroom door, with a slight grin—a bachelor amused at troubles of married man*]: Oh, never mind. [*Going off*] See yer Saturday.

TED [*turning and looking after him*]: That's right, yair. Saturday; the motion, yairs. [*Gets up, goes to back door. Looks after* DICK. *Comes back and stands at table for a moment, looking at bedroom door uncertainly. Goes toward bedroom door. Stops as he puts hand toward door knob. Looks back at table. Goes back to table. Picks up his half-*

emptied cup of tea. Goes over and pours it into sink. Puts cup and saucer down on bench beside sink. Hesitates, goes back to table. Does same with DICK'S *half-empty cup. Picks up* MRS. G.'S *untouched cup of tea, hesitates, puts it down again, covers it with saucer. Does all this clumsily, evidently not used to it. Hesitates again. Goes back to table. Looks at bedroom door again, not sure what to do. Wavers between sink and table for a moment, then puts bread and butter away in dresser. Hesitates. Goes toward bedroom door. Puts hand quietly on door knob. Looks back at table then at sink. Goes over to sink, rinse: cups and saucers under tap. Looks uncertainly round for tea-towel. At last sees it hanging over stove. Takes it down, dries cups and saucers clumsily. Puts them back on bench beside sink. Slings tea-towel on rail over stove with an impatient gesture that says "well, that's done". Turns away, then turns back; takes down tea-towel, folds it neatly twice lengthways, then hangs it carefully over rail, making sure that ends are even. Turns uncertainly and looks at bedroom door.]*

[MARY *enters by back door. Bare feet. Faded floral cotton dress, old hat of her father's. Tear in crown, hair showing through. General impression of beauty in rags.*]

[TED *starts guiltily.*]

MARY: Hullo, you got back?

TED: Yair, while ago.

MARY [*looking round from table to stove to sink*]: Where's [*hesitates*] . . . where's Mum?

TED [*looks helplessly at bedroom door*]: In there.

MARY [*looking at bedroom door, then at her father*]: She all right?

TED: Course she is. Leastways, I s'pose she is. I dunno. I just come home.

[MARY *looks from him to door.*]

Why?

MARY: Why what?

TED: Why'd yer ask?

MARY [*dodging the point*]: Ask what?

TED: She all right? Expect her ter be crook, or somethin'?

MARY [*hesitates*]: Aw, no.

TED [*slightly impatient*]: Why'd yer ask then?

MARY: What's she doin' in there?

TED: How do I know? Gettin' dressed I s'pose. [*A bit more im-*

patiently] Why?

MARY: Aw, nothin'.

TED [*flaring up*]: For Christ sake! Man comes home and it's trouble this and trouble that, and nothin' this and nothin' that. Man'll go crackers.

MARY: Well, you needn't all pick on me.

TED: Who's pickin' on yer?

[*No answer.*]

Who's pickin' on yer?

[*No answer.*]

[*Jerks his thumb at his chest*] Am I pickin' on yer? [*Pause.*] [*Jerks thumb at bedroom door*] Is she pickin' on yer?

MARY: Yes.

TED: She is?

MARY: Yes.

TED: What's she pickin' on yer for?

[MARY *suddenly flings herself down at table, buries her head in her arms, and bursts into tears.*]

[*Picking up chair by back and slamming it down on floor*] For Christ's sake. What are you blubberin' for?

[*No answer.*]

What's this about her pickin' on yer?

[*No answer.*]

What's she pickin' on yer for? Come on, what's it all about?

MARY [*half raises tear-stained face*]: Never you mind. [*Drops head in arms again.*]

TED: A man had any bloody sense he'd be in the madhouse. [*Stands with hands on back of chair, gazing down angrily at* MARY.]

[*Bedroom door opens.* MRS. G. *comes out, wiping eyes.*]

[*Wheeling around, pointing at* MARY] What's all this about?

[MRS. G. *doesn't answer. Goes over to stove. Lowers stove-door with corner of sugar-bag apron, looks at fire, closes door— watched in silence by* TED. *Lifts lid off saucepan and gives contents a stir with big spoon on side of stove. Puts back lid sideways on so it won't boil over. Puts saucepan to side of stove. Goes to table, still followed by* TED'S *angry glare. Takes her cup to sink, empties it. Rinses it out, dries with tea-towel. Flings tea-towel carelessly back over rail, spreads it out carefully to dry but with edges uneven. (Everything that* TED *did was wrong.) Gathers up cups and saucers—her own and those that* TED *had left on sink—and puts them carefully away in kitchen dresser. Looks round kitchen to see if anything else wants doing. Goes over to* MARY. TED *looking from one to the other in angry silence. Puts her hand on* MARY'S *shoulder.* MARY *shrugs it off.*]

MRS. G. [*to* MARY]: You'd better go and lie down.

[MARY *gets up, face covered with one arm. Goes to bedroom door on opposite side to other bedroom. Goes in and closes door behind her, watched by* MRS. G. *and* TED.]

[MRS. G. *looks round room again—goes to her bedroom door. Enters, closes door behind her.*]

[TED *looks, bewildered, from one door to other. Picks up chair by back again. Slams it down on floor. Stamps to back door, wrenches hat off peg, jams it on head. Gives a last angry look at closed bedroom door. Goes off down back steps.*]

(*End of Scene*)

ACT TWO

scene 2

Kitchen of Grant family. Late Saturday night. MRS. GRANT *seated at table (centre) lit by pressure lamp. Hurricane lamp (not alight) beside door, rear centre.* MRS. GRANT *dressed slightly better than previously. Has on pair plain spectacles, is doing fancy work, open flat (no handle) work-basket (or box) on table beside her. Glances up, while still going on with her fancy work, at (cheap) clock on kitchen mantelpiece over stove, which is alight. Holds up fancy work and looks at it in lamplight. Rummages in work-box for another coloured thread. Sound of car horn tooting (off). She glances at clock again. Sound of car engine revving up and moving off.*

VOICES [*off*]: Goodnight, Ted.

VOICES [*off*]: 'night.

VOICES [*off*]: 'night.

[MRS. G. *gets up. Takes off spectacles, puts fancy work and spectacles down on basket. Goes to stove. Lifts stove-lid and puts kettle on open fire to boil.* TED *comes up back steps, carrying sugar bag in one hand. He is dressed for "going out", white cotton open-neck shirt, no tie, not very new hat, odd trousers and coat.*]

MRS. G. [*still at stove, back to* TED, *over shoulder*]: Late, ain't yer?

TED [*coming up to table—rather tersely*]: Late? No. Same as usual.

[MRS. G., *without speaking, glances quickly sideways at him over her shoulder, trying to gauge his mood — nothing specific or dramatic about this, just a husband-wife interchange.* TED *puts bag down on floor at end of table. Clink of bottles. Takes off his coat, working his shoulders as though glad to be rid of it, and slings it over back of a chair. Takes off hat, puts it on corner of table (important).* MRS. G. *goes over, picks up coat and hangs it coathanger fashion on back of chair.*]

MRS. G.: Goner have a bit of supper?

TED [*takes bottle of beer out of bag puts on table*]: No, I'm right.

[Takes out another bottle.] Got this. *[Takes crab out of bag. Slings bag in corner beside dresser. Puts crab down on work basket.]*

MRS. G.: Oh, look out!

TED: Why, what?

MRS. G. *[picking up crab]*: Not on me fancywork!

TED: Fancy work! All right, put it there on the table. *[Looks at basket.]* What fancy work? *[Sits down facing footlights.]*

MRS. G.: Oh, just somethin' I'm doin'. *[Picks up work-basket and puts it on chair, down-stage of table so that it is in full view of audience.]* How'd it go?

TED: Meetin'? All right. Had it all our own way. Trust Dick for that. *[Gets up and gets enamel mug from dresser. Gets opener out of dresser drawer, opens bottle and pours out mugful.]* Goiner have some?

　[MRS. G. shakes head, no, and makes a moue.]

　[TED drinks it up in one gulp. Refills mug.] What's this about fancy work?

MRS. G.: Just a tray-cloth I'm doin'.

TED: Traycloth! Cripes. Gettin' flash, ain't we? How come?

MRS. G.: Mary showed one I'd done ter Mrs. Johnson. One I done before we was married. She reckoned it was good enough to win in the Show. Thought I'd do another.

　[TED goes silent at mention of MARY. Takes another pull at mug of beer. Reaches out and pulls a leg off the crab. Sits with leg of crab in hand, frowning and staring ahead of him. MRS. G. glances enquiringly at him. Goes to stove. Puts kettle to one side. Puts lid on stove. Glances again at TED.]

TED *[without looking up]*: Where is she?

MRS. G. *[hesitates]*: Who?

TED *[looking up]*: Mary.

MRS. G.: Over Mrs. Johnson's. Got her to sleep there for a couple of nights. Ain't too good.

TED: Who ain't?

MRS. G.: *She* ain't—Mrs. Johnson. Got ter see the Doctor again next week.

　[TED starts to shell crab-leg, takes a bite, then long silence as he looks broodingly before him again.]

Mary wants ter leave her. Get another job.

236

TED [*rather ominously*]: Does she? Why?

MRS. G.: I dunno. Sick of it—I s'pose. I dunno.

TED: Yer don't know? [*Pause.*] I do.

MRS. G.: Know what?

TED [*looking at* MRS. G.]: Why she wants ter leave.

MRS. G. [*still at stove, looking at* TED. *Hesitates*]: Why?

TED [*with suppressed violence*]: *You* know why?

MRS. G. [*looks anxiously at him*]: What d'yer mean? I know?

TED: Course yer know.

    [MRS. G. *takes down kitchen clock and winds it. Puts it back on mantelpiece.*]

TED: It's fast. Quarter've an hour.

    [MRS. G. *takes down clock again, turns hands back. Puts clock back on mantelpiece.*]

TED [*staring ahead, brooding again*]: Man bein' made a bloody fool of. [*Pause.*]

MRS. G.: What d'yer mean?

TED: Mean? They're all talkin' about it.

    [*Pause.*]

MRS. G.: About what?

TED: About him [*jerks head in direction of next door farm*] and her.

MRS. G.: Him and her? Who's talkin'?

    [*Pause.*]

TED: Makin' a fool of a man behind his back.

MRS. G. [*glancing at him, trying to weigh the situation up*]: Why, what happened?

TED: Happened? We comes outer the meetin' and that big yob Clarrie James sings out in front of the mob, "What's this about yer matin' up with them holy Joes out your way, Ted?" The mob laughs of course. Tryin' to make a fool of a man. I soon shut him up.

MRS. G. [*hesitates*]: What'd he mean?

TED: That's what I didn't know at first. Dick wised me up after. Seems she's been goin' inter the pictures with him. You know about it?

MRS. G.: With who?

TED [*jerks his head in direction of next door*]: Him. Their Charlie. You know about it?

[*Long pause.* MRS. G. *avoids looking at him.*]

TED: Well, *did* you know about it?

[*Pause.*]

MRS. G.: Yair. Had a go at her over it. Had a go at them, too [*jerks head in direction of next door*]. When they was gettin' the cow outer the well. Told him we didn't want his Charlie hangin' round.

TED: Had a go at her, did yer? That what she meant th' other day about you pickin' on her?

MRS. G. [*hesitating*]: Yair that an'—different things.

TED [*suspiciously*]: What things? What she start cryin' like that for?

MRS. G. [*heading him off*]: I told them to keep their cow off our place, and their Charlie too.

TED: I'd better look if they done any damage to the well, gettin' the cow out. What'd they do with the rope?

MRS. G.: I dunno. I never thought. I never stayed, after I said about their Charlie hangin' round. He went crook. Said it was her leadin' him on.

TED: Her? Leading *him* on? I'll take the gun to him, I see him hangin' round. When's she comin' home? I'll have a word with her, too. She knows well enough I won't have any of us mixin' with the likes of them. Makin' a fool of a man in front of the mob. D'you know how they been goin' inter the pictures?

MRS. G.: I never asked her.

TED: Robinson's car. Where'd he get the money, I'd like ter know? Pinchin' it off his boss, more'n likely.

MRS. G.: Robinson tell you they went in his car?

TED: Yair. They was muggin' up in the back seat.

MRS. G.: Muggin' up? He tell yer? Pity he couldn't mind his own business.

TED: I asked him. After what Dick told me. They all knew about it. Makin' a man look like a bloody fool. [*Pause.*] Anyway, what was she cryin' about the other day? Wasn't only you pickin' on her about that. What d'yer mean, different things?

MRS. G.: Oh, just somethin' we was talkin' about.

TED [*suspiciously*]: What was yer talkin' about?

[*Pause.*]

MRS. G. [*goes to stove, opens it, looks in to make sure fire is out. With back to him*]: I just wondered, that was all.

[*Pause.*]

TED: Wondered?

MRS. G.: Well, it was on account of her bein' out with him—gettin' home late an' that.

TED: After the pictures?

MRS. G.: Other times too. While you been away.

TED: Other times? So they ain't only been goin' to the pictures?

MRS. G.: No, other times too.

TED [*thinks this over for a while*]: And what was you wonderin' about?

MRS. G.: Oh, nothin'. Things didn't seem ter be goin' right, that was all.

TED: Not goin' right?

MRS. G.: Yair.

TED: How, not goin' right?

MRS. G.: Oh well, I may be wrong. P'raps it's all right. It was just— her wantin' to leave Mrs. Johnson's.

TED: Why did she want to leave?

MRS. G.: She said—she was all worked up—didn't know what she was sayin'.

[*Pause.*]

TED: What'd she say?

MRS. G. [*pause*]: She wanted—ter get married.

TED: *What*? Married?

MRS. G.: Yair.

TED: To get *married*?

MRS. G.: Yair.

TED [*incredulously*]: Did she say she want to—to—? Who'd she want to get married to?

[*Pause.*]

MRS. G.: Him [*jerks her head toward next door*].

TED: Him!

MRS. G.: Yair.

TED: Their Charlie, yer mean?

MRS. G.: Yair.

TED: That psalm-singin' mob! Them! To him! Does she think I'll let her get—us gettin'—her gettin'—the likes of us gettin' mixed up with *them*? You can tell her from me—

MRS. G.: You can tell her. I had my go.

TED [*glares across the table*]: She thinks she's gointer make that sorter fool of me in front of the mob—Clarrie James an' them—you had a go at her?

MRS. G.: Yair. I just told yer.

TED: What'd she say?

[MRS. G. *shrugs her shoulders.*]

[*Glaring across table, speaking to himself*] Married! That mob! Makin' a bloody fool of a man. [*Violently to* MRS. G.] Well, you can tell her from me—

MRS. G.: You tell her.

TED: Anyway, what put it into her head—gettin' married? A kid her age? Why she ain't [*pause—suddenly suspicious*]. What d'yer mean, married? Why she wanter get married?

[MRS. G. *turns away without answering.*]

[*Violently*] Why she wanter get married? She ain't gointer get married, she can take that from me. But why—? [*Pauses, looks quickly at* MRS. G.] What'd yer mean just now, things wasn't going right?

MRS. G.: I might be wrong about that.

TED: About what?

[MRS. G. *turns away without answering.*]

About what? [*violently*] D'yer mean—?

[*Jumps to feet, knocking over bottle of beer, which pours across table onto work-basket on chair. Table has been arranged on slight slope so that bottle rolls into right position over work-basket. His hat has been placed on table in such a position as to prevent bottle rolling any further.*]

MRS. G.: I may be wrong.

TED: You'd better be or I'll—I'll—

MRS. G.: Oh Ted, look out [*rushes to table and pulls work-basket from under dripping beer*].

TED: What's the matter?

MRS. G.: Yer beer. All over me tray-cloth.

TED: Well cripes, I never knew it was there.

MRS. G.: Oh Ted [*holding up dripping tray-cloth*]. Just look at it. It's ruined.

TED: Well don't take on about it. I'll buy yer another one. What d'yer mean, wrong?

MRS. G.: Buy one! I was gointer put it in for the Show. And look at it.

TED [*apologetically*]: Well cripes—[*Angrily*] But what d'yer mean—?

MRS. G.: Yer mighter thought what yer was doin!

TED [*apologetically*]: Well it was an accident; couldn't yer see? [*Angrily*] But look here—

MRS. G. [*takes up work-basket. Goes off into bedroom holding up dripping tray-cloth*]: Just look at it. Ruined!

[TED *slumps back onto chair and watches her leaving room. Sits there gazing at beer trickling off table. Suddenly makes a swipe and knocks beer bottle and mug off table onto floor. Gets up and slams back door shut with his foot. Picks up coat off back of chair. Slings it over shoulder. Picks up hat, looks at it, swishes beer off it. Starts toward bedroom door. Pauses. Glares uncertainly round kitchen for a moment—angry, frustrated, bewildered. Then with an air of violent determination strides toward bedroom door.*]

(*End of Scene*)

ACT TWO

scene 3

Kitchen of Dillon family—Saturday afternoon. Same as first Act. Rifle against wall beside back door. BERT *at stove stirring something in saucepan.* GRANDPA *in wheel-chair beside stove, facing back door, old grey blanket over knees.* MR. DILLON *seated at table with pencil and paper, sucking end of pencil, frowning at paper.*

MR. D. [*to* BERT *at stove*]: How many bags of beans did Smithy take?
BERT [*back to* MR. D., *still stirring saucepan*]: Twen-y eight. No, thirty, that's right.
MR. D.: What'd he think of the price?
BERT [*half turning*]: No good. Too many comin' in he reckoned.
MR. D.: Ummmm. Thirty bags, say sixpence a pound. [*Does some calculating on paper. Chews end of pencil again. Doesn't look too pleased with result.*] Funny thing. Man always seems to miss the market. Anyway next door won't do any good out of his, time he gets 'em picked. If he'd stop home, 'stead of goin' off workin' for others.

    [*Door left opens.* CHARLIE *comes out of his bedroom. Eighteen years of age. A different generation to* BERT 25 *and has had better schooling. More conscious of his clothes and appearance, particularly now that he has a job in a small grocery store in the local town. This being Saturday afternoon, he is dressed to go out. He walks towards back door, adjusting hat on head so as not to disturb freshly brushed and oiled hair.* MR. D. *and* BERT *both look up and watch him as he somewhat self-consciously crosses room.*]

MR. D.: Where're *you* goin'?
CHARLIE [*expecting some such question, but pretending not to, over his shoulder*]: Out.
MR. D.: Out? Out where?

CHARLIE [*about to open back door, turns round*]: Just out. Can't I go out if I want to of a Saturday afternoon?

BERT: Anyone'd think yer was gointer get married, dolled up like that.

GRANDPA: Married? Who's gettin' married?

CHARLIE [*turning to* BERT *like a terrier snapping back at bigger dogs baiting him*]: Well, they're my clothes, ain't they? I paid for them.

BERT: Fancy tie an' all.

MR. D.: You get too much money, that's what's the matter with you. All these awards.

CHARLIE: I oughter be gettin' half a crown more a week according to the award.

MR. D.: Who said so?

CHARLIE: Mr. Harrison.

MR. D.: Who? Dick Harrison? That agitator!

CHARLIE: He knows all about the award.

MR. D.: Don't you start talkin' about awards . . . You can leave that to the mob next door.

BERT [*to* MR. D.]: Seen Harrison over there, coupla times lately.

CHARLIE: Well, why shouldn't he? He's a friend of theirs.

MR. D.: That's another thing. Where'd you go Saturday night?

CHARLIE [*looking sullen, realizing what's coming*]: Nowhere—

BERT: Yes, yer did.

CHARLIE: All right, the pictures, if you want to know.

MR. D.: Pictures eh? D'yer know what Preacher says about the pictures?

CHARLIE: Well, I got to have some amusement, haven't I?

MR. D.: And another thing—

CHARLIE [*realizing that it's coming and trying to head it off*]: All the other chaps my age go to the pictures.

MR. D.: 'Course they do. But they don't belong to the Children of the Lord Resplendent. We're different. Let them go to the pictures if they want to, but us . . .

CHARLIE: I don't see any harm in it.

MR. D.: But anyway, who'd yer go to the pictures with? That's what I wanter know.

GRANDPA: Who's that? Who'd yer say?

CHARLIE: What d'yer mean, who with?

BERT [*turning to stir the saucepan*]: Huh!

CHARLIE [*turning to him*]: What's it got to do with you?

MR. D.: You answer my question. Who did you go to the pictures with?

[CHARLIE *hesitates.*]

Now, no lies. I know who you went with.

CHARLIE: Well, what'd you want to ask for?

MR. D. [*rising angrily*]: Because I'm not gointer have yer takin' *her* to the pictures, that's why.

CHARLIE [*becoming angry too now that he sees the issue can't be avoided*]: Who d'you mean, her?

BERT [*at stove*]: Huh!

[CHARLIE *turns angrily towards him.*]

MR. D.: You know well enough who I mean.

CHARLIE [*looking directly at him, challengingly*]: D'you mean Mary?

MR. D. [*refusing to use her name*]: I mean *her* [*jerks his head toward next door*].

CHARLIE: Well, what if I did take her to the pictures? It's my money, isn't it?

MR. D. [*to* BERT]: Listen to that. That's what comes of Preacher getting him a job. And with one of our own, too.

CHARLIE: I earn the money. I can spend it how I like, can't I?

MR. D.: Listen to that! Listen to that! When I was your age—

CHARLIE [*defiantly*]: And what's more, you can't stop me.

MR. D. [*approaching him threateningly, raising voice*]: Can't stop you. Talk to me like that—

BERT [*edging toward back door*]: I think I heard a crow at them chickens. See if I can get a shot. [*Picks up rifle, leaning against wall beside back door. Goes out.*]

[*As he approaches back door* CHARLIE *comes forward toward middle of room, and stands, back to stove, facing father.*]

GRANDAD: The crows, the crows.

[*This interlude has broken the mounting tension.*]

MR. D. [*sitting down at table again, picking up pencil and tapping it irritably on table*]: The bringin' up we've given you. Decent religious upbringin'. What Preacher'd say . . . the likes of them. A mob of agitators, them and their politics . . . And takin' *her* to the pictures.

CHARLIE: Well, anyway . . .

MR. D. [*anger rising again*]: Didn't I tell you before, I wouldn't have yer goin' with her . . .

CHARLIE [*his anger rising again too*]: Well, I may as well tell yer, we're gointer get married.

MR. D. [*leaping up*]: Yer *what*?

CHARLIE: Get married, that's what I said.

MR. D. [*taking a step toward him with each word*]: Married? . . . You? . . . to her . . .?

CHARLIE [*retreating toward his bedroom door and not quite sure of himself*]: I'm old enough to do what I want to do, aren't I?

MR. D. [*suddenly suspicious*]: Married? Eh? Married?

CHARLIE: That's what I said.

MR. D.: Married? What's put that idea inter yer head?

CHARLIE: I don't know what you're talkin' about. We're gointer get married, that's all.

MR. D.: Does *she* [*always with an inflection of contempt and jerk of his head next door*] want ter get married?

CHARLIE: Yes.

MR. D.: D'yer mean—d' you mean—

CHARLIE: I mean what I said, that's all. We're going to get married.

MR. D.: You answer me, and none of yer lies. [*Advancing threateningly.*]

CHARLIE [*retreating*]: What's it got to do with you? It's our business.

MR. D.: What's it got ter do with me? I tell you this, you think I'll let you marry a—a—the likes of her—one of the likes of them?

CHARLIE [*angrily*]: If you're speaking about Mary—

MR. D.: I'm speakin' about the whole mob of them. They're nothing but a lot of agitators. And if you think you're gointer marry that—that—

CHARLIE [*threateningly*]: Don't you say anything against Mary or I'll—

MR. D. [*advancing with closed fists*]: Don't you speak to me like that, you—you—

  [*The sound of a car pulling up outside, toot of horn.*]

GRANDPA: What's that? Who's that?

  [MR. D. *goes hastily to back door and looks out.*]

  [CHARLIE *slinks back towards his bedroom.*]

MR. D.: Cripes, it's Preacher. [*Hastens to table, picks up pencil and paper, puts them in his trousers pocket. Wipes some crumbs off table with palm of hand, which he then wipes on seat of his pants. Hitches up pants and tucks down shirt inside pants. Pushes chair square with table. Goes over to stove, takes dirty dishcloth that's hanging over string stretched across stove recess, throws it into wash-up basin. Straightens blanket on* GRANDPA'S *knees.*]

GRANDPA: What's that? What's that? Married?

[MR. D. *looks anxiously round to see if there is anything else he can do as* PREACHER *is seen coming through back gate.*]

PREACHER [*approaching steps*]: Are you there, Brother?

[CHARLIE *retreats hastily to bedroom and quietly closes door.*]

MR. D.: Is that you, Preacher? Come in, come in. I was wondering if you might be along this afternoon. Come in, come in.

[*The latter remark is unnecessary as* PREACHER *has already entered and is looking round with a proprietary air. His manner of speech is slow and deliberate, rather pompous and pulpitical—but do not overdo it—he is a genuine fanatic, not a figure of fun. Any comedy that comes out of him must be incidental to his realness. He is thin, intense, sharp-featured, dressed in black.*]

PREACHER: Well, Brother, how are you? And your grand old father there [*with a half-bow in* GRANDPA'S *direction*]. How are you sir? How are you?

MR. D. [*to* GRANDPA, *bending down to him*]: It's Preacher, he's askin' how you are?

GRANDPA: What's that? Yes. Married—got married.

PREACHER: And you, Brother, how are you?

MR. D.: Me? I'm well, Preacher. And how are you?

PREACHER [*looking earnestly at him*]: I'm far from well, Brother.

MR. D.: Sorry to hear that, Preacher.

PREACHER: And you, Brother, unless I am very much mistaken, are far from well too.

MR. D.: Well, I—I—feel all right.

PREACHER: Yes, Brother, you may feel all right. I may feel all right. In fact we may both be, bodily speaking, all right. But spiritually, brother, spiritually—no, we are all steeped in sin.

MR. D.: Oh, yes—I see—yes.

PREACHER: That is the common lot of man, Brother. But we know, we the Children of the Lord Resplendent, that *we* are not doomed to eternal damnation. We are the Lord's chosen. If we acknowledge our sins, *we* will be saved. [*With a quick change of tone*] But let us speak of other things. Your wife? Have you had word of her?

MR. D.: Yes. She's comin' home soon, Saturday I think.

GRANDPA: When's Joan comin' home?

PREACHER [*glances uncertainly at* GRANDPA]: It has been a great trial for you all. I saw her yesterday.

MR. D.: You did, eh?

PREACHER: I visited her in hospital.

MR. D.: How was she?

PREACHER: She was wonderfully, radiantly well, in beautiful abounding health.

MR. D. [*rather surprised*]: Is that so?

PREACHER: Spiritually, I mean, Brother. Illness is a chastening experience. I spoke to her for an hour of sin and suffering and the sorrows of human existence. It was beautiful to see her agony of remorse at all the man-made evil in the world. Illness can be an ennobling experience. And tell me, Brother, how are things with you? All is well, I hope.

MR. D.: Well, yes. I got me troubles, of course. [*Glances towards* CHARLIE'S *door.*]

PREACHER: Who of us is free from trouble? It is God's way of testing our will to do his bidding. Do you know the cure for trouble, Brother? It is Truth.

MR. D.: That's just the trouble.

PREACHER: What is, Brother?

MR. D. [*glancing again at* CHARLIE'S *door*]: Truth. It's the truth that's just the trouble.

PREACHER: No, Brother, the trouble is that Truth lies at the bottom of a well, and we, poor mortals, must draw it up with a leaky bucket. It is only with the guidance of the Resplendent One that we can achieve Truth. Brother, let us kneel in prayer together and give our souls to the Resplendent One. With his help all our troubles will be overcome. [*Closes eyes.*]

POLICEMAN [*mounting back steps with heavy tread that interrupts Preacher's eloquence and makes him open his eyes and look inquiringly at* MR. D.]: Anybody home? [*With a loud knock on the door he walks straight in.*]

MR. D.: Come in, come in, Constable.

POLICEMAN: Did I interrupt you? Sorry.

PREACHER: No, no, that's quite all right. I was just about to go in any case. [*To* MR. D.] Well Brother, it has been a great pleasure to see you and to commune with you [*looks toward* GRANDPA *and bows slightly*] and your grand old father. To commune with you [*looks uncertainly at* POLICEMAN]—spiritually, and to know that— [*glances again at* POLICEMAN]— . . . all is well with you. And now, if you'll excuse me [*nods to* MR. D. *and makes a sort of embarrassed half-bow to* POLICEMAN, *who nods in a severely official manner, as* PREACHER—*hat in hand*—*backs toward door*]—God's blessing on you both [*glancing at* GRANDPA]. On you all. [*He turns and hastens down the steps and out through the back gate.* POLICEMAN *and* MR. D. *looking after him.*]

GRANDPA: Who's that? What's that?

POLICEMAN [*recovering his official aplomb and getting down to business, somewhat brusquely to compensate for his previous feeling of uncertainty. Pulls out notebook*]: Mr. Dillon?

MR. D.: Yes, that's me.

POLICEMAN [*seating himself at table, back to door*]: Sit down, Mr. Dillon [*half an invitation and half an order*].

[MR. D. *pulls up a chair and sits down at end of table facing Grandpa.*]

[*Flicking pages of his notebook and licking point of pencil*] I'm making enquiries [*his eyes rove around the kitchen*], Mr. Dillon, [*he glances inquiringly at* GRANDPA] regarding a length of rope.

MR. D.: What?

POLICEMAN: A length of hemp rope.

MR. D.: Hemp *rope*?

POLICEMAN: Yes, hemp rope.

MR. D. [*sparring for time to think the situation out*]: A length of hemp rope?

POLICEMAN [*consulting notebook and placing finger on an item therein as he looks up with a searching glance at* MR. D.]: Thirty-five feet of three-quarter inch new hemp rope.

MR. D. [*with a momentary note of protest plus contempt in his voice*]:

New? It wasn't new—[*Then sees his mistake and alters tone to a placatory inquiry*] Thirty-feet of hemp rope?

POLICEMAN: Thirty-five feet of three-quarter inch rope.

MR. D. [*recovering his balance*]: And what's happened to it? Somebody lost it?

POLICEMAN: It's reported missing from a neighbouring farm. A new hemp rope.

MR. D.: New? [*Shakes his head.*] I don't know anybody about here's got a new hemp rope.

POLICEMAN: The fact is, Mr. Dillon—

GRANDPA: Truth, truth. Bottom of a well . . .

POLICEMAN: What's he say?

MR. D. [*getting up hastily*]: He ain't well. He's been real crook. That's why I had the Preacher here. To try to do something for him. [*Goes over to* GRANDPA. *Adjusts the old grey blanket around his knees. Bends down, looks anxiously at him*] You all right, Grandpa?

GRANDPA: Down the well . . . a leaky bucket.

POLICEMAN: What's he say?

GRANDPA: Cow down the well. A leaky bucket . . .

MR. D. [*looking at* POLICEMAN *and shaking head*]: He's gointer have a turn, I think. That's why I had the Preacher here. Wish he hadn't gone.

POLICEMAN: A turn? What d'you do for him?

MR. D.: Could you just stand by him for a moment? I'll get him a bit of fruit salts. Sometimes that pulls him round.

POLICEMAN [*going over to* GRANDPA *and looking sympathetically down at him, back to door*]: Poor old chap. Ought to be in hospital, you ask me.

[MR. D. *goes towards dresser. At this moment* BERT *appears at back door with rifle. Standing beside back steps he reaches in to put rifle against wall beside door where it originally stood. He sees* POLICEMAN, *who has his back to door. Glances hastily at* MR. D., *who makes pantomime with his hand and says with exaggerated lip movement, but no sound*]

MR. D.: The Rope.

[BERT *looks puzzled for a moment. Then shows sudden enlightenment. Glances at* POLICEMAN, *turns and disappears.* MR. D. *puts a spoonful of fruit salts in an enamel mug. Goes over to tap at washup bench and fills mug.*]

POLICEMAN: He seems all right now.

MR. D.: Yer can't tell how he is. Sometimes they pass off, the turns. I'll give him this anyway.

POLICEMAN: You should have put the water in first.

MR. D.: Should I?

POLICEMAN: You ought to know, if that's what you always give him.

MR. D.: That's right. I forgot. It's the wife generally gives it to him. She's in hospital.

POLICEMAN: That's where he ought to be, if you ask me. But he seems all right now.

GRANDPA [*with a great sigh*]: Truth lies—bottom of the well.

POLICEMAN [*looking down at* GRANDPA]: Funny old bloke. What's he talking about.

[MR. D. *glances quickly at back door to make sure* BERT *has gone to plant rope, goes over and stands beside* POLICEMAN *blocking any chance of his turning and seeing* BERT *through door.*]

MR. D.: I'll give him this.

POLICEMAN [*glancing at contents of mug*]: I wouldn't. You should have put the water in first. It isn't properly mixed. It'll fizz up inside him.

MR. D.: That's right. So it might. P'raps I'd better not give it to him. He seems all right anyway.

POLICEMAN [*dismissing the matter*]: He's all right. He was just having a bit of a yarn to himself, weren't you Daddy? [*Goes back to table.*] Well now . . .

MR. D. [*taking the initiative*]: A new rope you say? The only rope I know of is one belongs to this bloke next door [*with a jerk of head and tone of contempt*]. Not a new one though. Bought it secondhand. At Atkinson's sale. It was three-quarter inch, I think, about that. Yes of course [*with an air of extreme candour*] that's the rope we used gettin' a cow out of his well for him— well for his missus, he was away—always is for that matter. That's the only rope I know of in these parts, and it wasn't new. Fact, I said at the time, when we was usin' it, the way he'd left it lyin' around, out in the weather . . .

POLICEMAN: And where's that rope now? You say you were using it?

250

MR. D.: What—is it him reported his rope missin'?

POLICEMAN: Yes.

MR. D. [*indignantly*]: You don't mean to say he had the hide to say *we* . . . The hide of some people!

POLICEMAN: Well, as a matter of fact he mentioned that you were the last to use it. You used it, you said?

MR. D.: Course we did. Gettin' the cow out of his well. Lucky for him we was here to give his missus a hand. And that's the thanks a man gets.

POLICEMAN: And where is the rope now, Mr. Dillon?

MR. D. [*with an involuntary glance at back door*]: How would I know?

POLICEMAN: You haven't seen it since you used it?

MR. D.: No, haven't set eyes on it.

POLICEMAN: And you don't know where it is now?

MR. D.: I've just told you I don't. All I know is that if that lyin' mongrel next door has said I took his rope—

POLICEMAN: There's no need for that. You say you don't know where the rope is—

MR. D.: Here's my boy. He might know, I don't.

BERT [*entering, seems surprised to see* POLICEMAN]: Oh, hullo . . .

MR. D. [*to* BERT]: That mongrel next door says we took his rope.

BERT: His what?

MR. D. [*putting him au fait with the story he has told* POLICEMAN]: You know, the rope we pulled the cow out of his well with. Says it's a new rope.

BERT: New! He never owned a new rope in his life—nor anything else new.

POLICEMAN: Never mind about that. You assure me you don't know where the rope is now?

BERT: Where it is? It's lyin' round somewhere over there [*nods next door*] goin' rotten. He wouldn't know where it was. He don't know where anythin' is.

MR. D.: Don't know what he owns and what he don't own. I'll have the law on him, that's what I'll do. Accusin' us of takin' his lousy rope.

POLICEMAN [*rising, putting away pencil and notebook*]: Well, if it's still over there, that's the end of the matter.

MR. D.: No, by cripes, it ain't. He's gointer hear more about it, you can take that from me.

POLICEMAN: Well, that's your affair, Mr. Dillon. I'll see him and tell him to have another look round for it.

BERT: It might be down the well. He wouldn't know what he done with it.

POLICEMAN: Well, goodday. [*To* GRANDPA] So long, Daddy. [*To* MR. D.] He'll be all right. [*Over shoulder as he goes out back door*] You want to keep an eye on him though.

GRANDPA: Truth—lies—truth—lies.

[MR. D. *and* BERT *watch* POLICEMAN *go out through gate.*]

MR. D. [*drawing deep breath of relief*]: Cripes! [*Going to back door and peeping out.*] He's gone straight over to look round the well.

BERT: He won't find it there anyway.

[MR. D. *and* BERT *look significantly at one another.*]

I never seen him till I was halfway in the door. Then I never woke up ter what yer meant at first. That lousy mongrel [*nodding next door*]. Tryin' to put us in.

MR. D.: Yes, and the rope was just lyin' round over there rotting. Bet he never even knew where it was till we found it for him. That's the sort of neighbour we've got to put up with. And then that kid [*glares at* CHARLIE'S *door*] got the nerve to tell me he's gointer [*hesitates*] . . .

BERT: What'd he tell yer he was gointer do?

MR. D.: But I'll stop him. He's only eighteen. He can't do what he likes and I'll see that he don't.

(*End of Act Two*)

ACT THREE

scene 1

The well, same as before, night time. At curtain rise stage is almost blacked out— a cloud is over the moon. A mopoke is heard calling (two calls). As cloud passes, light increases. CHARLIE *is gradually disclosed sitting on coaming of well, a sweater slung over his shoulder. His head is in his hands. It is a picture of dejection. As moonlight increases, shadow of the gallows is thrown across the stage. The mopoke calls again (two calls).* CHARLIE *looks up. Sits for a while gazing into space. Looks at shadow of gallows. Looks over his shoulder at gallows. Presently starts, listens intently, gets up. Goes quickly to side of stage. Listens for a moment. Then whistles softly, a prearranged call. Listens again. Repeats whistle. Listens. Silence. Comes back toward well. Stops and looks at well. Looks up at gallows. A cloud shadow passes over moon again. Light fades. He is just a dim, uncertain figure in middle of stage. Cloud passes. Light increases. Throws his sweater with gesture of disgust on coaming of well. He walks despondently up and down a couple of times. Suddenly stops, listens. Goes to side of stage. Whistles—listens. Whistles again. Silence. Comes back to centre of stage. Stands irresolute for a moment. Looks back toward side of stage. Then walks slowly off, head low, despondent, leaving his sweater on coaming of well.*

(Above action to occupy 2-3 minutes.)

A cloud passes over moon. Mopoke calls. Keep stage blacked out for some seconds (half a minute). Then light slowly returns. As light increases MARY *comes running from direction to which* CHARLIE *has whistled.*

(This action might take about two or less minutes.)

MARY *comes running on. She is bareheaded. Her hair somewhat wild. She is wearing a pair of rather smart semi-high heel shoes which contrast with a very old and worn faded dress. (General effect to have maiden-in-distress appeal. She is to touch the audience's sympathies without sentimentality.) She stops in middle of stage and looks anxiously around. Then goes left and peers out listening. Pauses. Calls softly.*

MARY: Charlie. [*Whistles same two notes as* CHARLIE. *Pauses. Listens. Turns and walks back across stage. Pauses in front of well. Looks at shadow of gallows and then up at gallows. Looks anxiously and nervously around. Turns and goes back left. Peers out, calls softly*] Charlie, Charlie. [*A note of fear in her voice, then whistles. Pauses. Goes back to centre of stage. Looks shrinkingly up at gallows again. Then down at well—and sees* CHARLIE'S *sweater on coaming. With a cry of fear runs over, picks up sweater, clutches it to her and sinking on her knees on coaming peers down into well, grasping sweater to her as she does so. Looks terror-stricken up at gallows, then down into well again. Calls hysterically*] Charlie, Charlie, Charlie. [*Stands up. Turns back on well. Buries face in sweater and bursts into sobs.*]

CHARLIE [*enters left*]: Mary, Mary. [*Rushes toward her.*]

MARY [*falling into his arms*]: Oh Charl.

[*They stand for a moment without speaking,* MARY *sobbing,* CHARLIE *caressing her head. The shadow of the gallows lies across them.*]

CHARLIE: What is it? What's the matter? What happened?

MARY [*pulling his head down and kissing him excitedly*]: Oh Charl, I thought—I came as soon as I could and you weren't here— and I saw—oh! it was horrible. I saw your sweater lying there and I thought—Oh Charl, where were you?

CHARLIE: I waited. I whistled and whistled. I thought you weren't coming—you couldn't get out. I started to go home and then I didn't know what to do and I came back and—what happened? I must have left my sweater behind.

MARY: Oh it was awful. It was lying there on top of the well—and I couldn't see you anywhere—and oh, I don't know—it was silly of me—I thought—there'd been a row or something—at home— and you'd [*looks sideways at well and shudders*]—it was awful. If you hadn't come I think I would have—

CHARLIE [*glancing at well*]: It gives you the creeps, doesn't it, when you look down it. It's so dark, there doesn't seem to be any bottom to it. If you hadn't been here when I came back—why were you so late? What happened?

MARY: I couldn't—they wouldn't let me—I couldn't get away.

CHARLIE: They wouldn't let you?

MARY: I had to wait till he'd gone—Dad. He went to a meeting. Oh Charl, what are we going to do? It's like being in jail. Can't we—couldn't we—?

CHARLIE: I don't know. I feel like doing something desperate.

MARY: I don't care what it is, Charl, as long as we're together.

CHARLIE: That's the trouble. They want to separate us. They're at me all the time.

MARY: We mustn't let them, Charl, no matter what they do. Oh Charl, you do love me, don't you.

[MARY *snuggles up to him, he strokes her hair. They kiss passionately.*]

CHARLIE: Of course I do.

[*They gaze rapturously at one another.*]

MARY: Do you love me more than anyone has ever loved anybody before?

CHARLIE: Yes, more than anybody ever has.

MARY: And more than that, too.

CHARLIE [*playfully*]: Don't be silly. There can't be more than that.

MARY [*offended, drawing slightly away*]: I'm not silly. If that's all you think of me—

CHARLIE: Of course it isn't. You know I didn't mean it. Don't be silly.

MARY [*pushes him away*]: There you are you said it again.

CHARLIE: I did not.

MARY: You did.

CHARLIE: Of course I didn't. Don't be—[*Checks himself.*]

MARY: There you are, you see, you said it again, you do mean it.

CHARLIE: I didn't say it.

MARY: You did. You were just going to say it.

CHARLIE: Well, that's only going to. I didn't say it. You said so yourself.

MARY: Well anyway, you didn't mean it, did you?

CHARLIE: Course I didn't.

MARY: You didn't mean it at all?

CHARLIE: Not at all.

MARY [*half laughing*]: Not the teeniest weeniest bit?

CHARLIE [*stroking her hair*]: Not the weeniest, teeniest bit.

MARY [*snuggling up to him*]: And you won't say it again?

CHARLIE: No.

MARY: Never?

CHARLIE: Never.

MARY: Never ever.

CHARLIE: Of course I won't, silly.

MARY [*laughing*]: There you are, you've said it again—

CHARLIE [*protesting*]: I never did. I only said—well, I didn't mean to, I meant—

MARY [*laughing*]: There you are, you don't know what you mean. Don't try to make up excuses, silly.

CHARLIE [*laughing*]: There you are, you've said it yourself.

[*They hold one another at arm's length for a moment laughing, then fall into one another's arms. She rests her head on his chest. He ruffles her hair. Cloud passes over moon—they remain silent for a while. Light gradually returns.*]

Is that why you were late—they wouldn't let you out?

MARY: Yes, he made Mum take my clothes away. I had to wait till he'd gone. I knew you'd be waiting. I didn't know what to do. I climbed out through the window. That's why I'm wearing this old dress. It was hanging behind the door. Mum didn't see it. It's as old as the hills. It's miles too tight for me. [*She gets up and pivots round to show him how tight it is, displaying her contours.*]

CHARLIE: You've got your best shoes on, too. Why shoes? I like you best in your bare feet.

MARY: Do you? [*She kicks the shoes off.*] I had to put them on. I came the short cut across the cultivation. You should see the burrs. They're awful.

CHARLIE: That's what Dad says. He says he—your father—only grows burrs.

MARY [*leaping to the defence*]: Well, he's been away. He hadn't time to plant anything. And anyway, what about your father? Dad says—[*hesitates*].

CHARLIE: Go on, what does he say? Anyway, who cares what he says? He's nothing but a—

MARY: Well, if you want to know, he says your father isn't a farmer's bootlace.

CHARLIE: Oh does he? Well, Dad's as good a farmer as anybody else. Only he hasn't got any money, that's all. You can't do things without money.

MARY: Well, isn't that why Dad goes out working?—to get money.

CHARLIE: And never gets his crops in—only burrs.

MARY [*pushes him away and starts to cry*]: I wish I hadn't come. I'm going home. [*Starts to wriggle her toes into her shoes.*]

CHARLIE: Aw cripes! Look—I never meant it.

MARY [*stops wriggling into her shoes*]: Well, you said it, you must have meant it.

CHARLIE: Well, I didn't mean it. And anyway it was you said about the burrs first.

MARY [*getting out of her shoes again and coming up to him*]: Oh Charl, I did not.

CHARLIE: You did. You said the burrs were awful in the cultivation. That's why you had to put your best shoes on.

MARY: That wasn't why I had to put on my best shoes at all. It was because Mum took the other shoes away, he made her, Dad did. These were the only ones I could find.

CHARLIE: Well you look a sight, wearing those shoes and that dress —[*hastily*] a nice sight—I mean. But what about the dress I bought you? I was hoping you'd be wearing that.

MARY: It's—it's—I couldn't wear it.

CHARLIE: Why, because your mother took it away?

MARY [*hesitates*]: No. It's—oh Charl you mustn't get wild, but he—Dad—he—wouldn't let me have it.

CHARLIE: Wouldn't let you have it?

MARY: I tried to hide it. But Mum must have told him about it.

CHARLIE: Is she against you—against us—your mother?

MARY: She's frightened of him I think—Dad—what he might do. Oh Charl, you mustn't be wild. He—he burnt it. He put it under the copper.

CHARLIE: Burnt it! Well, the mean cow!

MARY: Now Charl, don't be wild, please.

CHARLIE: It was a good dress. It cost—

MARY [*taking hold of his two arms and looking appealingly up at him*]: Now Charl, please.

CHARLIE: And he went and burnt it.

MARY: Oh Charl, don't let's have a row about it, please. I wish I hadn't told you.

CHARLIE: I'm glad you did. Burnt it. The mean cow!

MARY [*almost in tears*]: Oh Charl! Not another row, please.

CHARLIE: All right. I won't say anything about it. But to do a thing like that—he's a—

MARY: Now Charl, please. You promised. Why do we have to have rows?

CHARLIE: All right. I won't say anything. I don't want a row. I hate rows. It's just—I suppose it's because—they're always having rows, and they sort of—we sort of get mixed-up in it too.

MARY: We can't help it. We're part of the row—us always wanting to be together. Oh Charl, what are we going to do?

CHARLIE: It's awful. I tried to tell Dad. I said to him—I told him—about us—wanting to get married. There was an awful row. I didn't know what to say.

MARY: Oh Charl! What did he say?

CHARLIE: They were both at me, Bert and him—Dad. I mean that was before. He—I mean Bert—he went out to shoot a crow or something. He always clears out when there's a row on. He started it—picking at me—and then cleared out. There were only the two of us in the room then, me and Dad. I kept thinking of Mum, her being in hospital, and all. I mean it wasn't *him*— I didn't care what I said to *him*, the way I felt, and him talking religion and the Preacher at me.

MARY: Religion with you and politics with us.

CHARLIE [*ruefully*]: There's always got to be something.

MARY: What did he—say—you know—about us—about us getting married?

CHARLIE: He said—he didn't say it to me—I mean he said it after the row—I heard him say it afterwards—the Preacher came— I didn't tell you about that—I cleared out, went to my room— and then the Policeman—I'll tell you about that after—and when they'd gone—I was still in my room—I'd got out of the way as soon as I heard him—the Preacher—coming, and when they'd gone I heard him say—Bert had come back, he'd been shooting crows—I heard Dad say something to him about me being only eighteen and he could stop me getting married.

MARY: Oh Charl. And would he?

CHARLIE: Yes. I heard him say. I know he would, the way he took on about it, and about—about your father. That was after the Policeman had been. It was about a rope. I heard them talking about it. He was abusing your father about it.

MARY: Oh, why do they hate one another? Why do people have to hate one another? Why can't they all love one another, instead of hating? Why isn't the world full of love?

CHARLIE: He said I couldn't do as I liked—and he'd see that I didn't.

MARY: Oh Charl, what are we going to do?

CHARLIE: I dunno. I'm fed up.

MARY: Charl, couldn't we . . . ? [*Hesitates.*]

CHARLIE: You mean . . . [*Hesitates.*]

MARY: It's awful, Charl, isn't it? Couldn't we . . .?

CHARLIE: You mean clear out or something?

MARY: But Charl, where could we go?

CHARLIE: I dunno. [*Dramatically*] We'll go somewhere. They needn't think they can treat us like a couple of kids.

MARY [*clutching his arm*]: Oh Charl, will we really?

CHARLIE: Too right we will. I'm not goin' ter let them—

MARY: But d'you think we could? How would we—?

CHARLIE: We could get Robinson's car—say on Saturday. There's a midday train. If I see Robinson. Tell him not to let on. We could—would you? the both of us could—

MARY: But wouldn't that be—couldn't they—I mean the police or something—couldn't they get them . . .?

CHARLIE [*slight tone of uncertainty*]: The police. What could the police do anyway? It's got nothing to do with them. It's our business, isn't it?

MARY: But if they *did* send the police after us?

CHARLIE: We would—I dunno—we'd think up something.

MARY: But if they found us, Charl, and brought us back—

CHARLIE [*more doubtfully still*]: Brought us back here?

MARY: If they did, Charl, would they—do they—I mean—would they—put the—what do they call them—you know—on us.

CHARLIE: You mean handcuffs?

MARY: Yes. Oh Charl.

CHARLIE: Of course they wouldn't silly. Getting married isn't the same as committing murder.

MARY: Married! But Charl—I mean you've got to—haven't you got to—?

CHARLIE: Get a permit or somethin', you mean? I suppose you have—I dunno what you've got to do.

MARY: But wouldn't you have to get that from the police?

CHARLIE: I wonder would you—I mean being under twenty-one—the both of us?

MARY: But—oh Charl, we couldn't go to the police. They'd—

CHARLIE [*his determination flagging*]: No, I suppose we couldn't. They'd—I dunno what they'd do. That's the trouble. We don't know enough—we don't know how to go about it. I don't know—I don't know what to do.

MARY [*making bold as* CHARLIE *begins to wilt*]: But Charl, we *will* go, won't we? We'll manage somehow.

CHARLIE: Yes, but how? That's the thing.

MARY: We can think about that afterwards. Once we get there.

CHARLIE: Yes, but where?

MARY: Somewhere. Anywhere. Wherever we go—we can make out—we can pretend—you know, until . . .

CHARLIE: Yes, but pretending isn't that easy. You've got to—well you've got to—you've got to stay somewhere—some place—with somebody.

MARY: Well there's always some place.

CHARLIE: And you've got to have luggage—you've got to have—well, all flash clothes and that—you've got to seem like you've just been married.

MARY: Well, you can always say—I dunno, we'd think of something.

CHARLIE: Yes, but you think of some old crone in a boarding-house, or something, stickybeakin' round. And that sort, too, she'd be sure to be in with the police. That sort always are.

MARY: Do you think so, Charl!

CHARLIE: Of course. They gotter be. The police won't give them a licence, or whatever they've got to have, if they aren't.

MARY [*beginning to realize the risks involved*]: And she'd go to the police you think?

CHARLIE: Yeh, ring up or something.

MARY: I suppose they'd know—I mean about us. They'd be on the look out—all the police would, as soon as we cleared out.

CHARLIE: Well your—your father'd put them on anyway. If he burnt that dress he'd—

MARY: It'd be your father by the sound of it—the way he took on when you told him.

CHARLIE: Dad would? Of course he wouldn't. He wouldn't go running to the police. But your Dad—

MARY [interrupting]: Dad would not. I know he wouldn't—well I don't think—I'm sure he wouldn't.

CHARLIE: Well it was him went to the police about—about—

MARY: About what?

CHARLIE: You know. About—he went running to the police about that rope. So that just shows—

MARY [indignantly]: Running to the police! Well, who took the rope anyway. It was your Dad—

CHARLIE: He never did.

MARY: Well, him or Bert.

CHARLIE: He never did—they never did. If your Dad hadn't gone running to the police . . .

MARY: Running to the police! If they didn't take the rope what happened to it? They were the last to use it . . .

CHARLIE: Helping your mother get a cow out of the well . . .

MARY: Yes, and whose cow was it?

CHARLIE: That doesn't matter. They had to use the rope, didn't they?

MARY: Yes, and what happened to it after?

CHARLIE: What happened to it before, you mean. Lying there just going rotten. I heard Dad say. If somebody hadn't looked after it—and your Dad gotter go running to the police.

MARY: Well they did take it, then?

CHARLIE: I never said they did.

MARY: Oh Charlie, you did.

CHARLIE: I never did.

MARY: Well you as good as . . .

CHARLIE: I did not. I only said—

MARY: You did not. You said . . .

CHARLIE: I didn't say anything of the kind. And anyway, if it comes to that . . .

MARY [*clutching his arm*]: Oh Charl! Please! Must we have a row about it?

CHARLIE: *I* wasn't having a row. But when you said—

MARY: Oh Charl!

CHARLIE: Oh, all right.

MARY [*starts to weep*]: It was you saying that Dad would—

CHARLIE: Look, I never said it. Well I never meant it. [*Strokes her hair. She leans her head on his shoulder.*] Don't cry . . . Cripes! I feel as if I could—oh, I don't know what to do.

MARY [*through her tears*]: Never mind, Charl, as long as we've got one another.

CHARLIE [*over her shoulder, pursuing his own thoughts*]: There doesn't seem to be anything we can do . . . And them all onto us . . . rows . . . pickin' at us.

MARY: Charl, never let us have another row again, never ever.

CHARLIE [*still pursuing his own thoughts*]: What's it got to do with us if they want to have rows with one another . . . preachin' and politics . . . But, oh, I don't know what to do. I feel as if I could [*pauses and looks towards well*]—
[*Pause.*]

MARY [*looking up at him*]: As if you could what, Charl?
[CHARLIE *doesn't answer. Looks at* MARY *and again at well.*]
[*Anxiously*] Charl, what? As if you could what?
[*Another pause.* MARY *looking anxiously up at him.*]

CHARLIE: The two of us could—you and I could—

MARY: What, Charl? What do you mean?
[*The mopoke calls.*]
[*Startled*] Oh, Charl, what was that?

CHARLIE [*abstractedly*]: That? It was just a mopoke.

MARY: Oh, it gave me such a fright.
[*Mopoke calls again.*]
There it is again [*draws closer to* CHARLIE, *who puts his arm protectingly around her.*] Oh Charl, I'm fright-ened. What are we going to do?

CHARLIE: We can't go on like this. [*Draws her toward well*] Couldn't

we, the two of us—? [*Peers down into well.*]—If we held hands—
[*takes her hand*] and closed our eyes—and—

MARY [*pulling away from him*]: Oh no, Charl, no, no. I'm frightened.
[*She backs away from him, her hands up as if cutting herself off
from the well.*]

[CHARLIE *stands beside well, irresolute.*]

[*Coming forward and taking his hand*] Let's get the car. Let's see
Robinson. We could—we could go somewhere—anywhere. Oh
Charl, please. [*Pulling him away from well*] I'm frightened of
that well. Let's go somewhere else, out on the reserve or somewhere. I'm frightened.

[*The mopoke calls again.*]

[*Clutching him*] Oh Charl.

CHARLIE: It's only the mopoke.

MARY: I know but—but I'm frightened.

[CHARLIE *puts his arm protectingly around her.*]

Come on, Charl.

[*They go off, arms around one another, leaving his sweater and
her shoes at well.*]

(*End of Scene*)

263

ACT THREE

scene 2

Outside back door of kitchen of Dillon family. Inside kitchen GRANDPA *can be seen in his wheel chair. This is only to help audience orient itself—*GRANDPA *takes no part in action. Action takes place in space between back steps and back gate (the latter not showing). Two steps up to kitchen.*

BERT *standing in doorway in typical leaning Australian attitude.* MR. DILLON *and* PREACHER *at foot of steps.*

MR. D. [*to* PREACHER]: If you would just talk to him. He oughter been here. I told him not ter go out. But he seems ter do what he likes.

BERT: Gets too much money. Gone to his head. That's what's the matter.

PREACHER: I should have arranged for Mr. Hobson to pay his wages to you. You could have given him enough for pocket money. It's too big a temptation to young people, so much money.

MR. D.: If he'd been here. You could've spoken to him. He might take notice of you. It's that girl next door. I won't have him marry her, no matter what happens. [*Glances sideways at* BERT.]

PREACHER: No, no. Most unfortunate—young people today—I don't know. But no, no. It wouldn't do at all. People like that. We of the Faith are apart from people like that. It wouldn't do at all.

MR. D.: If he'd only been here. [*To* BERT] What time did you say he went out?

BERT: Haven't seen him since first thing this morning. He's got his best clothes on, too. I had a look in his room.

MR. D.: His best clothes. That's funny. Why would he put on his best clothes, that time of the morning?

BERT: Hey, who's this comin?

MR. D. [*following* BERT'S *glance*]: It's them.

PREACHER: Who? Who are they?

264

MR. D.: Them. [*Jerks his head next door*] Next door.

BERT [*lowering voice as they come on*]: What do *they* want? The whole shebang of them.

[TED *and* DICK HARRISON *enter by back gate, which is out of sight. Followed by* MRS. G. *and* POLICEMAN.]

[BERT *leaves doorway and comes down one step.*]

PREACHER [*with half bow*]: Good-afternoon.

TED [*hardly glancing at him*]: Good-day. [*To* MR. D.] Look, where's that girl of mine? [*Leans forward aggressively.*]

POLICEMAN [*tapping* TED *on shoulder*]: Now I warned you, there's to be no rough stuff.

DICK: He's got his rights, same as anybody else.

TED [*slightly less aggressive*]: Where's that girl of mine?

MR. D.: How do I know where your girl is? What's she got to do with me?

[BERT *comes down another step.*]

PREACHER: Brother, Brother, gently, gently. [*To* TED] Let me explain that this gentleman [*half bowing to* MR. D.] doesn't know anything about your girl.

TED [*contemptuously*] Gentleman! Anyway who're you? What's it got to do with you? Who asked you to stick yer bib in?

POLICEMAN: Now take it easy, take it easy.

TED [*to* MR. D.]: Its *you* I'm talkin' to. Where's my girl? Where's that boy of yours?

MRS. G.: If she'd never met him. She was a good girl till he led her astray.

MR. D.: *He* did? I like that. If it hadn't been for her stringin' him on—

TED: Don't you say anythin' agen my girl or I'll knock your bloody block off [*advances threateningly*].

POLICEMAN: Now look, if you start talking like that somebody's going to finish up in the cells. Break it down.

DICK: It's his own daughter, isn't it? Yer can't stop a man from demandin' his rights.

MRS. G.: It was him leadin' her astray, that's what it was. [*She starts to cry.*]

TED [*to* MRS. G.]: You leave this to me. And don't start that for Christ's sake.

265

PREACHER: Brother, Brother. Take not the name of the Lord in vain.

TED [*to* PREACHER]: You can leave the Holy Joe stuff out of it. Where's my girl, that's what I want to know? She ain't been seen since this mornin'.

[MR. D. *and* BERT *look at one another.*]

MR. D.: What's it got ter do with us when yer seen her?

TED [*aggressive again*—POLICEMAN *takes a step forward*—DICK *steps up behind* TED *as if to back him up*]: It's got this much to do with yer, it's that boy of yours has cleared out with her, that's what he's done.

POLICEMAN [*waving a warning hand to* TED *to keep quiet*—*to* MR. D.]: Look, where is that boy of yours? Bring him here and let me have a word with him.

MR. D.: My boy? Charlie you mean—?

MRS. G.: Yes, him. It's him that's led her astray.

TED [*to* MRS. G.]: Now look, will yer keep out of it?

POLICEMAN: Yes, where is he? Let me have a word with him.

MR. D. [*to* BERT]: You seen Charlie about anywhere?

BERT: No, I haven't seen him this half-hour or more.

[*Looks apologetically at* PREACHER, *who walks a few steps away, as though preferring not to hear such untruths.*]

TED [*to* BERT]: Half an hour? You sure you seen him half an hour ago.

BERT: Well, it might a been an hour.

TED: Yer a bloody liar, yer ask me. Yer a mob of bloody liars, [*looks at* PREACHER *standing dignified, aloof*] the lot of yer, the parson included.

POLICEMAN: Break it down, break it down.

DICK: A man's entitled to express his opinion, isn't he?

TED: You never seen that boy of yours an hour ago, nor two hours, nor three either for that matter. He's taken that girl of mine away, that's what he's done.

MRS. G.: He has, he has. I know he has.

TED: Look here, Missus, will you keep out of it.

MRS. G. [*crying*]: Me own daughter and her a good girl till he led her astray. [*Wipes her eyes and nose with corner of sugar bag apron.*]

TED [*pushing* MRS. G. *aside*]: Will you keep quiet? [*To* MR. D.] He's gone off with her, that's what he's done, and you've encouraged him.

MR. D.: Me?

TED: But if he thinks he's gointer marry her—

MR. D.: *Marry* her? Huh.

DICK: Its abduction, that's what it is, her under twenty-one, [*to* POLICEMAN] isn't it?

POLICEMAN: Abduction? They're both under age, aren't they? But anyway you've got to have your facts before you start talking like that.

MR. D.: You needn't worry about him marryin' her. I'll see to it that he don't, never fear.

MRS. G.: He oughter be made to marry her.

TED [*to* MRS. G.]: Will you keep out of it, I say?

MRS. G.: A good girl, till she started goin' with him.

TED: For Christ's sake.

MRS. G.: Now Ted, yer know yourself, she's always been—

TED: I'm not sayin' she hasn't, am I? I'm sayin' she ain't gointer marry him that's what I'm sayin'.

MRS. G. [*starts crying again*]: But Ted now—

TED: Now look, Missus, will you keep out of this.

MRS. G.: But Ted . . .

POLICEMAN [*to* DICK *over last line*]: Look, we'd better leave them to it. This is their affair.

DICK: But a man's got his rights . . .

POLICEMAN: Come on, come on. [*To others*] But look no rough stuff, I've warned you, or it *will* be my affair. [*To* DICK] Come on. [DICK *goes off with him reluctantly*.]

TED [*to* MR. D.]: Y'haven't answered my question. When did you see that boy of yours last?

MR. D.: Oh, how do I know? I don't keep lookin' at the clock and lookin' where he is.

TED: It might'a been better for you, you had.

MRS. G.: It would'a been better for her. There's no knowin' where she is.

TED: Now Missus, didn't I tell you to keep quiet.
[MRS. G. *covers her face with apron again*.]

[*Frowning and kicking a jam tin on the ground. Half talking to himself*] If a man knew how long they'd gone . . .

HERBIE [*coming on looking nervously at group, in an urgent aside to* MRS. G. *and in obvious distress*]: Hey, Ma.
   [MRS. G. *continues crying into apron.*]
   Hey, Ma, Ma. [*Pulls at her skirt.*]

MRS. G. [*raising her face*]: You go away.

HERBIE: But Ma.

MRS. G.: Go away, I tell yer.

HERBIE: Ma—I come past the well and—there was his sweater and her shoes—I think—they've—they've—

MRS. G. [*grabs him by shoulder*]: What d'yer mean?

TED [*wheeling on them*]: What's he want? What's he doin' here?

MRS. G. [*ignoring* TED]: What d'yer mean? What did yer see?

HERBIE [*almost inarticulate with agitation*]: I seen—I seen—their things—by the well—I think they're—down the well—

MRS. G.: My God, Ted. They're—they're in the well.

TED: The well! I never thought.

MR. D. ⎫
BERT ⎭ : The well!

TED: Come on we might be in time. [*To* HERBIE *hastily*] Don't you come. You go back home.
   [TED, MR. D., BERT *rush off.*]

MRS. G.: Yes, Herbie, you go back home and wait there. Oh, Ted.
   [*She follows after the others.*]
   [PREACHER *comes forward. Puts arm across boy's shoulders, consoling him. They go off, in opposite direction to others.*]
   [*Almost at once* BERT *comes on again, looking back carefully over his shoulder to make sure that the others can't see him. As curtain comes down he is kneeling down and reaching under back steps.*]

(*End of Scene*)

ACT THREE

scene 3

The well. CHARLIE'S *sweater lying where* MARY *let it fall in Act Three, Scene One . . .* MARY'S *shoes lying where she kicked them off.* TED *comes running on. Goes down on his knees beside well, peers down, beckons urgently to others,* MR. DILLON *followed by* MRS. GRANT.

TED [*agitated*]: I'll have ter go down. We'll have ter have a rope. What're we going to do for a rope?

MR. D. [*in great distress, realizing the jam he is in--can't reveal where the rope is*]: Oh, the rope.

TED [*peers down well, shading his eyes with hand*]: I'll have to go down without a rope, somehow.

MRS. G.: Oh Ted, Ted, how can you? Oh be careful, Ted. [*Picks up Mary's shoes and clutches them to her bosom.*] Oh, Mary, Mary. [MR. D. *picks up Charlie's sweater, looks at it, drops it. Kneels down beside* TED, *peers down well shading eyes. They are close together, almost touching. The whole action here to be carried on at top speed, to have effect of bringing them together in their agitation and urgency.*]

TED: Too dark. Can't see. Haveter go down. We'll have ter have a rope. [BERT *comes running on, carrying coil of rope over his shoulder.*] The rope. Where'd you get it? [*Grabs it from him.*]

BERT: Back there [*nodding vaguely over his shoulder*]. Wonder yer never fell over it.

MR. D. [*looks quickly at* BERT: *then a half-glance at* TED *to see how he has taken it.*]: Musta been there all the time. [*From here on action is fast and urgent, obliterating all trace of hostility—they are just three blokes doing an urgent job together. During above* TED *has been tying rope onto drum of windlass.*] [MR. D. *grabs windlass handle and begins to wind on rope while* BERT *guides it onto drum. Nobody speaks, just the rhythmical*

269

creak of the windlass. (This effect worth providing for, as it is typical of seldom used windlass, and suggests death and danger. Could be provided by violin off-stage.)]

MRS. G.: Oh Ted, hurry, hurry!

[TED, *when all rope is wound on, puts foot in loop of rope, already provided, to maintain speed of action.*]

Oh Ted, be careful.

BERT: Better let me go.

MR. D.: Yair, he's younger than you.

TED: No, I know the lay of it.

MRS. G.: Oh quick, Ted. But be careful.

TED [*seats himself on coaming of well—puts his weight on rope*]: Yer got it?

[BERT *and* MR. D. *each take handle of windlass. They face opposite ways,* MR. D. *facing back-stage.*]

MR. D. [*as* TED *lowers himself into well*]: What's the depth?

TED [*as his head disappears below coaming*]: Twenty-five, about that —to the water.

MRS. G.: Oh Ted! Hurry!

[BERT *and* MR. D. *brace themselves to take strain on handles.*]

Be careful, Ted!

[*Pause.*]

Oh Ted.

[BERT, MR. D. *take strain as handles begin to turn.* TED'S *head disappears, then his hand off coaming. Windlass, having been out in weather, squeaks—two notes repeated for each turn of drum.* MRS. G. *peers anxiously down. When a few turns—about eight or ten (important for later business)—of rope left on drum*]

TED [*muffled, from below*]: Hold it.

[*Windlass stops turning. Rope goes slack.*]

MRS. G. [*kneeling down facing backstage and peering into well*]: He's on the stagin', I think. Yer all right, Ted?

MR. D. [*anxiously to* MRS. G.]: Stagin' sound?

MRS. G.: Yair. I think so. Yer all right, Ted? What can yer see?

TED [*muffled*]: Yair. On the stagin'—too dark. Can't see—I don't think—

[*Rope sways slackly as* TED *moves about on staging.* MR. D. *and* BERT *stand with one hand lightly on handle, other arm resting*] *on top bar of windlass, peering down into well.*]

MRS. G.: Can yer—oh, Ted—can yer—see—see anythin'?

TED: Anybody got any matches?—I can't see—but I don't think—matches? Any matches?

MRS. G. [*looking up*]: Oh, if we'd only thought to bring matches!

BERT: I got a box. [*Feels in one pocket and then the other, letting go handle (showing that* TED *on staging is independent of windlass). Produces box of matches*] Here y'are.

MRS. G. [*down well*]: Yer there, Ted. Here's some matches.

TED [*anxiously*]: Hold it, hold it. I can't see for the light in me eyes. That's better, now.

MRS. G. [*holding matches over well—still clutching shoes with other hand*]: Can yer see it?

TED: Yair, let it go. Now—

[MRS. G. *drops matches down well.*]

[*Agitatedly*] Aw! What'd yer wanter let 'em go like that for?

MRS. G.: Oh Ted! Have yer got them.

TED: No, I missed them. Yer should'a waited.

MRS. G.: Oh, Ted!

TED: They're in the water I think. I couldn't see them comin'!

MRS. G.: Oh Ted, what're yer gointer do?

TED: It don't matter. I can see better now.

[*Nobody speaks. They all peer anxiously down well. The whole action suspended for a moment, giving "spotlight" effect of tension. Then . . .*]

[CHARLIE *comes on backstage as*]

MRS. G.: Should I go an' get another box, Ted? [*Looks up, sees* CHARLIE] Oh God!

[CHARLIE *stops surprised, seems about to make a run for it. Looks back (offstage) over shoulder.*]

[MR. D. *and* BERT *look up at* MRS. G.'S *cry.*]

MR. D. [*seeing* CHARLIE]: For the Lord's sake!

BERT: Well, cripes!

TED [*answering* MRS. G.]: No, I'll manage. If I had a stick or somethin'! [*Trails off; nobody takes any notice of him.*]

[MARY *appears behind* CHARLIE. *Peers round him. They clutch hands. Both dressed in their Sunday best.*]

MRS. G. [*dropping shoes down well, running to* MARY, *who comes forward hesitantly*]: Oh, Mary, Mary!

TED: What's that? Something hit me.

[*Nobody takes any notice of him.* MARY *and* CHARLIE *come forward hesitatingly, hand in hand.*]

MRS. G. [*clasps* MARY *to her, crooning*]: Mary! Mary!

[MR. D. *and* BERT *let go windlass handles.*]

MR. D. [*goes up to* CHARLIE, *puts arms across his shoulder*]: Oh boy, I'm—I'm—it's—I [*gives him a sort of hug*].

[MARY *and* CHARLIE, *being hugged by* MRS. G. *and* MR. D. *respectively, still hand in hand, rather bewildered.*]

TED: Hey, can yer drop me down a stick or somethin'? Think I can see the matches.

[*No one takes any notice of him.*]

CHARLIE [*looking round, puzzled*]: What are you—? What's the matter?

TED [*bellowing*]: Did yer hear me up there? A stick or somethin'.

[*Nobody takes any notice, except* CHARLIE *and* MARY, *who look at well, at one another, and then at others.*]

MR. D.: Gosh, boy, I'm glad ter see you.

MRS. G.: Oh Mary! [*Starts to cry.*]

MARY: Why mother, what's the matter?

TED: Hey, what goes on up there?

[*Nobody takes any notice.*]

CHARLIE: What's the—? Why are you—?

MR. D.: We thought—we didn't know—we—[*stammers to a halt*].

TED: Pull me up. There's nothing down here.

BERT [*coming to* MR. D.'S *rescue*]: We—we—wondered where you was. Where yer been?

TED: Hey, pull me up, can't yer? What goes on up there? [*He gives the rope an angry shake.*]

CHARLIE [*looking sheepishly at* MARY, *who gives hand a nervous tug*]: I just—we just—we came back to get—we left our—my sweater and her shoes—we left them here.

TED [*shakes rope again more angrily*]: Pull me up, pull me up. What the hell!

CHARLIE: We came—we came back to, to get them.

[TED *pulls rope furiously. Windlass handles turn at great speed. Continue to spin till rope unwound.* MR. D. *and* BERT *turn and look*

at spinning handles. This is the first time they have remembered
TED.]

MRS. G.: Back? D'yer mean—was yer . . .?

[*Car tooting heard in distance.*]

MR. D. and BERT: What's that?

[CHARLIE *and* MARY *look at one another.*]

CHARLIE: It's—it's Robinson.

MR. D.: Robinson?

MRS. G.: Robinson?

MARY: We told him—we asked him—

CHARLIE: He said he'd—he'd wait for us if we—if—we weren't long. He's on the reserve, we came the back way.

MR. D.: Wait for yer?

CHARLIE: We asked him to—well—he said he'd—

MR. D.: Wait for you? You mean—?

BERT: Yer don't—has he gotter—d'yer want him—to wait for yer?

MR. D.: What d'yer mean wait? [*Car toots again repeatedly.*] You don't want him ter wait for yer [*half a question, half a statement.*] [*His arm round* CHARLIE'S *shoulder again. To* BERT] You go and tell him he needn't wait.

CHARLIE: I think he—perhaps he—he wants his money.

[BERT *looks at* MR. D.]

MR. D.: Well that's all right. [*To* BERT] You pay him—

BERT: But—

MR. D.: Slip over home. There's that money on top of the dresser.

BERT: But didn't—?

MR. D.: No, he never took it. That'll shut Robinson up.

[TED'S *head appears above coaming as he comes—puffing—hand over hand up rope which has been trembling from his exertion during above.*]

TED: What the hell!

[MR. D. *and* BERT *run forward, take him under arms, and help him up.*]

[MRS. G. *and* MARY *and* CHARLIE *come forward, hand in hand.*]
What the hell!

MRS. G.: It's all right, Ted. They're—they're—here they are.

TED [*indignantly*]: *Here they are!* I like that! And me—what I want ter know is—?

MRS. G.: Now Ted, that's enough of that. Here they are [*she steps in between* CHARLIE *and* MARY *and holds their hands*] and that's all that matters.

TED: But—but—

MRS. G. [*peremptorily*]: Ted, stop it. We're only too thankful they never, that they—that they're here and everything's all right. Come here and tell them—tell them—well, if Mary wants ter get married she's gointer. [*Glances at* MR. D.]

MR. D.: Well I—it's—the way it's turned out—well, they wanter get married, I don't see why they shouldn't.

MRS. G.: So there Ted, you just show them how thankful you are that [*hesitates*]—just show them how thankful you are.

[TED *comes hesitatingly forward. More toots, loud and long.*]

MR. D. [*to* BERT]: Whip over and get that money and shut Robinson up. He's gettin' on my nerves.

MRS. G. [*dropping their hands and clutching* TED's *arm*]: Oh, her shoes, her shoes.

TED: Her shoes?

MRS. G.: I dropped them—down the well.

TED: So that's what hit me. Well I'm damned if I'm goin' down to get them.

MRS. G.: But Ted, its her best pair.

TED: Well, they can stay there. I'm not goin' down that well again.

MRS. G.: But Ted—

TED: Now Missus, don't take on about it, I tell yer I'm not goin' down that well again. I'll buy her another pair—for a weddin' present.

(*The End*)